Summer Bridge Activities™

creation and design
Michele D. Van Leeuwen

exercise illustrations by
Amanda Sorensen

Fifth and Sixth Grade

written by
Julia Ann Hobbs
Carla Dawn Fisher

Summer Bridge Activities™ Contains:

Fun, skill-based activities in **reading, writing, arithmetic,** and **language arts** with additional activities in **geography** and **science** to keep your child busy, happy, and learning! SBA is divided into three sections for review and preview with pages numbered by day. Children complete their work quickly with the easy-to-use format, leaving lots of time for play!

A **Reading Book List** based on the Accelerated Reader Program.

Incentive Contracts to encourage summer learning and reward your child's efforts. **"Discover Something New"** lists of creative things to do are found on the back of each SBA Incentive Contract Calendar for when your child says the inevitable: "What can I do? I'm bored."

Comprehensive **Word Lists,** which contain words to sound, read and spell, challenge children and encourage them to build their vocabulary. SBA also contains a **Fraction Table, Napier's Bones, Yardstick, Inch Rulers, Centimeter Rulers,** and **Meterstick** to use for many of the activities.

Tear-out answer pages to help correct your child's work.

An official **Certificate of Completion** to be awarded for successfully completing the workbook.

Mr. Fredrickson

Ms. Hansen

Here are some groups who think our books are great!

SBA YOUTH EDUCATION EXCELLENCE 1993-99

NBP EDUCATION EXCELLENCE 1999

PARENTS' CHOICE APPROVED

Hey Kids and Parents!
Log on to www.summerbrains.com for more eye-boggling, mind-bending, brain-twisting summer fun...
It's where summerbrains like you hang out!
www.summerbrains.com

Summer Bridge Activities™
5th to 6th Grade

For information, write
Rainbow Bridge Publishing, Inc.
PO Box 571470
Salt Lake City, Utah 84157-1470
801/268-8887
www.summerbridgeactivities.com

Publisher
Scott G. Van Leeuwen

Associate Publisher
George Starks

Series Creator
Michele D. Van Leeuwen

Product Development Director
Dante J. Orazzi

Editorial Director
Paul Rawlins

Copy Editors and Proofreaders
Kathleen Bratcher, Suzie Ellison, Randy Harward, Jerold Johnson,
Jeanna Mason, Kirsten Swinyard, and Jennifer Willes

Additional Content
Clareen Arnold, Molly McMahon

Graphic Design and Layout
Andy Carlson, Robyn Funk, Zack Johnson, and Amanda Sorensen

Please visit our website at
www.summerbridgeactivities.com
for supplements, additions, and corrections to this book.

Ninth Edition 2003

For orders call 1-800-598-1441.
Discounts available for quantity orders.

ISBN: 1-887923-08-X

PRINTED IN THE UNITED STATES OF AMERICA
10 9

Table of Contents

Dear Parents,

Thank you for choosing Summer Bridge Activities™ to help reinforce your child's classroom skills while away from school. This year, I am proud to offer you this special edition, "Building Better Bodies and Behavior," to help your children develop not only their minds this summer, but their bodies and character as well. I hope you enjoy!

Your personal involvement is so important to your child's immediate and long-term academic success. No matter how wonderful your child's classroom experience is, your involvement outside the classroom will make it that much better!

I originally created Summer Bridge Activities™ because as a parent of a first grader, summer was quickly approaching and I was concerned that the skills he had worked so hard to develop would be forgotten. I was apprehensive about his adjustment to school after three months of play and wanted to help in any way I could. I spoke with his teacher, other school administrators, and parents and found I was not alone in my concerns. I was told by several educators that up to 80% of what children are taught in school can be lost, unless that knowledge is reinforced quickly and continuously! I certainly did not want this to happen to my son!

I looked for appropriate workbooks but could not find any that compared with the Department of Education curriculum guidelines and included all the basic skills in an easy-to-use format. So, as a concerned parent, I organized a team of award-winning teachers and informed educators to create a series of workbooks that would make reviewing classroom skills—including reading, writing, arithmetic, geography, and language arts—fun and rewarding. The end result was the Summer Bridge Activities™ workbook that you have in your hands right now! I am confident that you will enjoy using it with your child.

Thanks again for choosing this wonderful program to assist with your child's academic success. I wish you the best of luck in helping your child get the most out of his/her education. Also, we at RBP welcome you to **www.summerbrains.com** where you will find additional fun, interactive learning games, ideas, and activities for you and your child at no additional cost. We look forward to seeing you there! Have a great summer and happy learning!

Sincerely,

Michele D. Van Leeuwen

Michele D. Van Leeuwen
Creator of Summer Bridge Activities™

Ms. Hansen TAKES YOU INSIDE

Summer Bridge Activities™

The exercises found in Summer Bridge Activities™ (SBA) are easy to understand and are presented in a way that allows your child to review familiar skills and then be progressively challenged on more difficult subjects. In addition to academic exercises, SBA contains many other activities to challenge and reinforce reading comprehension, phonemic awareness, and letter, word, and number recognition.

Sections of Summer Bridge Activities™

★ There are three sections in Summer Bridge Activities™; the first and second review, the third previews.

★ Each section begins with an SBA Incentive Contract Calendar.

★ Each day your child will complete an activity in reading, writing, arithmetic, and language skills. The activities become progressively more challenging.

★ Each page is numbered by day.

★ Your child will need a pencil, ruler, eraser, and crayons to complete the activities.

Books Children Love to Read

📘 SBA contains a Reading Book List with a variety of titles, including many that are found in the Accelerated Reader Program.

📘 RBP recommends that parents read to their pre-kindergarten and kindergarten–1st grade children 5–10 minutes each day and then ask questions about the story to reinforce comprehension. For higher grade levels, RBP recommends the following daily reading times: grades 1–2, 10–20 minutes; grades 2–3, 20–30 minutes; grades 3–4, 30–45 minutes; grades 4–5 and 5–6, 45–60 minutes.

📘 It is important that the parent and child decide an amount of reading time and write it on the SBA Incentive Contract Calendar.

SBA Incentive Contract Calendars

✏️ Calendars are located at the beginning of each section.

✏️ We suggest that the parent and child sign the SBA Incentive Contract Calendar before the child begins each section.

✏️ When your child completes one day of Summer Bridge Activities™, he/she may color or initial the pencil.

✏️ Refer to the recommended reading times. When your child completes the agreed reading time each day, he/she may color or initial the book.

✏️ The parent may initial the SBA Incentive Contract Calendar once the activities have been completed.

✏️ Let your child explore and experiment with the "Discover Something New" activities found on the back of each SBA Incentive Contract Calendar.

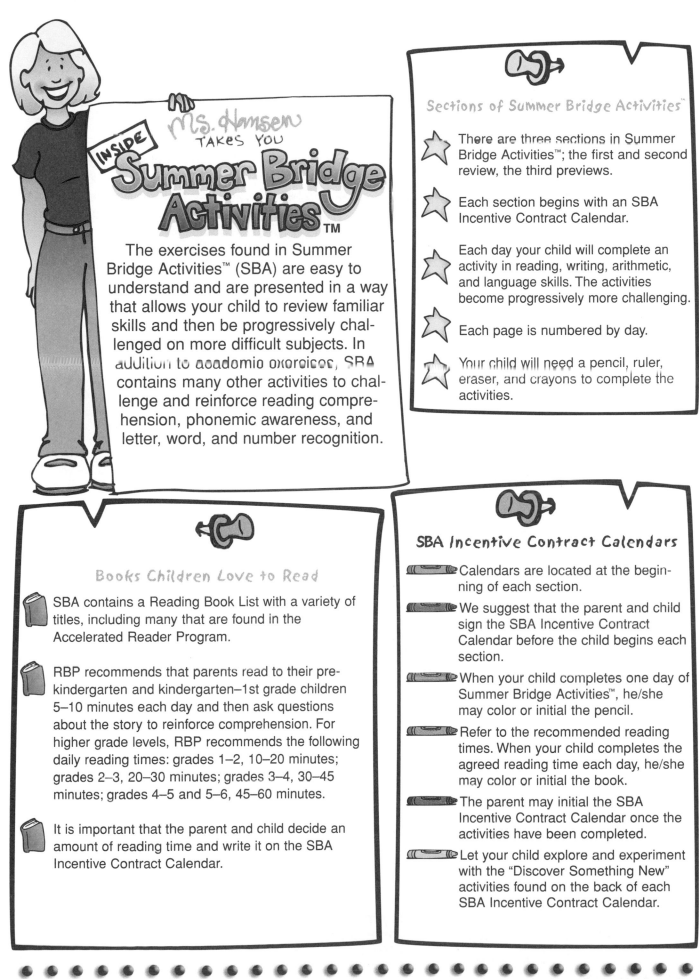

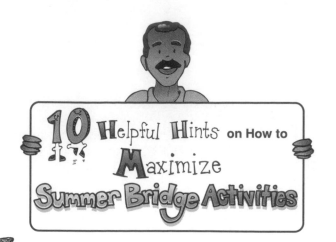

1 First, let your child explore the book. Flip through the pages and look at the activities with your child to help him/her become familiar with the book.

2 Help select a good time for reading or working on the activities. Suggest a time before your child has played outside and becomes too tired to do the work.

3 Provide any necessary materials. A pencil, ruler, eraser, and crayons are all that are required.

4 Offer positive guidance. Children need a great deal of guidance. Remember, the activities are not meant to be tests. You want to create a relaxed and positive attitude toward learning. Work through at least one example on each page with your child. "Think aloud" and show your child how to solve problems.

5 Give your child plenty of time to think. You may be surprised by how much children can do on their own.

6 Stretch your child's thinking beyond the page. If you are reading a storybook, you might ask, "What do you think will happen next?" or "What would you do if this happened to you?" Encourage your child to name objects that begin with certain letters or count the number of items in your shopping cart. Also, children often enjoy making up their own stories with illustrations.

7 Reread stories and flip through completed pages occasionally. Completed pages and books will be a source of pride to your child and will help show how much he/she accomplished over the summer.

8 Read and work on activities while outside. Take the workbook out in the backyard, to the park, or to a family camp out. It can be fun wherever you are!

9 Encourage siblings, babysitters, and neighborhood children to help with reading and activities. Other children are often perfect for providing the one-on-one attention necessary to reinforce reading skills.

10 Give plenty of approval! Stickers and stamps, or even a hand-drawn funny face, are effective for recognizing a job well done. When your child completes the book, hang his/her Certificate of Completion where everyone can see it. At the end of the summer, your child can feel proud of his/her accomplishments and will be eager for school to start.

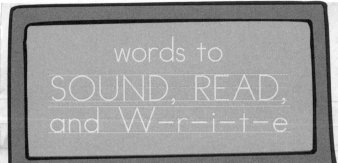

words to SOUND, READ, and W–r–i–t–e

A t the end of each section are words to sound out, read, and spell.

Together you and your child can...

Write your favorite words on flashcards. Make two sets and play the matching game (in order to keep the two matching cards, you have to know their meaning or spelling).

Draw pictures of exciting words.

Use as many words as you can from the list to make up five questions, statements, or explanations.

Write a story using as many words as you can from the word list.

Write a list of words you find while traveling to the grocery store, on vacation, or on the way to a friend's house.

Write a list of colors.

Write a list of words you have a hard time spelling.

Write a list of action verbs.

Practice writing each word five times.

Reading is the primary means to all learning. If a child cannot read effectively, other classroom subjects can remain out of reach.

You were probably the first person to introduce your child to the wonderful world of reading. As your child grows, it is important to continue encouraging his/her interest in reading to support the skills being taught in school.

This summer, make reading a priority in your home. Set aside time each day to read aloud to your child at bedtime or after lunch or dinner. Encourage your child to take a break from playing and stretch out with a book found on the Summer Bridge Activities™ Summer Reading Book List. Choose a title that you have never read, or introduce your child to some of the books you enjoyed when you were his/her age. Books only seem to get better with time!

Visit the library to find books that meet your child's specific interests. Ask a librarian which books are popular among children of your child's grade. Take advantage of summer storytelling activities at the library. Ask the librarian about other resources such as stories on cassette, compact disc, and the Internet.

Encourage reading in all settings and daily activities. Encourage your child to read house numbers, street signs, window banners, and packaging labels. Encourage your child to tell stories using pictures.

Best of all, show your child how much YOU like to read! Sit down with your child when he/she reads and enjoy a good book yourself. After dinner, share stories and ideas from newspapers and magazines that might interest your child. Make reading a way of life this summer!

Reading Book List

Adler, C.S.
Always and Forever Friends

Alexander, Lloyd
The Black Cauldron
The Drackenberg Adventure

Armstrong, William Howard
Sounder

Avi
Windcatcher

Babbitt, Natalie
Tuck Everlasting

Banks, Lynne Reid
The Adventures of King Midas
Indian in the Cupboard

Bawden, Nina
Henry

Bellairs, John
The Lamp from the Warlock's Tomb

Brittain, Bill
The Wish Giver: Three Tales of Coventree

Burch, Robert
Ida Early Comes over the Mountain

Butterworth, Oliver
The Enormous Egg

Byars, Betsy Cromer
The Summer of the Swans
The Pinballs

Cannon, A. E.
Amazing Gracie

Cassedy, Sylvia
Behind the Attic Wall

Conrad, Pam
Prairie Songs

Cooney, Caroline B.
The Face on the Milk Carton

Cooper, Susan
Over Sea, Under Stone

Coville, Bruce
Jeremy Thatcher, Dragon Hatcher
The Ghost Wore Gray

Dahl, Roald
James and the Giant Peach

DeAngeli, Marguerite
The Door in the Wall

DeFelice, Cynthia C.
Weasel

De Jong, Meindert
The Wheel on the School

Drucker, Malka
Jacob's Rescue: A Holocaust Story

Estes, Eleanor Ruth
The Hundred Dresses

Ferguson, Alane
Cricket and the Crackerbox Kid

Fitzhugh, Louise
Harriet the Spy

Fleischman, Paul
I Am Phoenix: Poems for Two Voices

Fleischman, Sid
Bull Run

Gardiner, John Reynolds
Stone Fox

Gates, Doris
Blue Willow

George, Jean Craighead
Julie of the Wolves

Grahame, Kenneth
The Wind in the Willows

Gray, Elizabeth Janet
Adam of the Road

Greer, Gery
Max and Me and the Time Machine

Henry, Marguerite
King of the Wind

Hahn, Mary Downing
Stepping on the Cracks

Hesse, Karen
Letters from Rifka

Hunt, Irene
Up a Road Slowly

Hobbs, Will
Bearstone

Hopkins, Lee Bennet
Dinosaurs

Irving, Washington
The Legend of Sleepy Hollow

Juster, Norton
The Phantom Tollbooth

Keith, Harold
Rifles for Watie

Konigsburg E.L.
From the Mixed Up Files of
    Mrs. Basil E. Frankweiler

Krumgold, Joseph
...and Now Miguel

L'Engle, Madeline
A Wrinkle in Time

Lawson, Robert
Rabbit Hill

Le Guin, Ursula K.
A Wizard of Earthsea
Lenski, Lois
Strawberry Girl
Levetin, Soria
Journey to America
Lewis, C.S.
Chronicles of Narnia Series
Lowry, Lois
Number The Stars
The Giver
MacBride, Roger Lea
Little House on Rocky Ridge
MacLachlan, Patricia
Sarah, Plain and Tall
McKinley, Robin
The Blue Sword
Mills, Claudia
Dinah In Love
Dynamite Dinah
Moody, Ralph
Little Britches: Father and I
Were Ranchers
Murphy, Jim
Across America on an
Emigrant Train
Naylor, Phyllis Reynolds
The Agony of Alice
Nixon, Joan Lowery
Land of Hope
O'Brien, Robert C.
Mrs. Frisby and the Rats of
NIMH
O'Dell, Scott
Streams to the River, River to
the Sea
Park, Barbara
Operation: Dump the Chump
Skinnybones
Paterson, Katherine
The Great Gilly Hopkins
Paulsen, Gary
Hatchet
Peck, Richard E.
Voices after Midnight

Peck, Robert Newton
Soup
Soup's Goat
Pevsner, Stella
Me, My Goat, and My Sister's
Wedding
Pinkwater, Daniel Manus
Lizard Music
Pitts, Paul
The Shadowman's Way
Racing the Sun
Prelutsky, Jack
Tyrannosaurus Was a Beast
Raskin, Ellen
The Westing Game
Rawls, Wilson
Where the Red Fern Grows
Roberts, Willo Davis
The Pet-Sitting Peril
The View from the Cherry Tree
Rinaldi, Ann
The Fifth of March
Rostkowski, Margaret I.
After the Dancing Days
Ruckman, Ivy
Night of the Twisters
Who Invited the Undertaker?
Rylant, Cynthia
Every Living Thing
Sachar, Louis
There's a Boy in the Girls'
Bathroom
Seredy, Kate
The White Stag
Smith, Doris Buchanan
The Pennywhistle Tree
Smith, Robert Kimmel
The War with Grandpa
Snyder, Zilpha Keatley
The Egypt Game
The Velvet Room
Sorensen, Virginia Eggertsen
Miracles on Maple Hill
Speare, Elizabeth George
Calico Captive
The Witch of Blackbird Pond

Springer, Nancy
Colt
Sperry, Armstrong
Call It Courage
Stolz, Mary
The Dog on Barkham Street
Taylor, Mildred D.
Roll of Thunder, Hear My Cry
Taylor, Sydney
All-of-a-Kind Family
Taylor, Theodore
Timothy of the Cay
Terban, Marvin
Hey, Hay! A Wagonful of Funny
Homonym Riddles
Tolkein, J.R.R.
The Hobbit
The Lord of the Rings
Travers, P.L.
Mary Poppins
Twohill, Maggie
Valentine Frankenstein
Uchida, Yoshiko
Journey to Topaz
Ullman, James Ramsey
Banner in the Sky
Voight, Cynthia
Wings of a Falcon
Wallace, Bill
Beauty
Never Say Quit
White, E. B.
Trumpet of the Swan
Willard, Nancy
A Visit to William Blake's Inn:
Poems for Innocent and
Experienced Travelers
Winthrop, Elizabeth
The Castle in the Attic
The Battle for the Castle
Wyss, Johann David
The Swiss Family Robinson
Yep, Laurence
Dragonwings
Dragon's Gate

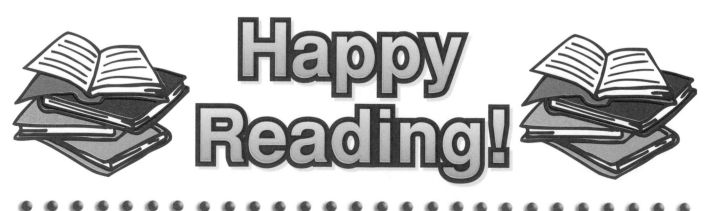

Summer Bridge Activities™

Incentive Contract Calendar

Month _____

My parents and I decided that if I complete 15 days of
Summer Bridge Activities™ and read _____ minutes a day,
my incentive/reward will be:

_____

Child's Signature _____
Parent's Signature _____

Day 1   📖 ⭐ —

Day 2   📖 ⭐ —

Day 3   📖 ⭐ —

Day 4   📖 ⭐ —

Day 5   📖 ⭐ —

Day 6   📖 ⭐ —

Day 7   📖 ⭐ —

Day 8   📖 ⭐ —

Day 9   📖 ⭐ —

Day 10   📖 ⭐ —

Day 11   📖 ⭐ —

Day 12   📖 ⭐ —

Day 13   📖 ⭐ —

Day 14   📖 ⭐ —

Day 15   📖 ⭐ —

Child: Color the ⭐ for daily activities completed.
Color the 📖 for daily reading completed.

Parent: Initial the _____ for daily activities and reading
your child completes.

1. Describe what you look like and write it down.

2. Make a picnic lunch for two and invite a friend over for a picnic in your backyard.

3. Feed the birds.

4. Ask your mom or dad for an old map and plan a trip. Decide on a destination and highlight your route. Figure out how many days it would take, where you would stop, and what you would like to see. Use the legend on the map to help you make these decisions.

5. Find some old socks, buttons, yarn, and needle and thread. Turn them into puppets and name them. Then find a cardboard box and paint it. Cut a hole in the front to put the puppets through and put on a puppet show for younger children.

Fun Activity Ideas to Go Along with the First Section!

6. Polish a pair of your mom's or dad's shoes and put a love note inside.

7. Visit a sick neighbor, friend, or relative.

8. Hold a fire drill in your home.

9. Start a diary.

10. Learn how to do something you have always wanted to do, like play the guitar, cross-stitch, rollerblade, cook pizza, train your dog, etc.

11. Write a story about your friend.

12. In the evening, look at the sky. Find the first star and make a wish.

13. Learn how to make one of your favorite foods.

14. Have a watermelon bust.

15. Make a pitcher of lemonade or punch and sell it in front of your house.

Use the following information to solve problems dealing with <u>place value</u>.

billions			millions			thousands					
hundred-billions	ten-billions	billions	hundred-millions	ten-millions	millions	hundred-thousands	ten-thousands	thousands	hundreds	tens	ones

<u>Remember</u>: Commas separate millions, thousands, etc.

Write the following in expanded form. The first one is done for you.

1. 72,584,361

   70,000,000 + 2,000,000 + 500,000 + 80,000 + 4,000 + 300 + 60 + 1
2. 37,126,489

3. 56,487,320,960

4. 90,675,409,783

Write the following using the correct word form. The first one is done for you.

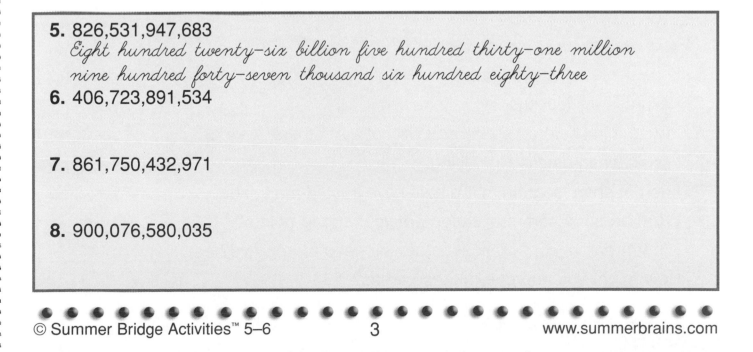

5. 826,531,947,683
   Eight hundred twenty-six billion five hundred thirty-one million nine hundred forty-seven thousand six hundred eighty-three
6. 406,723,891,534

7. 861,750,432,971

8. 900,076,580,035

Write a sentence showing what the underlined words below mean. Use the underlined word in your answer. Look the words up in a dictionary if you don't know what they mean.

1. Was John <u>elated</u> when he won first prize?

   _____

2. Why was there so much <u>turmoil</u> at the party?

   _____

3. Is it <u>mandatory</u> for you to go to school until you are eighteen?

   _____

4. Why is the little boy crying so <u>dolefully</u>?

   _____

5. Did the people raise enough money to <u>renovate</u> the old church?

   _____

6. Were the Scouts <u>intrepid</u> campers?

   _____

7. What was making the kitten <u>quiver</u> so hard?

   _____

8. Do you think Mr. Brown is a <u>corpulent</u> man?

   _____

9. How <u>palatable</u> are artichokes to you?

   _____

10. Were the police <u>inquisitive</u> about the cause of the accident?

    _____

Communication Skills. Communication skills are very important. Read the sentences below. Rate yourself between 1 (lowest) and 5 (highest) on how well you communicate. Then answer the following questions.

Your rating: _____

1. I speak clearly and loudly so others can hear what I am saying.   yes   no
2. I express my feelings.   yes   no
3. I try to think before I speak so I will not hurt others' feelings.   yes   no
4. I listen when others are talking.   yes   no
5. I do not share secrets that others have trusted me to keep.   yes   no

- What areas of communication are your strong points? _____
- What areas of communication do you need to improve? _____
- How might you improve in these areas? _____

What's in a Number? Write a definition and some examples of the following number words or terms.

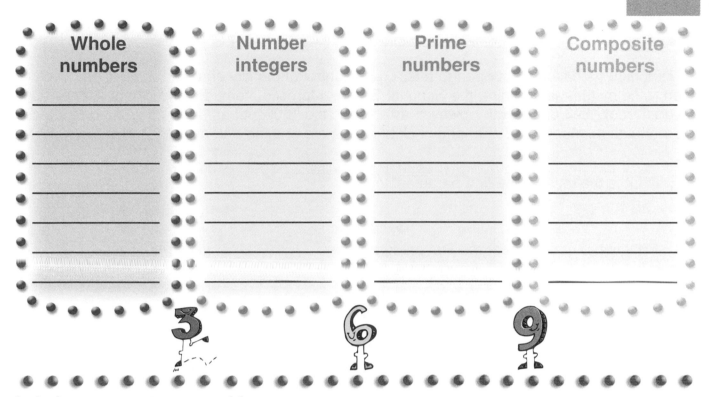

Whole numbers	Number integers	Prime numbers	Composite numbers
_____	_____	_____	_____
_____	_____	_____	_____
_____	_____	_____	_____
_____	_____	_____	_____
_____	_____	_____	_____
_____	_____	_____	_____

Label as many states on this map as you can.

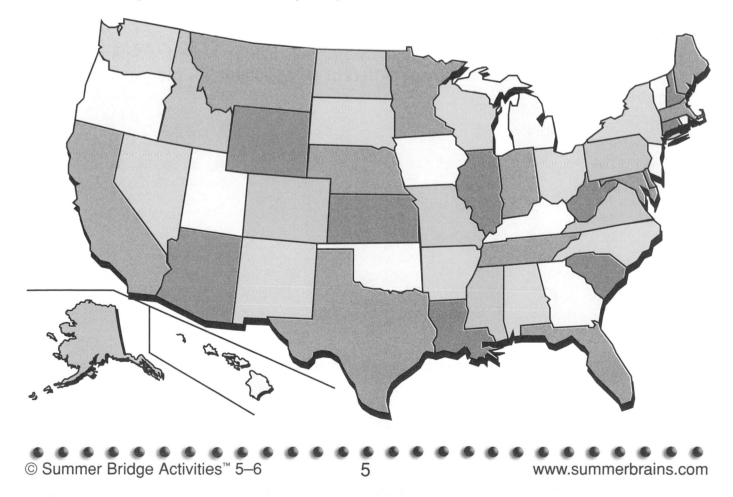

Read the following paragraphs and answer the questions.

Timbuktu is a small trading town in central Mali. It was established around A.D. 1100 and is located near the southern edge of the Sahara Desert. It was a trading post for products from North and West Africa. Camel caravans from the north traded salt, cloth, cowrie shells, and copper. The dealers in Timbuktu exchanged the goods for gold, kola nuts, ivory, and slaves that they got from the south.

Timbuktu's location left it open to attack, and control of the city changed many times. It has been ruled by the Mali Empire, the Songhai Empire, Morocco, nomads, and others. France controlled it from 1893 until 1960. However, as early as the 1600s it has declined in importance and population. Many of its mud and brick buildings are eroding and are half-buried in the sand.

1. What is the topic of the first paragraph?

2. What is the main idea of the first paragraph?

3. What is the topic of the second paragraph?

4. What is the main idea of the second paragraph?

Investigate the life of Sir Francis Drake. Compare the different ways Spain and England felt about Drake. Write these different perspectives on the T-chart below.

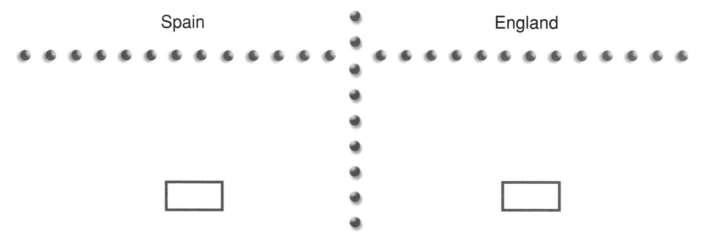

Spain   England

Choose a color that would describe the feelings of each country towards Drake. Put the color in the appropriate box.

Front-End Estimation in Addition.
Estimate each sum by using your knowledge of rounding off numbers.

1. 45 + 32

_____

2. 74 + 23

_____

3. 91 + 57

_____

4. 37 + 83

_____

5. 389 + 412

_____

6. 278 + 582

_____

7. 222 + 387

_____

8. 625 + 371

_____

9. 519 + 750

_____

10. 432 + 929

_____

11. 351 + 476

_____

12. 948 + 511

_____

13. 999 + 808

_____

14. 1,243 + 3,569

_____

15. 2,735 + 4,960

_____

16. 5,429 + 2,099

_____

17. 10,364 + 3,910

_____

18. 22,100 + 30,439

_____

19. 7,896 + 49,637

_____

20. 34,433 + 16,377

_____

21. 110,345 + 7,630

_____

22. 205,933 + 460,362

_____

23. 711,393 + 202,501

_____

24. 473,926 + 410,345

_____

Match the correct capital with each state.

____ Alabama	____ Nebraska	**a.** Montpelier	**n.** Salem
____ Arizona	____ New Hampshire	**b.** Honolulu	**o.** Boston
____ California	____ New Mexico	**c.** Hartford	**p.** Pierre
____ Connecticut	____ North Carolina	**d.** Lincoln	**q.** Sacramento
____ Florida	____ Ohio	**e.** Columbus	**r.** Frankfort
____ Hawaii	____ Oregon	**f.** Madison	**s.** Montgomery
____ Illinois	____ Rhode Island	**g.** St. Paul	**t.** Augusta
____ Iowa	____ South Dakota	**h.** Springfield	**u.** Raleigh
____ Kentucky	____ Texas	**i.** Phoenix	**v.** Austin
____ Maine	____ Vermont	**j.** Des Moines	**w.** Concord
____ Massachusetts	____ Washington	**k.** Providence	**x.** Tallahassee
____ Minnesota	____ Wisconsin	**l.** Olympia	**y.** Jefferson City
____ Missouri		**m.** Santa Fe	

Look up the word <u>dramatize</u> in a dictionary and answer the following questions.

1. What are the guide words on the page?

2. How many meanings are listed for the word?

3. Write the word. Show the special spelling.

4. How many syllables does the word have?

5. What does dramatize mean in this sentence?
Do you always have to <u>dramatize</u> everything, Annie?

6. Write the other forms of the word given in the dictionary and tell what part of speech they are.

7. List two other words on the same page as dramatize. Show the special spelling.

"I" Messages. A way to share feelings is to use an "I" message. An "I" message includes an action, effect, and feeling. For example, a friend is coming to your house so you can go to a show. He or she is late. You might say to your friend, "Because you were late [action], I thought we would miss the show [effect]. I was angry [feeling]."

Read the scenarios below and write an "I" message.

1. You find out that a friend is telling lies about you.
[action]
[effect]
[feeling]

2. Your parents have given you a special present.
[action]
[effect]
[feeling]

3. You thought your friend was to meet you at 2:00, but he didn't come until 3:00.
[action]
[effect]
[feeling]

4. Your friend tells you that you have hurt her/his feelings.
[action]
[effect]
[feeling]

Field Trip.

The students at Franklin Elementary School are going on a field trip to the Museum of Natural History. Three thousand sixty-eight students are going on Wednesday, and 2,864 are going on Thursday. Mr. Rand, the principal, wants to order special school name tags that come in packs of 1,000. Each package cost $5.25.

How many packages does Mr. Rand need to order? _____

What steps did you use to solve the problem?

Could you have used any of these ways or a combination of ways to find the answer?

a. mental math	**d.** subtraction
b. estimation	**e.** place value
c. addition	**f.** guessed

What information was essential to know before you solved the problem?

What information was not necessary to know?

Restate the problem, changing one or more of the facts without altering the solution or outcome of the problem.

Match the correct capital with each state.

____ Alaska	____ Nevada	**a.**	Salt Lake City	**n.**	Helena
____ Arkansas	____ New Jersey	**b.**	Lansing	**o.**	Cheyenne
____ Colorado	____ New York	**c.**	Bismarck	**p.**	Topeka
____ Delaware	____ North Dakota	**d.**	Annapolis	**q.**	Richmond
____ Georgia	____ Oklahoma	**e.**	Nashville	**r.**	Trenton
____ Idaho	____ Pennsylvania	**f.**	Juneau	**s.**	Boise
____ Indiana	____ South Carolina	**g.**	Harrisburg	**t.**	Albany
____ Kansas	____ Tennessee	**h.**	Dover	**u.**	Jackson
____ Louisiana	____ Utah	**i.**	Carson City	**v.**	Columbia
____ Maryland	____ Virginia	**j.**	Little Rock	**w.**	Baton Rouge
____ Michigan	____ West Virginia	**k.**	Indianapolis	**x.**	Atlanta
____ Mississippi	____ Wyoming	**l.**	Denver	**y.**	Charleston
____ Montana		**m.**	Oklahoma City		

Write a sentence for each compound word below.

- •levelheaded
- •hand-me-downs
- •halfhearted
- •lifesaver
- •sightseers
- •well-balanced
- •self-addressed
- •wholesale

1. _____

2. _____

3. _____

4. _____

5. _____

6. _____

7. _____

8. _____

The Skeletal System. Study the chart of the skeletal system below. Go outside with a partner. Lie flat on the sidewalk and have your partner outline your body. Draw the skeletal system in the outline of your body. Label as many bones as you can.

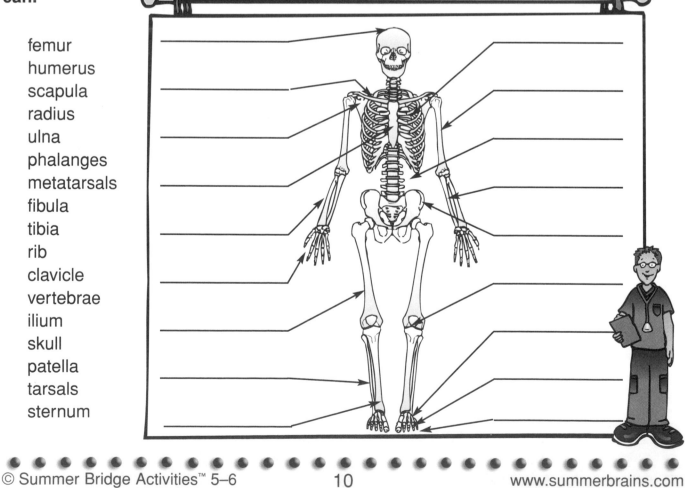

femur
humerus
scapula
radius
ulna
phalanges
metatarsals
fibula
tibia
rib
clavicle
vertebrae
ilium
skull
patella
tarsals
sternum

Estimation with Sums and Differences.
Estimate the sum or difference first; then find the actual sum or difference.

1. 8,666 +9,346	2. 7,543 +2,396	3. 3,693 +1,690	4. 54,561 +36,287
estimate_____ actual_____	estimate_____ actual_____	estimate_____ actual_____	estimate_____ actual_____
5. 34,865 +62,444	6. 47,267 +55,085	7. 65,639 +53,263	8. 28,790 +83,964
estimate_____ actual_____	estimate_____ actual_____	estimate_____ actual_____	estimate_____ actual_____
9. 5,394 -2,587	10. 3,368 -2,139	11. 69,293 -22,887	12. 125,394 -69,831
estimate_____ actual_____	estimate_____ actual_____	estimate_____ actual_____	estimate_____ actual_____
13. 25,689 -13,798	14. 417,937 -409,986	15. 709,723 -337,251	16. 876,259 -395,828
estimate_____ actual_____	estimate_____ actual_____	estimate_____ actual_____	estimate_____ actual_____

Below are the stressed syllables of some spelling words. Write the other syllables, and then write the words in cursive. Each blank stands for a letter. The first one is done for you.

practice	purchaser	glamorous	trillion
measure	refund	~~January~~	appearance
improvement	magazine	diamond	manager
amazement	chosen	attention	causing

1. Jan´ u a r y   *January*

2. ___ ten´ _____   _____

3. pur´ _____   _____

4. re´ _____   _____

5. tril´_____   _____

6. mea´_____   _____

7. ___pear´___   _____

8. cho´_____   _____

9. di´_____   _____

10. mag´_____   _____

11. man´_____   _____

12. caus´_____   _____

13. __maze´_____   _____

14. glam´_____   _____

15. prac´_____   _____

16. ___prove´_____   _____

Cause and Effect.
Some sentences have a clue word to help show the cause-effect relationship. Fill in the blanks with clue words. Then write the cause and effect.

Our school was closed today <u>because</u> of the bad snowstorm we had last night.

Cause: *Bad snow storm.*

Effect: *School was closed.*

1. It snowed all day, _____ the ground was white.
   Cause: _____
   Effect: _____

2. Our electricity went off last night, _____ we went out to dinner.
   Cause: _____
   Effect: _____

3. _____ Joe left the gate unlatched, all the cattle were out in the road.
   Cause: _____
   Effect: _____

4. Scott woke up with the flu today; _____ , he had to miss school.
   Cause: _____
   Effect: _____

5. _____ I know how much Judy loves to read, I got her a set of books for her birthday.
   Cause: _____
   Effect: _____

Science—Structure of the Earth.
Label the different layers of the earth with the terms below. Use the same terms to complete the sentences below.

center of the earth	**crust**	**inner core**
mantle	**lithosphere**	**outer core**

1. The core of the earth has two parts.
   The _____ is liquid.
   The _____ is solid.

2. One reason the crust and _____ are brittle is because they are the outermost and coldest layers of the earth.

3. The top layer of the earth is the _____

4. The _____ is extremely hot and is the thickest layer.

5. As the _____ is approached, pressure and temperature increase.

Mental Math for Multiples of 10, 100, and 1,000. Remember to use mental math!

1. 7 x 10 = _____
2. 16 x 10 = _____
3. 10 x 92 = _____
4. 100 x 8 = _____
5. 50 x 50 = _____
6. 7 x 600 = _____
7. 500 x 200 = _____
8. 5 x 900 = _____
9. 70 x 60 = _____
10. 30 x 400 = _____
11. 200 x 300 = _____
12. 400 x 600 = _____
13. 8 x 1,000 = _____
14. 9 x 3,000 = _____
15. 30 x 5,000 = _____
16. 900 x 200 = _____
17. 800 x 600 = _____
18. 10 x 1,800 = _____
19. 9,000 x 700 = _____
20. 7,000 x 50 = _____
21. 60 x 8,000 = _____
22. 700 x 800 = _____
23. 900 x 900 = _____
24. 1,000 x 19 = _____
25. 52 x 2,000 = _____
26. 400 x 300 = _____
27. 5,000 x 50 = _____
28. 250 x 200 = _____
29. 15,000 x 30 = _____
30. 200,000 x 40 = _____

Healthy Lifestyles.
Fill in the chart of acts and consequences. Using the last two lines, fill in two acts that you may do in a day and what consequences follow.

Acts	Consequences
1. Do not eat breakfast	
2. Cheat on test	
3.	Get an A in spelling
4. Comfort a friend	
5.	Feel good about yourself
6.	You have a lot of energy
7. Take a shower every day	
8. Adult catches your friend smoking	
9.	Get sick
10. Visit the elderly	
11. Say NO to drugs	
12.	
13.	

Syllables. Show the syllables by leaving a space between them. Then write <u>long</u>, <u>short</u>, <u>schwa</u>, or <u>silent</u> for the vowel sound in each syllable. Remember, the schwa sound is usually heard in the unstressed syllable. Use a dictionary if you need help.

EXAMPLE: terrific   *ter ri fic* *schwa short short*

1. jackal _____

2. liable _____

3. volcano _____

4. that _____

5. attraction _____

6. billow _____

7. paralysis _____

8. identify _____

9. mold _____

10. victory _____

11. lesson _____

12. referee _____

The Muscular System and Nervous System. Fill in the blanks with the correct word.

cerebrum	involuntary muscles	medulla
nervous system	voluntary muscles	cerebellum
contracts	spinal cord	

1. Muscles you can control are called _____.

2. When one muscle in a pair _____, or shortens, the other muscle relaxes.

3. _____ are muscles that work automatically, such as the heart.

4. The _____ is the network of cells that receive and send messages to and from the brain and spinal cord to every part of your body.

5. The part of your brain that controls your learning and memory is the_____.

6. The _____ controls how your muscles work together.

7. The part of your brain that controls your heart rate and breathing is the _____.

8. The _____ extends from the base of the brain down your back and is involved with all senses.

Multiplying by 2- and 3-Digit Numbers.
Remember:

```
   218          429           293
 x  36        x 375         x 704
 1308         2145          1172
  654         3003           000
 7848         1287          2051
            160875        206272
```

1. 826 x 47	2. 584 x 29	3. 249 x 63	4. 973 x 51
5. 670 x 94	6. 776 x 68	7. 845 x 77	8. 392 x 82
9. 628 x 274	10. 831 x 347	11. 609 x 149	12. 586 x 781
13. 196 x 175	14. 594 x 739	15. 854 x 837	16. 697 x 507

Possessive and plural forms of many nouns sound alike but are different. An 's can make the base word noun become a singular possessive. For example: All the <u>players</u>' (plural) coats looked the same, but one <u>player's</u> (singular possessive) coat was ripped in the back. In the following sentences, cross out the plurals and possessives that are incorrect. Write them correctly at the right of the sentences. If they are right, just write "correct."

1. All the news <u>reporter's</u> decided to stay at the Brookgreen Inn. _____

2. Ten <u>driver's</u> went out on the job this morning, but only nine returned on time. _____

3. One <u>drivers</u> truck was stuck in a huge snowdrift. _____

4. The <u>announcer's</u> voice sounded awful this morning. _____

5. Many <u>authors</u> had a convention last year to come up with

   new ideas for books. _____

6. The <u>authors</u> new book sold 1,000 copies in four hours. _____

7. The <u>organizer's</u> of this party can be proud of themselves. _____

Sequence.

Read this paragraph; then write the main points in the correct order. The third one is done for you.

Traveling Spiders

The baby wolf spider rides on its mother's back. Jumping spiders travel by ballooning. They raise their abdomens so the wind can pull silk threads from their spinnerets. The wind then lifts the little spiders into the air like balloons on strings. Fisher spiders are very lightweight, so they can travel by walking on water. Crab spiders walk backwards and sidewards. All spiders can make and travel on a dragline (a silk thread).

1. _____

2. _____

3. *Fisher spiders can walk on water.*

4. _____

5. _____

Digestive System.

Put the steps of the digestive process in the proper sequence.

_____ Food moves to the small intestine.

_____ The tongue pushes food down the esophagus.

_____ Undigested food passes out of the body through the anus.

_____ Villi in the small intestine absorb digested food into the bloodstream.

_____ Teeth and saliva start to change food.

_____ Undigested food moves to the large intestine, or colon.

_____ Food goes to the stomach where it is further broken down.

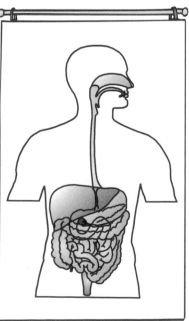

Add, subtract, or multiply. Find the answer to each of the following story problems and tell which operation you used to solve the problem.

1. A person can make 36 single-dipped ice cream cones out of one gallon of ice cream. If you have 12 different flavors of one-gallon ice cream containers, how many cones do you need to use all of the ice cream? _____

2. Mrs. Stone hand-dipped 425 chocolates the first of May, 592 the middle of May, and 143 the last part of May. How many chocolates did she make in May? _____

3. Farmer Tim sold 4,987 pounds of potatoes last year and 12,709 pounds this year. Next year he hopes to do even better. How many more pounds of potatoes did he sell this year than last year? _____

4. Denim shorts sell for $27.59 a pair at Lornet Department Store. Its regular denim jeans sell for $12.18 more than its denim shorts. How much do the store's regular denim jeans cost?
_____

5. Mirror Park has 73 ducks on its lake. An average of 670 people visit the ducks each day. If each person fed the ducks 3 pieces of bread each day, how many pieces of bread would each duck get each day? _____

6. If each person in the United States drank 42 gallons of milk a year, and each gallon cost $1.98, how much would each person spend on milk a year? _____

7. Vicki planted 136 red tulip bulbs, 734 white bulbs, and 400 yellow bulbs. How many flowers will she have if each bulb blooms? _____

8. Gloria bought 25 pairs of socks at $5.80 a pair. If her mother gave her $500, would she have enough money left to buy 6 pairs of shoes at $30.00 each? _____

9. Grayson came home with 12 popsicles that cost him $3.00 a dozen. He sold 2 popsicles to his sister, Denise, at 50¢ each and 4 popsicles to his brother, Tanner, at 50¢ each. How much profit will Grayson make after he sells the rest to his Grandma Dorothy at 50¢ each?
_____

Look in an atlas. Which states contain the following latitude and longitude?

1. 40° N, 110° W _____

2. 35° N, 110° W _____

3. 35° N, 120° W _____

4. 40° N, 83° W _____

5. 33° N, 87° W _____

6. What is the latitude and longitude of one corner of your state? _____

7. What is the latitude and longitude of your city or town? _____

Context clues help you learn new words and their meanings. Use the context clues in the following sentences to tell what the underlined words mean.

1. Mary <u>feigned</u> surprise when her friends had a birthday party for her.

   feigned— _____

2. My <u>colleagues</u> and I work together on many new projects.

   colleagues— _____

3. Maurice looks at his watch often to make sure he is always <u>punctual</u>.

   punctual— _____

4. Joseph, a <u>philatelist</u>, has a large collection of stamps.

   philatelist— _____

5. The pig napping in the mud was hardly able to <u>bestir</u> itself for its dinner.

   bestir— _____

• •

Read the following passage and answer the questions below.

Englishman Sir Walter Raleigh wanted to start a colony in the New World (North America). In 1585, Raleigh sent colonists to what is now North Carolina. The colonists did not want to work and almost starved to death. They were taken back to England. Two years later a second group of colonists sailed over to the same place as the previous colonists. They worked very hard to survive.

Because of a war involving England, Raleigh lost track of the colonists. In 1591, a ship from England finally arrived to check on the colonists, but the colonists had disappeared! There was no sign of life. All the sailors found were some empty trunks, rotted maps, and the word CROATOAN carved on the doorpost of the fort. Croatoan was an island 100 miles south of The Lost Colony. No one knows if the colonists were attacked by the Croatoan Indians or if the settlers went to live on Croatoan Island. The Lost Colony has been a great mystery in American history.

1. How many years has it been since the first colony settled in North Carolina?

2. What year did Raleigh send the second set of colonists to North Carolina?

3. How many years did it take Raleigh to send a ship to check on the second set of colonists?

4. Why was this colony called The Lost Colony?

5. State what you think might have happened to The Lost Colony.

6. Think of a title that would be appropriate for this passage.

• •

Find the quotient when dividing whole numbers.

EXAMPLE:

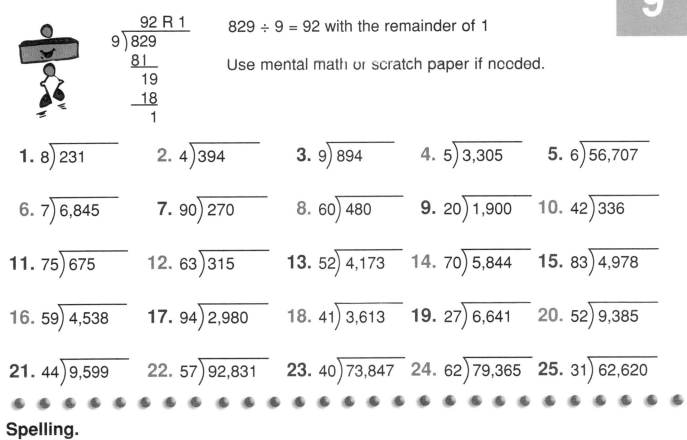

$$9\overline{)829} = 92 \text{ R } 1$$

$829 \div 9 = 92$ with the remainder of 1

Use mental math or scratch paper if needed.

1. $8\overline{)231}$ 2. $4\overline{)394}$ 3. $9\overline{)894}$ 4. $5\overline{)3,305}$ 5. $6\overline{)56,707}$

6. $7\overline{)6,845}$ 7. $90\overline{)270}$ 8. $60\overline{)480}$ 9. $20\overline{)1,900}$ 10. $42\overline{)336}$

11. $75\overline{)675}$ 12. $63\overline{)315}$ 13. $52\overline{)4,173}$ 14. $70\overline{)5,844}$ 15. $83\overline{)4,978}$

16. $59\overline{)4,538}$ 17. $94\overline{)2,980}$ 18. $41\overline{)3,613}$ 19. $27\overline{)6,641}$ 20. $52\overline{)9,385}$

21. $44\overline{)9,599}$ 22. $57\overline{)92,831}$ 23. $40\overline{)73,847}$ 24. $62\overline{)79,365}$ 25. $31\overline{)62,620}$

Spelling.

Find the word that is misspelled in each row and spell it correctly. Use a dictionary if you need help.

1.	refund	remodel	decode	previw	_____
2.	deposet	pretend	deflate	pace	_____
3.	mold	respond	brutel	revise	_____
4.	fiction	grieff	unsafe	equip	_____
5.	transfer	defend	truthful	penlty	_____
6.	prdict	decide	gossip	fragile	_____
7.	beware	precice	porches	capital	_____
8.	leashes	cipher	volt	climack	_____
9.	month	friendly	wrench	businiss	_____
10.	jiant	angle	guest	greet	_____
11.	surgery	magnit	usually	bearish	_____
12.	slogan	gigantck	beast	galley	_____

Day 9

Prefixes. Remember, prefixes are added to the beginning of base words. Add prefixes to these base words. Use as many prefixes as you can with the base words and see how many you can make. Use prefixes <u>mis</u>-, <u>re</u>-, <u>un</u>-, <u>non</u>-, and <u>pre</u>-.

EXAMPLE: view – <u>pre</u>view   <u>re</u>view

Base words:

join	_____	trace	_____
name	_____	heat	_____
spell	_____	cut	_____
treat	_____	turn	_____
stop	_____	read	_____
sure	_____	fit	_____
call	_____	place	_____

Choose one word for each of the prefixes and write a sentence for it.

mis   1. _____

re   2. _____

un   3. _____

non   4. _____

pre   5. _____

Circulatory System. Label the different parts of the heart with the terms listed. Color the side of the heart that has oxygen-rich blood red. Color the side of the heart where the blood is lacking oxygen blue.

- *aorta*
- *left ventricle*
- *tricuspid valve*
- *cardiac septum*
- *left atrium*
- *aortic valve*
- *pulmonary valve*
- *right ventricle*
- *right atrium*
- *bicuspid valve*
- *pulmonary artery*
- *pulmonary vein*

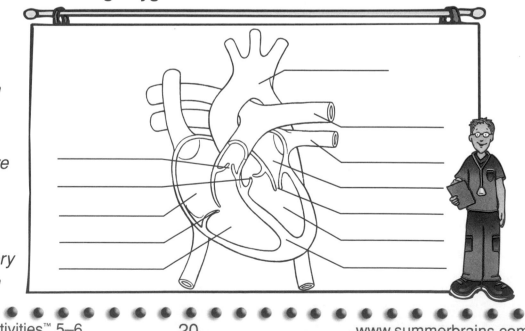

Mixed Practice. Be sure to watch the signs. You can use mental math or scratch paper if needed.

1. 684 ÷ 9 = _____ 2. 356 ÷ 8 = _____ 3. 793 x 27 = _____

4. 469 ÷ 7 = _____ 5. 7,133 ÷ 8 = _____ 6. 4,036 x 9 = _____

7. 143 + 973 = _____ 8. 72,483 + 56,774 = _____

9. 8)9,696 = _____ 10. 63,459 - 21,365 = _____

11. 90)48,713 = _____ 12. 569,040 ÷ 8 = _____

13. 53,907 x 6 = _____ 14. 483 x 175 = _____

15. 763,947 - 244,398 = _____ 16. 45)29,705 = _____

17. 14,008 ÷ 60 = _____ 18. $678.14 + $990.27 = _____

19. 297 x 47 = _____ 20. 3,046 x 70 = _____

21. 34,148 + 95,228 = _____ 22. 49,375 ÷ 71 = _____

23. 573 + 4,935 + 7,340 = _____ 24. 75)566,212 = _____

25. 456,350 ÷ 32 = _____ 26. 3,804 x 43 = _____

Matter. Matter exists in three states: solid, liquid, and gas. Put the following words in the appropriate categories.

butter	lava	oxygen	water
box	dust	ice	radon
milk	juice	nitrogen	vapor

Solid	Liquid	Gas

Water can be in three different states: liquid-water, solid-ice, gas-vapor. See if you can come up with some items in your home that can be in more than one state.

Solid	Liquid	Gas

You have taken two kinds of tests in the past year: <u>essay</u> and <u>objective</u> tests. When you take an <u>essay</u> test you write out the answers. When you take an an <u>objective</u> test you have multiple-choice, true-false, matching, and completion questions. When you take a test, read the directions carefully before you begin. Think about how much time you should take for each question and then begin. Answer the following questions and tell what kind of test they would be on. Also, if the question is from an objective test, write the type of question.

1. Match the words below to their meaning.

equip	confused noise
clatter	to make whiter
penalty	to ask for advice
bleach	furnish
consult	punishment

Kind of test _____   Kind of question_____

2. Write a paragraph about the produce grown in the state where you live.

_____

_____

_____

Kind of test _____   Kind of question _____

3. Fill in the blanks.

   a. Most cars run on a fuel called _____.

   b. _____ is candy made with milk, sugar, chocolate, and butter.

   c. _____ _____ is famous for his animated movies.

   d. This state does not border any other state or nation. It is _____.

   e. A sombrero is a kind of _____.

   Kind of test _____   Kind of question _____

4. Write <u>F</u> for false, <u>T</u> for true.

   a. All mammals live on land. _____

   b. After the Industrial Revolution, many people moved to the cities. _____

   c. Eli Whitney invented the cotton gin. _____

   d. A census worker helps find out how many people live in the United States. _____

   Kind of test _____   Kind of question _____

Multiples and Common Multiples.

Remember: A <u>multiple</u> is a number exactly divisible by another number.
6 12 18 24 30 are multiples of 6.

List 5 or 6 multiples for the following numbers.

1. 5 _____

2. 9 _____

3. 7 _____

4. 2 _____

5. 10 _____

6. 12 _____

7. 3 _____

8. 8 _____

List 3 common multiples for these numbers.

Remember: The common multiples for 2 and 4 are 4, 8, 12, or other "numbers in common."

9. 3 and 4_____

10. 5 and 10 _____

11. 8 and 12 _____

12. 2 and 9_____

13. 4 and 7_____

14. 6 and 8_____

15. 8 and 10 _____

16. 5 and 6_____

17. What is the least common multiple for 2 and 9? _____

18. For 5 and 6? _____ **19.** For 3 and 4? _____ **20.** For 8 and 10? _____

Refusal Skills. Refusal skills help a person say NO to risky behaviors and situations. Here are some refusal skills you can use:

• Say No firmly and clearly.

• Walk away if a person continues to pressure you.

• Suggest an alternative activity.

• Tell an adult you trust if you are continually pressured.

• Explain the consequences.

Read the following situations below. How would you respond to each situation? Use some of the refusal skills listed above.

1. Your friend's older sister has a pack of cigarettes in her bedroom. Your friend dares you to try one.

2. While at the store, you see a video that your really want to watch. A friend suggests you hide the video in your coat and take it home.

3. Your friend didn't study for the test today. He wants you to let him look at your paper during the test.

4. A group of friends tell you that to be in their club, you need to make fun of other students.

Writing Complete Sentences. <u>Remember</u>: A complete sentence expresses a complete thought. If it does not express a complete thought it is called a sentence fragment. A complete sentence needs to tell whom or what the sentence is about and what happened to the whom or what.

Match the sentence fragments to make complete sentences.

1. Folklore is passed	on your head?
2. The early cattle ranchers	escaped from its cage.
3. Jodie rides her	drove their cattle to the market.
4. The snake in the science corner	from generation to generation.
5. Can you balance a book	bike to school most days.

For each of the following, write F if it is a sentence fragment or S if it is a complete sentence.

1. All of my friends like spaghetti. _____

2. Went camping last summer. _____

3. A turkey buzzard is a dark-colored vulture. _____

4. Collects signatures for the P.T.A. _____

5. Answered the most questions. _____

6. Mr. Able turned on the lights. _____

7. Is Dr. Gold going to put? _____

8. Rummy is the name of a card game. _____

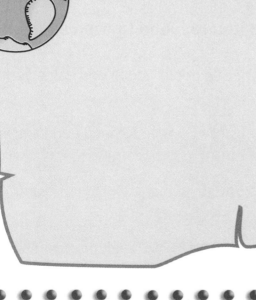

Colonies in the New World.

Many colonists came over by boat to settle in the New World. Make a list of the supplies these adventuresome colonists would need. Write them on the scroll. Try to write as many items as you can!

Analyze the list you made. Circle in red the most important supplies one would need. Underline in blue the supplies that are of medium importance. Cross out in green the supplies that would not be necessary.

Adding and Subtracting with Decimals. <u>Remember:</u> The first step when adding or subtracting decimals is to line up the decimals. If the number of decimal places is not the same, you can attach zeros to the end of a number to make it easier.

EXAMPLE: $3.45 + 5.923 = 3.450$
$$\begin{array}{r} 3.450 \\ + 5.923 \\ \hline 9.373 \end{array}$$

Solve the problems.

1. $18.91 + 11.5 = $ _____
2. $3.806 + 5.29 = $ _____
3. $5.619 + 3.041 = $ _____
4. $76.453 + 82.5 = $ _____
5. $437.7 + 13.906 = $ _____
6. $42.881 + 8.96 = $ _____
7. $49.07 - 36.05 = $ _____
8. $65.007 - 6.3 = $ _____
9. $34.09 - 9.407 = $ _____
10. $185.04 - 165.9 = $ _____
11. $379.76 - 37.435 = $ _____
12. $224.00 - $116.98 = $ _____
13. $49.071 + 23.015 = $ _____
14. $85.089 - 34.12 = $ _____
15. $377.76 + 59.94 = $ _____
16. $365.50 - 54.935 = $ _____

Analogies. Analogies show relationships between words, such as <u>preview</u> is to <u>previewed</u> as <u>decide</u> is to <u>decided</u>, or <u>hear</u> is to <u>ear</u> as <u>talk</u> is to <u>mouth</u>.

Write an analogy for each of the following comparisons.

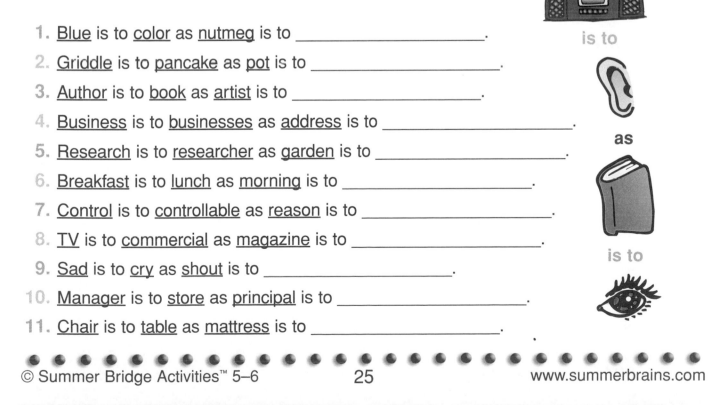

1. <u>Blue</u> is to <u>color</u> as <u>nutmeg</u> is to _____.
2. <u>Griddle</u> is to <u>pancake</u> as <u>pot</u> is to _____.
3. <u>Author</u> is to <u>book</u> as <u>artist</u> is to _____.
4. <u>Business</u> is to <u>businesses</u> as <u>address</u> is to _____.
5. <u>Research</u> is to <u>researcher</u> as <u>garden</u> is to _____.
6. <u>Breakfast</u> is to <u>lunch</u> as <u>morning</u> is to _____.
7. <u>Control</u> is to <u>controllable</u> as <u>reason</u> is to _____.
8. <u>TV</u> is to <u>commercial</u> as <u>magazine</u> is to _____.
9. <u>Sad</u> is to <u>cry</u> as <u>shout</u> is to _____.
10. <u>Manager</u> is to <u>store</u> as <u>principal</u> is to _____.
11. <u>Chair</u> is to <u>table</u> as <u>mattress</u> is to _____.

Complete Subjects and Predicates. The subject tells what or whom the sentence is about. The predicate tells about the subject.

Listed below are some complete predicates. Write a complete subject to go with them.

1. _____ know how to operate the computers.

2. _____ fascinated Megan.

3. _____ misplaced his new pocket knife.

4. _____ need water.

5. _____ collapsed suddenly.

6. _____ crashed into the ditch.

Listed below are some complete subjects. Write a complete predicate to go with them.

7. The package _____.

8. A team of horses _____.

9. The famous actor _____.

10. Sarah and Julie _____.

11. Anthills _____.

12. Nobody _____.

Research the settling of the Puritans and Pilgrims in the New World. Fill in the Venn diagram with their similarities and differences.

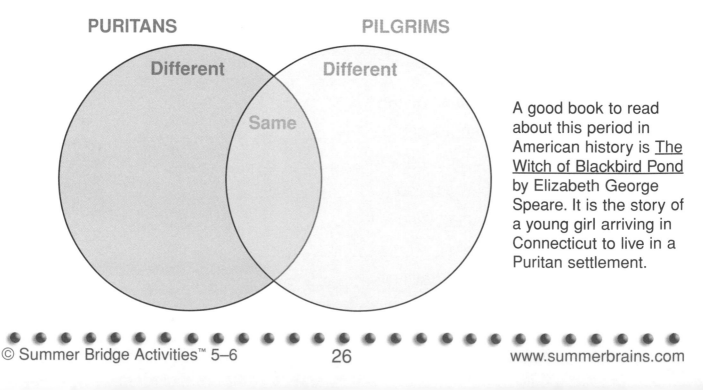

PURITANS   PILGRIMS

Different   Different

Same

A good book to read about this period in American history is <u>The Witch of Blackbird Pond</u> by Elizabeth George Speare. It is the story of a young girl arriving in Connecticut to live in a Puritan settlement.

Multiplying Whole Numbers and Decimals. Remember to put the decimal point in the correct place in the product.

Day 13

| 1. | 0.12
x 6 | 2. | 0.08
x 7 | 3. | 4.6
x 3 | 4. | 5.05
x 8 | 5. | 2.9
x 5 | 6. | 2.71
x 4 |

| 7. | 6.5
x 13 | 8. | 1.906
x 28 | 9. | 7.0216
x 52 | 10. | 6.65
x 77 | 11. | 5.364
x 93 | 12. | 0.0352
x 49 |

| 13. | 3.613
x 84 | 14. | 40.35
x 38 | 15. | 7.735
x 47 | 16. | 9.546
x 68 | 17. | 7.263
x 87 | 18. | 9.634
x 54 |

| 19. | 359.073
x 24 | 20. | 5.9081
x 71 | 21. | 12.504
x 99 | 22. | 8.709
x 56 | 23. | 27.035
x 93 | 24. | 7.893
x 32 |

25. Jan works delivering pizza and gets paid $37.40 a night. She works 23 nights each month. How much does Jan earn each month? _____

26. Jake works at a grocery store. He gets paid $8.65 an hour for each hour he works. He usually works 37 hours a week. How much does he earn in a week? How much would he earn in a 4 weeks? _____

Chemical Change. With chemical change, two or more substances are combined to form a completely new substance. For example, iron plus oxygen makes rust. Physical change occurs when a substance changes but no new substance is formed (e.g., water to ice).

Read the list below. Determine if a physical change and/or chemical change has occurred. Then come up with some of your own ideas!

Activity	Physical Change	Chemical Change	Own Ideas
Chopping wood			
Baking cookies			
Burning wood			
Painting a door			
Making ice cubes			
Cutting tomatoes			
Making ice cream			

Day 13

Two Kinds of Verbs: Action Verbs and State-of-Being Verbs.

Action verbs tell about an action you can see (<u>ran</u>) or an action you cannot see (<u>hear</u>).

State-of-being verbs tell what something or someone is (<u>is</u>, <u>are</u>, <u>am</u>, <u>appear</u>, <u>look</u>, etc.).

    Make a design by coloring the action verbs orange and the state-of-being verbs green. Color the empty spaces any color you like, except orange or green.

			walk	has been			
			sound	call			
			dance	are			
			will be	sit			
	caught		laugh	been		honked	
			smell	plays			
see			wore	feel			seem
	being		will	gather		were	
		dive	jump	won	dive		
asking	rolled	wiggled	be	is	wiggled	read	eat
writing	cheer	buzzing	are	am	buzzing	barking	selling
		climbs	skiing	paint	cry		
	become		built	have been		was	
remain			has	carried			has had
			bake	felt			
	practice		became	blew		clapped	
			watched	wants			
			have	mopped			
			cooking	had			
			had been	hit			

Measuring with Metrics.

1 centimeter = 10 millimeters

1 decimeter = 10 centimeters

1 decimeter = 100 millimeters

1 meter = 10 decimeters

1 meter = 100 centimeters

1 meter = 1,000 millimeters

1 kilometer = 1,000 meters

Estimate and then measure the following using the metric system. If you need a metric ruler, there is one in the back of this book.

	Estimation	Measurement (Use more than one term of measurement.)
a book		
toaster		
width of a drawer		
your little finger		
a can of soup		
a necklace		
a spatula		
an eraser		
bathroom floor		
garbage can		
flashlight		
Choose things that you would like to measure.		

Day 14

Pronunciation and Spelling.

Do you remember that **g** and **c** both have a hard and soft sound? **G** as in su**g**ar (hard) and **g** as in **g**iant (soft), **c** as in **c**amel (hard) and **c** as in **c**ity (soft). In the first column of blanks, put **S** or **H** after each word to tell if the **c** or **g** is soft or hard. In the second column, match the hard or soft **c** and **g** words to the word or words that mean about the same.

EXAMPLE:

1. geyser	H	attracting		
2. music		writing instrument		
3. cyclone		produce		
4. generate		schedule		
5. slogan		operation		
6. calico		melody, harmony		
7. pencil		violent contact		
8. regulate		grain		
9. picture		refusal, not positive		
10. magnet		painting		
11. country		hot spring	1	
12. gelatin		motto		
13. pillage		without pretense		
14. process		recommendation		
15. surgery		messenger		
16. against		jelly-like substance		
17. collide		territory/land		
18. angel		hurricane		
19. calendar		adjust		
20. sincere		illusions		
21. magic		cloth		
22. cereal		transform		
23. negative		in contact with		
24. advice		looting		

Equal Metric Measures. Use the metric measure information on page 29 if you need help to do this activity.

Change each measurement to millimeters.

1. 25 cm   2. 3 m   3. 9 dm   4. 10 dm   5. 12 m   6. 17 cm

_____mm   _____mm   _____mm   _____mm   _____mm   _____mm

Change each measurement to centimeters.

7. 8 m   8. 50 mm   9. 100 m   10. 4 km   11. 400 mm   12. 5 km

_____cm   _____cm   _____cm   _____cm   _____cm   _____cm

Use greater than (>), less than (<), and equal (=) signs.

13. 37 m ☐ 370 cm   14. 51 m ☐ 5 dm   15. 216 cm ☐ 216 mm

16. 40 cm ☐ 400 mm   17. 5 m ☐ 15 km   18. 80 km ☐ 80,000 m

An Experiment with Chemical and Physical Change.

Materials: 5 pennies, 1 nickel, 1 dime, and 1 quarter
salt
vinegar, water, milk
aluminum foil

Directions: Fold foil into a pan with sides turned up.
Place coins in pan.
Pour salt (about 1 tsp.) over coins.
Pour vinegar over each coin.
Observe.

Questions:

1. What happened to each coin?

2. Why did this happen?

3. Predict what would happen if you did this experiment with water or milk.

   Water:

   Milk:

4. Repeat the experiment with the water and milk.

5. Was your prediction right?

6. Which experiment demonstrates chemical change?

   Which experiment demonstrates physical change?

7. Experiment with different liquids to determine if they cause a physical or chemical change.

Day 15

The six sentences below tell the sequence of events in a story. They are in order. Write a story to go with them. Make sure the events in your story are in this order. Give your story a title. Write in cursive.

1. On Saturday, Mom and I went to a professional basketball game.
2. We rode the crowded subway to the game.
3. The Coliseum was even more crowded than the subway.
4. Mom and I traded seats because I couldn't see very well!
5. We both wanted our home team to win.
6. Because we were so tired after the game, we took a taxi home.

Title: _____

_____

_____

_____

_____

_____

_____

_____

_____

_____

_____

_____

_____

_____

_____

_____

_____

_____

_____

_____

Words to Sound, Read, and Spell

abandon	biography	criminal	factories
abscess	bleating	customs	failure
abuse	boastful	data	famous
acceptance	bracing	deadline	fearsome
accompany	brash	decree	feat
adapted	brazen	defied	flared
affection	brilliant	democracy	flax
agility	busily	desert	forehand
agriculture	canoeist	desolate	foresee
ailing	capable	desolation	formal
alias	caper	despairingly	founded
allergy	captivity	destruction	frantic
amazing	caravan	determine	frequently
ancestors	carpentry	determined	fret
angrily	casual	dictionary	frightening
animation	changeable	diggings	frustration
animator	characteristic	dignity	generators
aphids	circulate	directory	generosity
appalled	circulation	disaster	gladden
apprenticed	citrus	discipline	gloomily
approaches	claim	dismally	gopher
assassinate	clownish	displeasure	governor
assurance	clues	distribution	grief-stricken
asterisk	coastline	doer	groves
astonishing	collapsed	doubtful	guarantee
astounded	colony	embarrassing	hazel
astrology	comedian	encyclopedia	headquarters
astronaut	companionship	endear	hemisphere
atmosphere	compliment	engineers	heroine
attracted	conceited	enthusiasm	hoist
audition	concoctions	entrap	homogenized
autobiography	confidence	environment	horizon
autograph	confidential	equator	humorous
automatic	conquer	escapade	hydrant
awaken	conquered	escort	hydroplane
awestruck	constantly	evaporation	idioms
awkwardness	contacts	excavation	illusion
bachelor	convicted	excellent	impatient
bail	convinced	excitement	improvement
barren	convincing	expanse	inattention
bellowing	cowering	expedition	incident
bicyclist	crazily	experienced	inconsiderate
billow	credit	explanation	independence

Words to Sound, Read, and Spell

indignant	nuisance	reflect	tenants
indignantly	obliged	refuge	therapist
information	obvious	relieved	thermometer
inhabited	occasionally	repel	thought
inspired	occupation	reservoir	thoughtless
instincts	opportunity	respect	threat
insulated	ordeal	respectfully	threatened
insulation	organs	retrieve	tilted
intelligent	ostrich	revived	tolerance
intended	outlandish	rhinoceros	tonsils
intention	overcoming	ridiculous	torrents
interest	overcrowded	rouse	touchy
interlock	panel	rugged	traditions
irrigated	particular	sarcastically	transplanting
kennel	personification	schemed	trespass
larvae	personal	scholar	trespassing
laughingstock	personnel	scornfully	trigger
logical	phantom	script	triumph
loitering	photograph	scriptwriter	typist
loyal	physical	self-praising	unappreciative
manufacturing	pollution	sharpened	unattainable
measurement	popularity	shelter	unchecked
merchant	porcupine	shirker	unconscious
method	praise	solemnly	undertow
methods	prey	solution	unoccupied
microscope	profit	specialists	urge
migration	program	species	venture
migratory	progress	spirits	vessel
mime	prosper	spunk	vicinity
misfortune	prosperity	stalked	victorious
mistrustful	prosperous	starvation	violent
momentous	protest	stethoscope	virus
mountainous	purchase	stock	volts
narration	radar	stunned	wheeze
narrator	rarely	suspicious	whimsical
nimbleness	ravage	swap	whisking
nitrogen	ravine	swindled	wicker
noise	reconstruct	sympathetic	wither
notebook	recovered	telephone	worthless
notice	recovery	tempered	

Summer Bridge Activities™

Incentive Contract Calendar

Month _____

My parents and I decided that if I complete 20 days of
Summer Bridge Activities™ and read _____ minutes a day,
my incentive/reward will be:

_____

Child's Signature _____
Parent's Signature _____

Day 1   📖 ⭐ ____   Day 11   📖 ⭐ ____

Day 2   📖 ⭐ ____   Day 12   📖 ⭐ ____

Day 3   📖 ⭐ ____   Day 13   📖 ⭐ ____

Day 4   📖 ⭐ ____   Day 14   📖 ⭐ ____

Day 5   📖 ⭐ ____   Day 15   📖 ⭐ ____

Day 6   📖 ⭐ ____   Day 16   📖 ⭐ ____

Day 7   📖 ⭐ ____   Day 17   📖 ⭐ ____

Day 8   📖 ⭐ ____   Day 18   📖 ⭐ ____

Day 9   📖 ⭐ ____   Day 19   📖 ⭐ ____

Day 10   📖 ⭐ ____   Day 20   📖 ⭐ ____

Child: Color the ⭐ for daily activities completed.
Color the 📖 for daily reading completed.

Parent: Initial the _____ for daily activities and reading
your child completes.

Fun Activity Ideas to Go Along with the Second Section!

1. Get a piece of paper that is as long and as wide as you are. Lie down on it and have someone outline you with a marker. Then get up and color in the details—eyes, ears, mouth, clothes, arms, hands, etc.

2. Make a "Happy Birthday" card for your friend who is celebrating a birthday soon and give it to your friend on his or her special day.

3. Invite your friends over for popcorn and vote on your favorite movie. Watch it, then take parts and act it out in your own way.

4. Visit the library and attend story time.

5. With bright colored markers, draw a picture of your favorite place to go. Paste it to a piece of posterboard and cut it into pieces for a jigsaw puzzle.

6. Give your dog a bath, or ask your neighbor or friend if you can give their dog a bath.

7. Pack a lunch and go to the park.

8. Roast marshmallows over a fire or barbecue.

9. Draw the shape of your state and put a star where you live. Include a drawing of the state flower, motto, and bird.

10. Make a batch of cookies and take them to a sick friend, neighbor, or relative.

11. Plant some flower or vegetable seeds in a pot and watch them grow.

12. Organize an earthquake or fire drill for your family.

13. Pick one of your favorite foods and learn how to make it.

14. Write a poem that rhymes.

15. Get your neighborhood friends together and make a card of appreciation for the firefighters closest to you. Then all of you deliver the card and take a tour of the fire station.

16. Prepare a clean bed for your pet.

17. Make a kite and fly it.

18. Read to younger children in your family or neighborhood.

19. Invent a new game and play it with your friends.

20. Surprise a family member with breakfast in bed.

Negative and Positive Numbers.

A negative number has a quantity less than zero. A positive number, on the other hand, is a number greater than zero.

Illustrate and/or explain positive and negative numbers using a number line, a countdown at Cape Canaveral, and a thermometer.

Write a story problem to go with one of the illustrations and/or explanations you used above.

Facts from the Colonies in the 1600s and 1700s.

The Southern Colonies. From the list below, choose the word that means almost the same as the underlined word or phrase in the sentences.

indigo	indentured servants	proprietor
slaves	cash crops	

_____ 1. George Calvert was the first <u>owner</u> of a colony.

_____ 2. A lot of Southern farmers grew <u>crops that they could sell for money</u>.

_____ 3. In the 1740s, Eliza Lucas developed <u>a blue dye made from a plant</u>.

_____ 4. Originally, <u>people who agreed to work five or seven years to pay their passage to America</u> labored on Southern farms. These people were eventually replaced by <u>people captured from Africa who were forced to work for nothng</u>.

The Middle Colonies. Circle all the colonies considered to be the Middle Colonies.

New Jersey	Georgia	Rhode Island
Delaware	New York	Pennsylvania

The New England Colonies. Circle the correct answer to complete each statement.

1. A person who wanted to purify the church was called a
   a. Programmer   **b.** Puritan   **c.** Convert
2. A person whose expertise is shipbuilding is called a
   a. carpenter   **b.** cartwright   **c.** shipwright
3. Usually in the center of town was a grassy area called a
   a. field   **b.** common   **c.** meadow

Word Meanings.
Fill in the blanks from the word list below.

inland	suspicious	desert	escorts	conduct
frank	allergy	knead	margin	impression
inlets	stethoscope	appalled	subscribe	owing

1. All the _____ around the lake were crowded with boats.

2. Everyone in the class had a chance to listen to my heart through the _____.

3. The night watchman became _____ of the two men parked near the back door of the building.

4. We _____ to at least four different newspapers.

5. Did you leave a _____ on both sides of your paper?

6. Ted spends too much money. He is always _____ for something.

7. She was _____ in telling me she did not like my new dress.

8. Use both hands when you _____ the bread dough.

9. My _____ acts up every time I go to the theater because I'm allergic to perfume.

10. Toby's _____ at the party was rude and inexcusable.

Here is a list of words you should know how to spell. Put the words in alphabetical order.

stranger	pottery	individual	journey	rely
toiletry	reunite	robbery	adventure	delay
subscription	alleys	cemetery	identify	unnecessary
announcement	celery	victorious	enemy	grocery
hurried	deciding	toil	misplaced	

1. _____

2. _____

3. _____

4. _____

5. _____

6. _____

7. _____

8. _____

9. _____

10. _____

11. _____

12. _____

13. _____

14. _____

15. _____

16. _____

17. _____

18. _____

19. _____

20. _____

21. _____

22. _____

23. _____

24. _____

Deposits and Deductions.

Amanda opened a checking account on May 15th with $500.25. On May 31st she deposited another $496.80. On June 4th she withdrew $145.00 to buy a bicycle. On June 15th she deposited $435.20. On June 30th she deposited $600.00. On July 1st she withdrew $400.00 to go to Camp Rockland, plus she also needed $63.00 for a sleeping bag. On July 15th she deposited $110.00. On July 24th she withdrew $900.00 to buy a compact TV with a built-in VCR.

Use the chart below to record Amanda's checking account record.

DATE	DEPOSITED	WITHDREW	TOTAL $
May 15	$500.25		$500.25
May 31			
June 4			
June 15			
June 30			
July 1			
July 15			
July 24			

Remember, when you deposit money you add, and when you withdraw money you subtract.

Use Amanda's checking account record to graph the total dollar amounts.

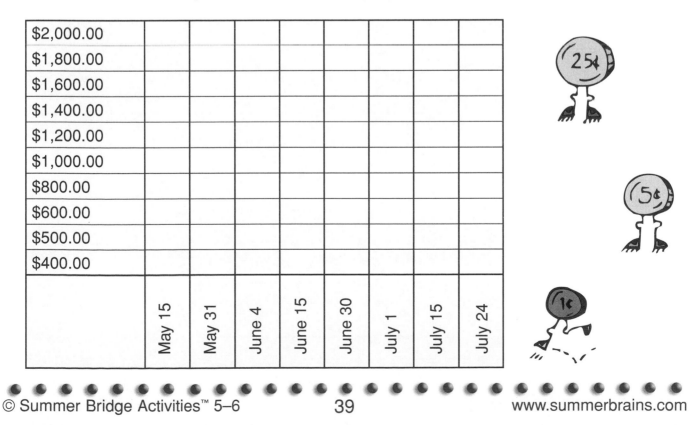

	May 15	May 31	June 4	June 15	June 30	July 1	July 15	July 24
$2,000.00								
$1,800.00								
$1,600.00								
$1,400.00								
$1,200.00								
$1,000.00								
$800.00								
$600.00								
$500.00								
$400.00								

Day 2

Topic Sentences.
Remember: The topic sentence expresses the main idea of the paragraph. Underline the topic sentences of these paragraphs.

1. The beginning of his life was very unusual. He was born in Texas into a large family. He fell out of a covered wagon and was not missed for many days because he had so many brothers and sisters. His parents couldn't find him, so he was raised by coyotes. He thought he was a coyote until he discovered he didn't have four feet and a tail.

2. Nuclear energy is the most awesome power that exists. It produces tremendous heat and light. It has been used to produce hydrogen and atomic bombs. It results from changes in the core of atoms. One important use of nuclear energy is in producing electricity. Scientists believe that if it were fully developed, nuclear energy could produce all the world's electricity for millions of years.

Now it's your turn! Write a topic sentence for these two paragraphs. Try to make it interesting so others will want to read the paragraph.

3. _____
They are among the world's oldest and largest living things. Some are thousands of years old and over 200 feet tall. Some of them are about 100 feet around at the base. You can see them in California and Oregon. They are the giant sequoia and redwood trees.

4. _____
It ranges from great works like Michelangelo's carvings to African masks. A piece of sculpture can be very large, like the Statue of Liberty, or small enough to sit on a table or hold in your hand. It has always played an important part in the history of man. Sculpture is an excellent way to express your own ideas and feelings.

Fill in the vowels for these spelling words. Then write each word three times in cursive.

1. r h __ n __ c __ r __ s _____ _____ _____

2. c h __ m __ c __ l _____ _____ _____

3. s t __ m __ c h _____ _____ _____

4. r h __ b __ r b _____ _____ _____

5. s c h __ l __ s t __ c _____ _____ _____

6. r h __ t h m _____ _____ _____

7. l __ g g __ g __ _____ _____ _____

8. r __ m __ __ n d __ r _____ _____ _____

9. __ m __ t t __ d _____ _____ _____

10. m __ l __ t __ r __ _____ _____ _____

Fractions. Remember: When talking about fractions, the denominator names the number of equal parts of a whole amount, and the numerator names the number of parts being taken from the whole.

Write the fraction that tells what part is shaded.

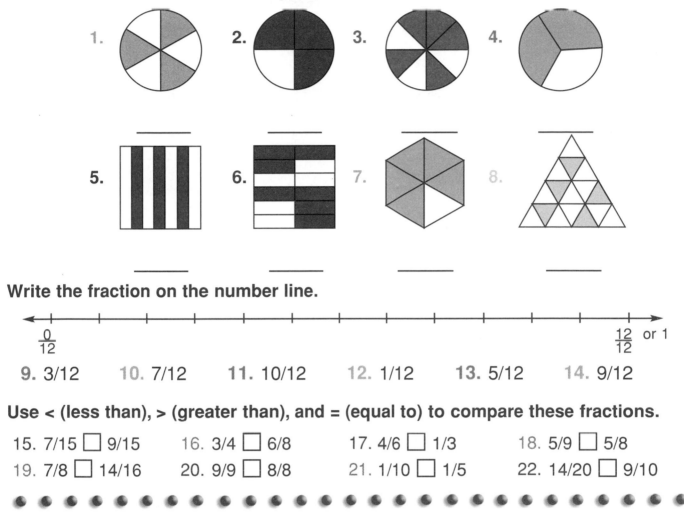

1.   2.   3.   4.

5.   6.   7.   8.

Write the fraction on the number line.

$\frac{0}{12}$ $\frac{12}{12}$ or 1

9. 3/12   10. 7/12   11. 10/12   12. 1/12   13. 5/12   14. 9/12

Use < (less than), > (greater than), and = (equal to) to compare these fractions.

15. 7/15 ☐ 9/15   16. 3/4 ☐ 6/8   17. 4/6 ☐ 1/3   18. 5/9 ☐ 5/8

19. 7/8 ☐ 14/16   20. 9/9 ☐ 8/8   21. 1/10 ☐ 1/5   22. 14/20 ☐ 9/10

1700s Communication. Improved roads, mail service, and newspapers improved communication between the Colonies in the 1700s. Fill in the chart below. List some things that have helped present-day communications. Predict what types of communication we might have in the next one hundred years.

1700s	Present Day	100 Years
mail service		
improved roads for coaches		
newspapers		

Day 3

Read a book or story of your choice and do the following.

1. Write the names of four characters and tell why they were important to the story.

   a. _____

   b. _____

   c. _____

   d. _____

2. What are some important details or events of the story you read? List at least three.

   a. _____

   b. _____

   c. _____

   d. _____

3. How did the story end?

4. Would you like it to end differently? If so, how would you have it end?

Plate Tectonics. Circle the seven major plates of the earth's surface. On the world map below, divide the earth into the seven plates. See if you can label them correctly. Check the answers in the back to see how close you came!

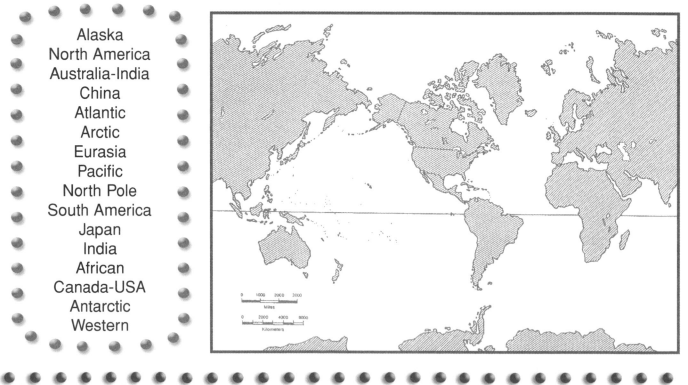

Alaska
North America
Australia-India
China
Atlantic
Arctic
Eurasia
Pacific
North Pole
South America
Japan
India
African
Canada-USA
Antarctic
Western

Divide to find the fraction of a number.

1. 1/2 of 10 = _____ 2. 1/8 of 24 = _____ 3. 1/6 of 48 = _____ 4. 1/5 of 45 = _____

5. 1/4 of 32 = _____ 6. 1/3 of 60 = _____ 7. 1/7 of 56 = _____ 8. 1/12 of 36 = _____

Divide to find the equivalent fractions.

9. $\frac{3}{4} = \frac{\_}{8}$ 10. $\frac{5}{8} = \frac{\_}{16}$ 11. $\frac{10}{25} = \frac{2}{\_}$ 12. $\frac{4}{9} = \frac{\_}{36}$

13. $\frac{7}{12} = \frac{28}{\_}$ 14. $\frac{6}{6} = \frac{12}{\_}$ 15. $\frac{3}{4} = \frac{\_}{20}$ 16. $\frac{7}{15} = \frac{\_}{45}$

Multiply to find the equivalent fractions.

17. $\frac{9}{12} = \frac{36}{\_}$ 18. $\frac{2}{3} = \frac{10}{\_}$ 19. $\frac{3}{10} = \frac{18}{\_}$ 20. $\frac{1}{3} = \frac{3}{\_}$

21. $\frac{5}{8} = \frac{\_}{72}$ 22. $\frac{2}{5} = \frac{8}{\_}$ 23. $\frac{5}{12} = \frac{\_}{36}$ 24. $\frac{11}{24} = \frac{11}{\_}$

Reduce the fractions to the lowest terms that make whole or mixed numbers.

25. $\frac{56}{6} =$ 26. $\frac{14}{4} =$ 27. $\frac{38}{8} =$ 28. $\frac{51}{8} =$

29. $\frac{17}{2} =$ 30. $\frac{35}{5} =$ 31. $\frac{14}{6} =$ 32. $\frac{10}{8} =$

Health—Communicable Diseases. Answer T for true or F for false to the following statements. If false, correct the sentence so it is true.

_____ 1. Pathogens are people who build roads.

_____ 2. Communicable diseases are spread by contact with an infected person.

_____ 3. The common cold, flu, and sore throat are considered communicable diseases.

_____ 4. Pathogens cannot spread by touch or through the air.

_____ 5. Washing hands does not reduce the risk of pathogens entering the body.

_____ 6. Medicines that kill some pathogens are called antibiotics.

Imagine you are principal of your school. As principal, you must write some rules that would help the school be free from the spread of pathogens that can cause communicable diseases. Write five rules you would enforce.

Day 4

Main Verbs and Helping Verbs. **Remember:** The verb in a sentence may be one word or a few words. Some words can be either a helping verb or a main verb. Underline the complete verb in these sentences.

EXAMPLE: Jack <u>was</u> in town. Or, Jack <u>was working</u> in town.

1. Joseph is walking to the park with his friends.

2. My mother has been working at Sears for many years.

3. I might have called if I had known you were home.

4. The snowstorm yesterday buried all the beautiful flowers.

5. Jim does enjoy sports.

6. Mark is playing outdoors with Sam.

7. David does his homework every day.

8. Misty and Courtney are watching television.

9. The hikers were thirsty and hungry.

10. I have been thinking about the play all day.

Liberty Bell. Read the following report on the Liberty Bell and correct the ten facts that are inaccurate.

The Liberty Bell was rung at noon on July 4, 1776, to announce the adoption and signing of the Bill of Rights. Its inscription, "Proclaim Liberty throughout all the land unto all the inhabitants thereof," is from Shakespeare (1564–1616). The bell originally had a different name. It was first called Independence Bell. The province of Pennsylvania paid about $300 for it in 1752. The Liberty Bell weighs more than 2,080 tons. The Liberty Bell was cast in Spain. It broke in ringing after its arrival and was recast in New York City from the same metal but with a different inscription in 1753. It rang at each successive anniversary of the Adoption of the Declaration of Independence until 1935. The Liberty Bell is no longer rung, since it broke, but it has been struck on special occasions. On June 6, 1944, when the Allied forces landed in France, Philadelphia officials struck the bell. pecial sound equipment picked up the tone and broadcast it to all parts of the United States. Officials rang a larger bell in the steeple of Independence Hall to announce America's entry into World War III.

Corrections:

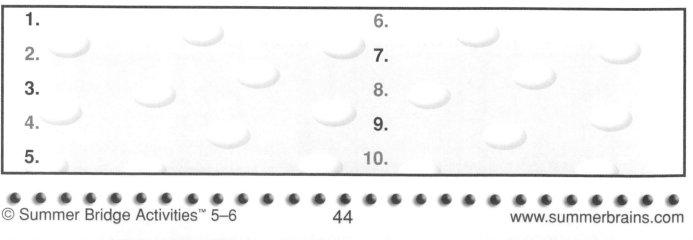

1.	6.
2.	7.
3.	8.
4.	9.
5.	10.

Mixed Practice.
Estimate first, then solve the problem to see how close you got.

EXAMPLE:

		Est.							
1.	6,525	7,000	**2.**	1,236	**3.**	74,652	**4.**	28,746
	3,910	4,000		4,253		75,843		93,009
	+2,335	2,000		+7,237		+18,284		+88,537

actual __12,770__

estimate __13,000__ 13,000

5. 365,244	**6.** 866,533	**7.** 904,568	**8.** 350,859
-79,087	-278,184	-578,179	-126,388

actual _____

estimate _____

9. 533	**10.** 975	**11.** 4,675	**12.** 342,250
x 24	x 53	x 85	x 27

actual _____

estimate _____

13. 24)164	**14.** 80)286	**15.** 62)190	**16.** 73)1,494

actual _____

estimate _____

George Washington. Below are some sentences about our first president, George Washington. Read the sentences and put them in the correct chronological order.

_____ When his father died in 1743, Washington went to live on a plantation known as Mount Vernon.

_____ George Washington was born in 1732 in Virginia.

_____ Washington married Martha Dandridge Custis in 1759.

_____ After the Revolutionary War, Washington was elected first president of the United States in 1789.

_____ During his childhood years, Washington enjoyed reading about battles and war heroes.

_____ In 1758 Washington became a member of the Virginia House of Burgesses.

_____ George Washington died in 1799.

_____ Beginning his military career at age 21, Washington served in the French and Indian War from 1754–1758.

_____ During the Revolutionary War, Washington won victories at Trenton in 1776 and Yorktown in 1778.

_____ Washington believed America needed independence from England. In 1778, he was chosen to lead the Continental Army against the British soldiers.

"Washington" is the name of our nation's capital, a state, thirty-one counties and at least sixteen cities. Why do you think so many places are named after George Washington?

Day 5

Syllables. Write your telephone number down the side of the paper. Include your area code. For each digit, write a word that has that number of syllables. Look in the dictionary for help. If you have numerals over 5 you can use two words to total the number. If your phone number has a zero, leave the line blank.

_____ _____

_____ _____

_____ _____

_____ _____

_____ _____

_____ _____

_____ _____

_____ _____

_____ _____

_____ _____

The following words are names of birds. Some are water birds, some are land birds, and some are tropical birds. Some can't even fly!

If you want to be a bird-watcher, you will need to know the names of birds. Unscramble these words and you will be on your way! The first letter is underlined.

1. aayrcn _____
2. wiik _____
3. dirnaalc _____
4. eonhr _____
5. rlekelid _____
6. unpiegn _____
7. hgldinocf _____
8. hbdrmuimgni _____
9. onol _____
10. idnmcgkriob _____

11. nacuot _____
12. icosrht _____
13. dkheaciec _____
14. nfoacl _____
15. tsnahape _____
16. peatreak _____
17. geela _____
18. maiofgln _____
19. prworas _____
20. elehovsr _____

Grocery Store Estimation in Weight and Cost.

Before you go to the grocery store, estimate how much you think certain produce will weigh. Make a chart showing your results; then go to the grocery store and actually weigh the produce. Chart these results. <u>Remember</u>: Most scales in the United States will be in pounds and ounces, whereas other countries use grams and kilograms.

EXAMPLE:

produce	estimated weight	actual weight	estimated cost	actual cost
6 apples	3 pounds	2 pounds 3 oz	$3.00	$3.15

Precursors to the Revolutionary War. Answer the following questions. Use the time line.

1754	1763	1765	1770	1773	1774	1775
French and Indian War	King George III gives proclamation to limit western settlement	Stamp Act	Boston Massacre	Boston Tea Party	Intolerable Acts	Battles fought at Lexington and Concord

1. How many years after the French and Indian War did the Boston Massacre occur? _____

2. Which events occurred in Boston? _____, _____

3. Which occurred first—the Stamp Act or the Intolerable Acts? How many years are there between these events? _____, _____

4. Choose four events on the time line. Draw and color four pictures in the rectangles below that show the sequence of those events.

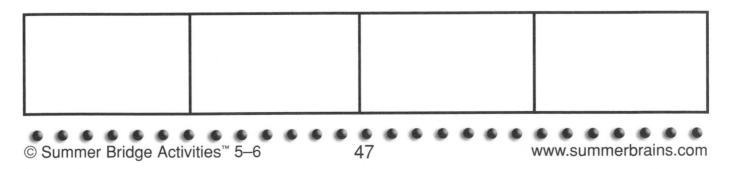

Day 6

Verbs. Circle the correct form of the _be_ verb.

1. I (be, am) guessing the number of pennies in the jar.
2. What (is, be) your favorite month of the year?
3. The workmen (been, were) repairing the road in front of our house.
4. Carla (was, were) laughing very loud.
5. (Is, Are) you the team leader?
6. My Uncle Clint (been, has been, have been) an astronaut, an explorer, and is now a teacher.
7. The haunted house (is being, are being) torn down.
8. We (be, will be) playing in the orchestra on Saturday night.

Now write a sentence for each of these words. Make sure your sentences are different from the ones above.

9. were _____

10. has been _____

11. was being _____

12. are _____

Plate Movement. Match the type of plate boundary with the correct synonyms and definitions.

<u>Synonyms</u>	<u>Definitions</u>
1. sliding	**a.** plates push against each other
2. spreading	**b.** plates move away from each other
3. colliding	**c.** plates slide by each other

<u>Synonyms</u>	<u>Definitions</u>	<u>Type of Plate Boundary</u>
_____	_____	divergent boundary
_____	_____	convergent boundary
_____	_____	transform boundary

Look at the pictures below. Determine which picture represents each type of plate boundary listed above.

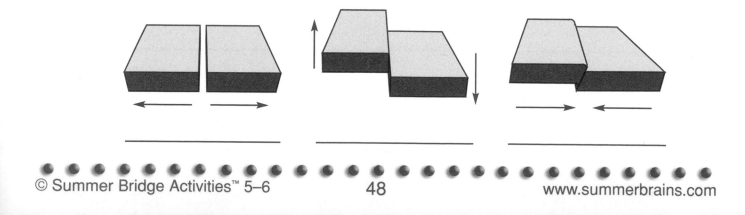

_____   _____   _____

Understanding Geometric Lines. Match the terms with their definitions.

_____ segment

_____ ray

_____ angles

_____ perpendicular lines

_____ parallel lines

_____ congruent

_____ symmetric

_____ congruent segments

_____ circumference

_____ radius

_____ diameter

_____ AB or BA

a. A figure that can be folded and both parts fit perfectly.

b. Lines that never meet.

c. Has an end point or a starting point and can go from there in one direction.

d. A part of a line that can be named by its endpoints.

e. Lines that intersect to form right angles of 90 degrees.

f. Rays with the same endpoint.

g. Ways of labeling endpoints on a segment.

h. Figures having the same shape and size.

i. Segment that passes through the center of a circle and has both endpoints on the circle.

j. A line connecting the center of a circle to a point on the outside of a circle.

k. The distance around a circle.

l. Have equal lengths.

Illustrate each of these geometric terms.

1. segment

2. ray

3. angle

4. perpendicular lines

5. parallel lines

6. congruent

7. symmetric

8. congruent segments

9. circumference

10. radius

11. diameter

12. AB or BA

Fill in the blanks. Writing is a process of steps.

Step one:	Prewriting should include these activities: _____ ideas that you want to write about, _____ a topic, _____ ideas, and _____ ideas.
Step two:	Write some paragraphs about your topic.
Step three:	Kinds of information you can include about the topic are _____, _____, _____, _____, and _____.
Step four:	Describe things about the topic in the _____ order.
Step five:	Proofread and check for mistakes in _____, _____, and _____.
Step six:	Rewrite and _____.

Read this part of the Declaration of Independence and answer the questions below.

We hold these truths to be self-evident, that all men are created equal, that they are endowed by their Creator with certain unalienable Rights, that among these are Life, Liberty and the pursuit of Happiness.

That to secure these rights, Governments are instituted among Men, deriving their just powers from the consent of the governed.

That whenever any Form of Government becomes destructive of these ends, it is the Right of the People to alter or to abolish it, and to institute new Government, laying its foundation on such principles and organizing its powers in such form, as to them shall seem most likely to effect their Safety and Happiness.

1. What are the basic rights of all people in accordance to the Declaration of Independence?

2. Why are governments "instituted," or created?

3. If people feel the government is not acting in their best interest, what should they do?

4. On what principles will the new American government be founded?

5. Draw and color a flag below that expresses the feelings and beliefs of the Declaration of Independence.

Earth's Magnetic Field. Read the following passage and answer the questions below.

The earth is like a huge magnet. It has a magnetic field. Its magnetism is the strongest at the North and South Poles. When rock forms, any magnetic particles will align themselves with the earth's magnetic field. They will point towards either the North or South Poles. There are some rocks that do not point to the current North and South Poles. Scientists conclude that either the North and South Poles have moved, or the rocks themselves have moved since they were formed. Most feel the rocks and continents have moved. Geologists use this information to determine how the continents have moved over time.

1. Why is the earth compared to a magnet?

2. Where are the earth's strongest points of magnetism?

3. How can geologists study the movements of the continents?

4. How might the magnetism of the earth affect a compass?

5. What would happen to a ship and its compass if the earth's magnetic strong area became the western part of the earth and NOT the North Pole?

Find the Perimeter. <u>Remember</u>: To find the perimeter, you have to add the lengths of each side.

15 in.

8 in.   8 in.

15 in.

1. _____ inches

4 cm

4 cm   4 cm

4 cm   4 cm

4 cm

2. _____ centimeters

5 yd.

4 yd.   4 yd.

8 yd.

3. _____ yards

26 m   26 m

36 m   22 m

4. _____ meters

17 ft.

3 ft.

3 ft.

20 ft.

17 ft.

20 ft.

5. _____ feet

30 dm

15 dm

32 dm

6. _____ decimeters

Find the Area. <u>Remember</u>: Area is measured in square units.
Area = length x width.

Remember:
1/2 x base x height
for triangles

5 cm

4 cm

7. _____ cm² (square centimeters)

8 yd

8 yd

8. _____ square yards

12 in.

36 in

9. _____ square inches

4 in.

6 in.

10. _____ square inches

4 in.

6 in.

10. _____ square inches

16 m

13 m

11. _____ m²

70 dm

24 dm

12. _____ dm²

The Revolutionary War. Answer T for true or F for false to the following statements. If false, correct the statement so it will be true.

_____ 1. Loyalists supported the colonists.

_____ 2. Thomas Paine convinced many colonists to break from Great Britain with his pamphlet <u>Common Sense</u>.

_____ 3. The British had no struggle in taking Breed's Hill, known as the Battle of Bunker Hill.

_____ 4. The Declaration of Independence was written by John Adams on July 4, 1775.

_____ 5. The patriots had support from many American women when fighting their battles.

_____ 6. Mary Ludwig Hays, known as Molly Pitcher, carried pitchers of water to men who were fighting in battles.

Earthquakes.

Many earthquakes occur at the plate boundaries. Study the following map of earthquake epicenters and answer the questions below.

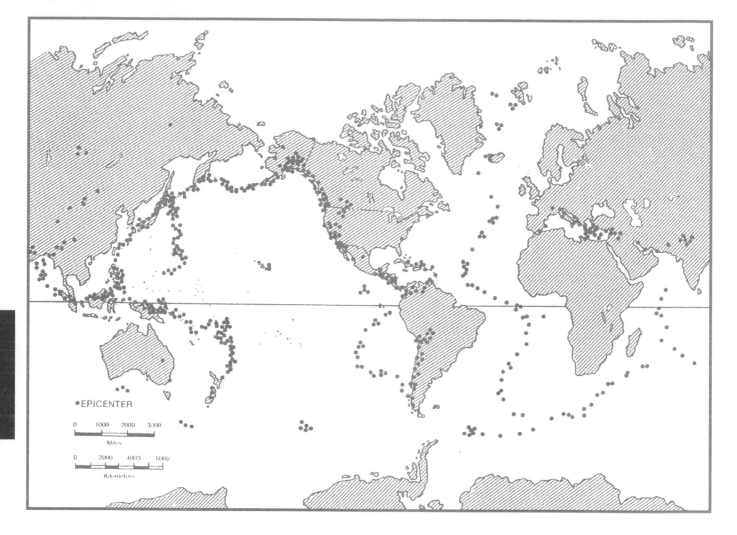

• EPICENTER

0   1000   2000   3000
Miles

0   2000   4000   6000
Kilometers

1. Color the areas with the most earthquake activity. What pattern do you see?

2. Review the map on plate boundaries on page 42. What is similar about these boundaries and earthquake activity?

3. Explain how you came up with your answer for question 2.

4. Observe the earthquakes that occur in the interior of the plates (e.g., China, U.S., and Australia). How is the distribution of these earthquakes different from that of earthquakes along the plate boundaries?

Write the rest of the number families. The first one is done for you.

1. 78 x 42 = 3,276

42 x 78 = 3,276

3,276 ÷ 42 = 78

3,276 ÷ 78 = 42

2. 39 x 56 = 2,184

_____

_____

_____

3. 95 x 37 = 3,515

_____

_____

_____

4. 49 x 76 =

_____

_____

_____

5. 141 x 27 =

_____

_____

_____

6. 3,762 ÷ 38 =

_____

_____

_____

7. 26,320 ÷ 47 =

_____

_____

_____

8. 48,306 ÷ 83 =

_____

_____

_____

9. 194 x 92 =

_____

_____

_____

10. 16,019 ÷ 83 =

_____

_____

_____

11. 2,650 x 54 =

_____

_____

_____

12. 876,600 ÷ 360 =

_____

_____

_____

Respiratory System.

There are a lot of ways you can take care of your respiratory system. Some ways are exercising regularly, not smoking, and not inhaling chemicals produced by products such as paint or glue. Look at some old magazines and ask your parents if you can cut out pictures of people caring for their respiratory system. If you don't have any old magazines, draw and color pictures.

Day 9

Read these paragraphs. Remember to ask yourself:

1. Does the paragraph have one main idea?
2. Do all the sentences in the paragraph tell about the main idea?
3. Is every sentence in the paragraph a complete sentence?

Draw a line through the sentence or sentences that do not belong in the paragraph. Tell why.

1. Water in the ocean never stops moving. The most well-known movements are waves. Waves are set in motion by earthquakes, winds, and the gravitational pull of the sun and moon. Ocean water is also very salty. On shore, we see waves caused by the wind. Their size depends on whether they come from far across the ocean or are caused by winds from nearby storms.

2. The beaver is a furry animal with a flat, wide tail that looks like a paddle. There are more beavers in the U.S. and Canada than anywhere else. The beaver's strong front teeth are used for cutting down trees. They use the branches to build dams and homes, but they eat the bark from them first. Beavers almost always seem. We often call people who work hard "eager beavers."

3. Write a paragraph. Try to remember the three rules as you write.

Earthquakes. Read the paragraph and fill in the blanks with the words listed.

seismologists	earthquake	seismic waves	energy
epicenter	fault	above	fracture
focus			beneath

An _____ is sudden shaking of the ground that happens when

_____ stored in rock is released. A _____ is a break, or

_____, in the Earth's crust. As rock breaks, stored energy moves along the fault.

The hypocenter, or _____, is where an earthquake begins. This occurs

_____ the Earth's surface. The point on the Earth's crust which is directly

_____ the focus is called the _____. ._____, or shock

waves, move out from the focus and cause the ground to shake. _____ study and

record these shock waves and determine the size of the earthquake.

Multiplying with "Napier's Bones."

In 1617, John Napier used a method of multiplying with rods marked with numbers. Some people call it "Napier's Bones," or "lattice" multiplication. When placing the appropriate "bones" side by side, you read the product of multiplication.

Use the "lattice" approach by multiplying the digits of the two factors. Write them on the lattice form, then add along the diagonals, carrying the remainder to the next diagonal.

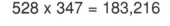

EXAMPLE:

528 x 347 = 183,216

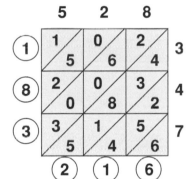

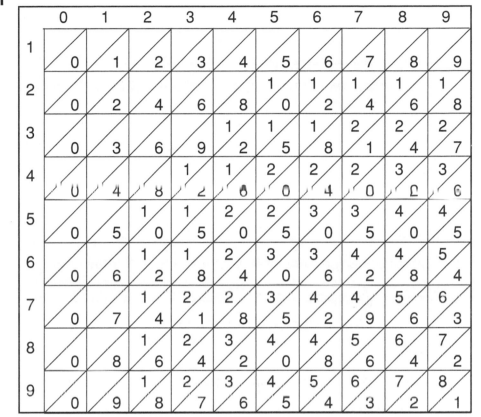

1. 476 x 304 = _____

2. 722 x 436 = _____

3. 821 x 569 = _____

4. 835 x 321 = _____

5. 605 x 843 = _____

6. 349 x 275 = _____

7. 652 x 872 = _____

8. 349 x 731 = _____

9. 644 x 590 = _____

10. 863 x 182 = _____

11. 295 x 452 = _____

12. 524 x 604 = _____

13. 466 x 459 = _____

14. 989 x 329 = _____

15. 916 x 334 = _____

16. 827 x 373 = _____

17. 881 x 705 = _____

18. 518 x 367 = _____

19. 1,073 x 272 = _____

20. 1,855 x 146 = _____

21. 4,312 x 9,403 = _____

22. 1,283 x 474 = _____

23. 9,190 x 355 = _____

24. 5,963 x 540 = _____

Some key words and punctuation marks signal that an author is giving a context clue. These include dashes, commas, parentheses, and phrases like <u>which is</u>, <u>in other words</u>, <u>for instance</u>, and <u>etc</u>. In these sentences write what the underlined words mean. Then write the key words or punctuation marks that helped you tell the word's meaning.

EXAMPLE: The candidate shouted through a <u>megaphone</u> (large funnel-shaped horn) so the crowd could hear him.
megaphone *Large funnel-shaped cone;*   *parentheses*

1. I feel <u>torpid</u>—sluggish and lazy—in the hot summer weather.

   torpid _____

2. Paul Bunyan used an <u>adze</u>, which is a flat-bladed ax, to cut down the forest.

   adze _____

3. The cook made <u>ragout</u>, a highly seasoned stew, every day for the ranch hands.

   ragout _____

4. Jason mashed his <u>patella</u>, in other words, his kneecap.

   patella _____

5. The silver <u>jubilee</u> anniversary, that is, the 25th anniversary, was celebrated for ten days.

   jubilee _____

6. David can play a <u>marimba</u> (a xylophone).

   marimba _____

For 7 and 8 use the above words and write your own sentences. Use context clues in each one. Use a dictionary to find the meanings.

7. _____

8. _____

Add a prefix or a suffix to the following base or root words. Then choose six of the words you made and write a sentence with them.

1. ____agree
2. ____capable
3. delay____
4. hazard____
5. ____necessary
6. marvel____
7. ____comfort____

8. ____placed
9. avoid____
10. ____number____
11. care____
12. smart____
13. ____verb
14. ____plant

15. ____respect____
16. ____change
17. loyal____
18. ____depend____
19. thought____
20. ____mature
21. act____

Mixed Practice. Find the missing factors.

1. 67 x ____ = 536

2. 96 x ____ = 864

3. ____ x 77 = 385

4. ____ x 84 = 924

5. 2,210 ÷ ____ = 85

6. 5,518 ÷ ____ = 62

7. 29 x ____ = 1,972

8. 19,347 - ____ = 18,470

9. 23,432 + ____ = 24,089

10. 32 x ____ = 6,400

11. ____ x 75 = 11,250

12. 4,905 ÷ ____ = 327

13. 56,993 - ____ = 55,598

14. 4,266 ÷ ____ = 711

15. 33 x ____ = 17,886

16. ____ + 34,561 = 40,090

17. 307 x ____ = 18,113

18. 741 x ____ = 61,503

19. 50,000 ÷ ____ = 1,250

20. ____ x 56 = 16,016

21. 40,572 ÷ ____ = 126

22. 19,263 + ____ = 66,390

23. 73,477 - ____ = 62,305

24. ____ - 80,399 = 110,099

25. ____ x 48 = 64,800

26. 83,037 ÷ ____ = 933

27. ____ ÷ 19 = 773

28. ____ ÷ 49 = 192

29. 932 x ____ = 355,092

30. 5,396 + 3,217 + ____ = 10,990

Endocrine System. Read the phrases below. Determine whether the pituitary gland or thyroid gland is responsible. Write P for pituitary and T for thyroid.

1. _____ A person's height

2. _____ Influences the reproductive system

3. _____ Rate at which the body uses food

4. _____ Helps control growth rate

5. _____ May affect the weight of a person

Day 11

Irregular Verbs. Change the present form of the verb at the first of the sentence to the past form. Write the past form in the blank.

EXAMPLE: <u>wear</u>   I ___*wore*___ an old coat to school.

<u>ring</u>   1. The telephone _____ ten times before she answered it.

<u>build</u>   2. The contractor _____ a new apartment building every year for five years.

<u>feed</u>   3. Aunt Dawn _____ her cats three times a day.

<u>choose</u>   4. We each _____ a friend to go with us to Disneyland.

<u>spend</u>   5. My brother _____ all of his allowance on ice cream.

<u>spin</u>   6. The top _____ for five minutes.

<u>run</u>   7. Our family _____ in a marathon two summers ago.

<u>eat</u>   8. The monkey _____ four bananas.

<u>shake</u>   9. I was so afraid of the dark that I _____ all over when the lights went out.

<u>hold</u>   10. Kit _____ his breath for one minute.

<u>bleed</u>   11. My nose _____ for half an hour last night.

<u>draw</u>   12. The class _____ pictures showing what they did on their field trip.

<u>ride</u>   13. Alexander _____ his Shetland pony in the rodeo parade last summer.

<u>teach</u>   14. Julie's mother _____ us how to jump double dutch with our new jump ropes.

<u>fight</u>   15. My sisters and I _____ a lot when we were children.

Quotes.

Make a list of favorite or frequently used quotes among your family and friends. Have your family and friends help you compile your list.

EXAMPLE: If wishes were fishes we'd all take a swim.

Simplifying Fractions. Simplify the fractions down to the lowest term possible.

EXAMPLE:

1. $\frac{5}{10} = \frac{1}{2}$

2. $\frac{8}{12} =$ ___

3. $\frac{6}{9} =$ ___

4. $\frac{15}{25} =$ ___

5. $\frac{9}{27} =$ ___

6. $\frac{50}{75} =$ ___

7. $\frac{16}{20} =$ ___

8. $\frac{9}{72} =$ ___

9. $\frac{18}{45} =$ ___

10. $\frac{60}{100} =$ ___

11. $\frac{24}{32} =$ ___

12. $\frac{75}{100} =$ ___

13. $\frac{36}{45} =$ ___

14. $\frac{16}{24} =$ ___

15. $\frac{16}{72} =$ ___

16. $\frac{30}{80} =$ ___

17. $\frac{8}{64} =$ ___

18. $\frac{15}{40} =$ ___

19. $\frac{27}{45} =$ ___

20. $\frac{18}{24} =$ ___

21. $\frac{10}{35} =$ ___

22. $\frac{4}{18} =$ ___

23. $\frac{9}{15} =$ ___

24. $\frac{14}{21} =$ ___

25. $\frac{21}{28} =$ ___

26. $\frac{8}{40} =$ ___

27. $\frac{45}{120} =$ ___

28. $\frac{32}{48} =$ ___

29. $\frac{144}{180} =$ ___

30. $\frac{18}{144} =$ ___

31. $\frac{150}{200} =$ ___

32. $\frac{32}{40} =$ ___

33. $\frac{81}{135} =$ ___

34. $\frac{280}{420} =$ ___

35. $\frac{72}{96} =$ ___

Heroes in America. Match these people with the important contributions they made during America's fight for independence.

_____ George Washington

_____ Thomas Jefferson

_____ Patrick Henry

_____ Benjamin Franklin

_____ Thomas Paine

_____ John Paul Jones

_____ Mary Ludwig Hays

_____ Francis Marion

_____ Deborah Sampson

a. "Swamp Fox," guerrilla warfare

b. commander of American ship *Bonhomme Richard*

c. dressed in men's clothing and joined the army

d. crossed the Delaware River on Christmas Eve

e. "Gentlemen, we must all hang together, or most assuredly we shall all hang separately."

f. carried pitchers of water to soldiers

g. "Give me liberty or give me death!"

h. Common Sense

i. wrote the Declaration of Independence

Choose one of these people and do a small report on him/her. After giving so much of themselves to gain independence for America, how do you think they would feel if they saw America today? What do you think they would say?

Direct objects are nouns or pronouns that complete or receive the action of the verb. They follow action verbs only. Circle the verb and underline the direct objects in these sentences. Use the direct objects to complete the puzzle.

EXAMPLE:

1. John Smith (guided) the <u>colonists</u> in the new world.
2. The robber threw the jewels into the bag and ran.
3. Sarah bought some groceries at the supermarket.
4. The crowd begged the musicians to play more.
5. We captured the tarantula in an old glass jar.
6. The sun melted the icicles that were on the house.
7. My brother, the quarterback, made a touchdown.
8. The movers loaded the furniture into the truck.
9. Loryn watches movies with her friends.
10. Trenton sold fifty tickets for the drawing.
11. Julia cut the watermelon into a dozen pieces.
12. The tangled string ruined my kite.
13. Allie borrowed my new umbrella.

Complete the puzzle.

```
_ _ _ _ _ D _ _ _
        _ I _ _
      _ _ R _ _ _ _ _
    _ _ _ _ _ E _ _
        _ _ _ C _ _
      _ _ _ T _
    _ _ _ _ O _
      _ _ B _ _ _
        _ J _ _ _
      _ _ E _ _ _
        _ C _ _ _ _ _
    _ _ _ _ _ _ T _
  _ _ _ _ _ _ _ _ S
```

Mysterious Division Power. Choose any 2-digit number. Write it 3 times to make a 6-digit number. Divide it by 13; then divide the answer by 21, and divide that answer by 37.

EXAMPLE: 14 $141{,}414 \div 13 = 10{,}878 \div 21 = 518 \div 37 = 14$ MAGIC!

1. <u>56</u> $565{,}656 \div 13 = \underline{\hspace{2cm}} \div 21 = \underline{\hspace{1.5cm}} \div 37 = \underline{\hspace{1cm}}$

2. <u>35</u> $353{,}535 \div 13 = \underline{\hspace{2cm}} \div 21 = \underline{\hspace{1.5cm}} \div 37 = \underline{\hspace{1cm}}$

3. <u>73</u> $737{,}373 \div 13 = \underline{\hspace{2cm}} \div 21 = \underline{\hspace{1.5cm}} \div 37 = \underline{\hspace{1cm}}$

4. <u>29</u> $292{,}929 \div 13 = \underline{\hspace{2cm}} \div 21 = \underline{\hspace{1.5cm}} \div 37 = \underline{\hspace{1cm}}$

5. <u>80</u> $808{,}080 \div 13 = \underline{\hspace{2cm}} \div 21 = \underline{\hspace{1.5cm}} \div 37 = \underline{\hspace{1cm}}$

Now use your own 2-digit numbers.

6. $\underline{\hspace{1cm}}$ $\underline{\hspace{2cm}} \div 13 = \underline{\hspace{2cm}} \div 21 = \underline{\hspace{1.5cm}} \div 37 = \underline{\hspace{1cm}}$

7. $\underline{\hspace{1cm}}$ $\underline{\hspace{2cm}} \div 13 = \underline{\hspace{2cm}} \div 21 = \underline{\hspace{1.5cm}} \div 37 = \underline{\hspace{1cm}}$

8. $\underline{\hspace{1cm}}$ $\underline{\hspace{2cm}} \div 13 = \underline{\hspace{2cm}} \div 21 = \underline{\hspace{1.5cm}} \div 37 = \underline{\hspace{1cm}}$

9. $\underline{\hspace{1cm}}$ $\underline{\hspace{2cm}} \div 13 = \underline{\hspace{2cm}} \div 21 = \underline{\hspace{1.5cm}} \div 37 = \underline{\hspace{1cm}}$

10. $\underline{\hspace{1cm}}$ $\underline{\hspace{2cm}} \div 13 = \underline{\hspace{2cm}} \div 21 = \underline{\hspace{1.5cm}} \div 37 = \underline{\hspace{1cm}}$

11. $\underline{\hspace{1cm}}$ $\underline{\hspace{2cm}} \div 13 = \underline{\hspace{2cm}} \div 21 = \underline{\hspace{1.5cm}} \div 37 = \underline{\hspace{1cm}}$

12. $\underline{\hspace{1cm}}$ $\underline{\hspace{2cm}} \div 13 = \underline{\hspace{2cm}} \div 21 = \underline{\hspace{1.5cm}} \div 37 = \underline{\hspace{1cm}}$

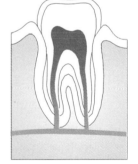

Teeth. Match the appropriate term and definition.

_____ crown

_____ root

_____ enamel

_____ dentin

_____ pulp

_____ cementum

a. soft tissue that contains nerves and blood vessels in center of tooth

b. part of tooth above the gum

c. hard tissue that covers the root

d. part of tooth that holds it in the jawbone

e. hard tissue that forms body of tooth

f. hard tissue that covers the crown of tooth

Write a short story titled "The Tale of Tooth City." Have a villain whose name might be "Wicked Wizard Plaque." Be creative with your story. Have a happy ending with healthy teeth.

_____

_____

_____

_____

Day 13

Syllables. Read these sentences; then write the underlined word on the line, leaving a space between the syllables. Use the dictionary if you need help.

1. We used some old <u>wicker</u> chairs on our patio. _____

2. <u>Lavender</u> is a shade of the color purple. _____

3. My brother, who is six feet six inches tall, has <u>enormous</u> feet. _____

4. In the spring, my favorite flowering bush is the <u>lilac</u>. _____

5. We use <u>natural</u> gas to heat our house. _____

6. If you want to be a doctor of <u>dermatology</u>, you would study about skin diseases. _____

7. I could hear a <u>whispering</u> voice behind me. _____

8. Have you ever been to <u>San Francisco</u>? _____

9. The <u>coauthor</u> of my new book is Carla Powers. _____

10. We think it's fun to visit cities that have <u>cobblestone</u> streets. _____

11. How old were you when you learned the <u>alphabet</u>? _____

12. Allen acted like a <u>zombie</u> after being up all night. _____

13. The comedian's <u>originality</u> was amusing. _____

14. Jay was in <u>misery</u> for a long time after the accident. _____

Analogies. Analogies are similar relationships between two pairs of words. Write an analogy to finish each sentence.

EXAMPLE:

1. <u>Tree</u> is to <u>lumber</u> as <u>wheat</u> is to _____flour_____.

2. <u>Page</u> is to <u>book</u> as _____ is to the <u>United States</u>.

3. <u>Brake</u> is to <u>stop</u> as <u>engine</u> is to _____.

4. <u>Mechanic</u> is to <u>motors</u> as <u>plumber</u> is to _____.

5. <u>Bird</u> is to <u>nest</u> as _____ is to <u>den</u>.

6. <u>Bricks</u> are to a <u>wall</u> as <u>fingers</u> are to _____.

7. <u>Finger</u> is to <u>hand</u> as <u>toe</u> is to _____.

8. <u>Penny</u> is to <u>dime</u> as inch is to _____.

9. <u>Space</u> is to <u>rocket</u> as _____ is to <u>boat</u>.

10. <u>Stage</u> is to <u>actor</u> as <u>pit</u> is to _____.

11. <u>Diamond</u> is to <u>jewel</u> as <u>steel</u> is to _____.

12. <u>Fame</u> is to <u>famous</u> as <u>study</u> is to _____.

Chart the graph point by point. The first number tells how far to go to the right. The second number tells how far to move up. The distance between the grid lines represents 2 units.

Day 14

1. Place the dot and letter on the point called for. The first one is done for you.

(2, 2) dot A
(12, 16) dot H
(16, 12) dot J
(6, 4) dot P
(14, 10) dot K
(10, 14) dot G
(4, 6) dot B
(8, 12) dot F
(8, 6) dot O
(12, 8) dot L
(8, 10) dot D
(10, 8) dot N
(13, 13) dot I
(6, 8) dot C
(10, 11) dot E
(11, 10) dot M
(16, 4) draw a ☆
(4, 14) draw a ☆
(2, 18) draw a ☆
(16, 8) draw a ●
(2, 10) draw a ●
(10, 18) draw a ●

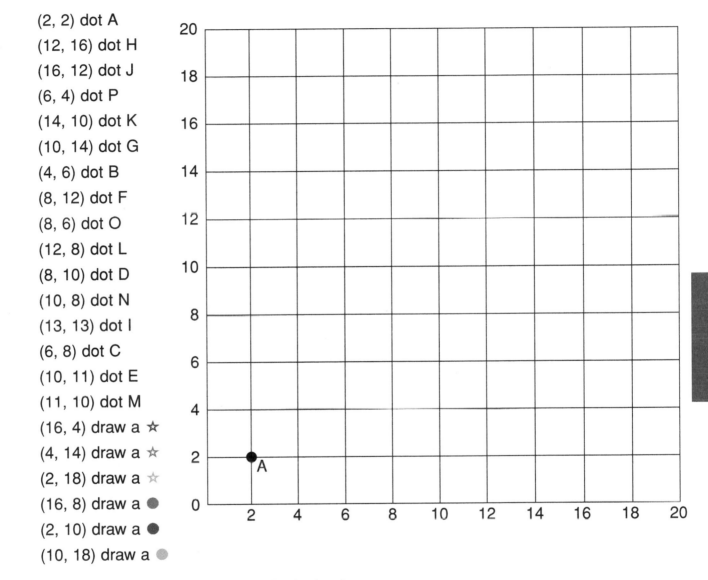

2. Connect dots A through P in alphabetical order.

3. Connect dot P to A.

4. Connect dots E to I and I to M.

Make a "point by point" direction course and have a friend or family member see if they can graph it. You could make a design, picture, or map. Use your imagination and have fun.

Circle the correct noun.

1. The (Farmers', Farmers) Market was only open on Friday.

2. That (mountain, mountains) peak is too hard for me to climb.

3. (Ed White's, Ed White) was the first astronaut to walk in space.

4. We saw a herd of (deer, deers) along the side of the road.

5. Why do (goose, geese) have webbed (foot, feet)?

Write the plural form of each noun to fill in the blanks.

potato
man
trout
party
elf

6. The _____ on our farm were the best!

7. The nurse took the pulses of the _____.

8. My father caught ten rainbow _____ that day.

9. The _____ we went to were all fun.

10. Many _____ worked on the shoes for the queen.

Fill in the blanks with proper nouns.

11. We live very close to the _____ Mountains.

12. _____ comes in the month of October.

13. The _____ Islands are very beautiful.

14. Judge _____ went on vacation as soon as the trial was over.

15. _____ favorite basketball team is the _____.

Practice writing and spelling these words three times each. Then have someone give you a test on them. Use another piece of paper for the test.

1. practicing _____

2. guesses _____

3. manufacture _____

4. poisonous _____

5. loafer _____

6. vigorous _____

7. boundary _____

8. prejudice _____

Exchange and Share $906.00. You have $906.00 to share among 7 family members. Find out if you can share it equally. To begin with, you have nine $100 bills, no $10 bills, and six $1 bills. Share and exchange down.

1. You have nine $100 bills. How many $100 bills does each family member get? _____ How many are left? _____

2. Exchange the $100 bills you have left for _____ $10 bills.

3. Each family member gets _____ $10 bills. How many are left? _____

4. Exchange your $10 bills for _____ $1 bills. How many $1 bills do you have altogether? _____

5. Each family member gets _____ $1 bills. How many are left? _____

6. Each family member gets _____ $100 bills, _____ $10 bills, and _____ $1 bills.

7. How much money does each family member get? _____

8. What could you do with the amount left over? _____

9. Is there another way to share the money equally? Show us!

Make up your own "Exchange and Share" situation or use the following: $504 among 21 people. Use the above method.

The Bill of Rights is the name given to the first ten amendments added to the Constitution. Other amendments also have been added. Read the passages below and determine which situations are constitutional or unconstitutional. Then write down which amendment would support your decision.

1. In the 1960s, a group of black students walked around with signs that said "Down with segregation!"

2. A city police department would not allow women to join the police force.

3. A person accused of a serious crime refuses to give evidence against himself.

4. A town does not like the religious beliefs of a particular group, so it forbids that group to build a place where they can worship.

5. A woman accused of a serious crime wants a trial with a jury. The government says she doesn't have enough money for this type of trial.

6. A group of students who just turned eighteen want to vote for whom they would like as the next president of the United States.

7. The president of the United States wants to run for office again. This would be his/her third term.

Day 15

Contractions. Words like <u>let's</u> (let us), <u>you'll</u> (you will), etc., are contractions. Contractions that have the word <u>not</u> in them are called negatives. The rule is NEVER use double negatives when you write or speak. Other words like <u>nothing</u>, <u>never</u>, and <u>nobody</u> are also negatives. In these sentences, find the double negatives and rewrite the sentence in cursive, using the correct word.

EXAMPLE: The fight didn't solve nothing. *The fight didn't solve anything.*

1. The team didn't want no trouble. _____

   _____

2. Haven't you never seen Yellowstone Park? _____

   _____

3. There weren't no eggs left in the carton. _____

   _____

4. I haven't never been happier to finish a school year. _____

   _____

5. This path doesn't lead nowhere. _____

   _____

6. Can't no one in this class solve the puzzle? _____

   _____

7. Richard didn't have nothing to read. _____

   _____

8. Nanette said that she hadn't never thought of that idea. _____

   _____

9. Don't spill none of the juice on the carpet. _____

   _____

10. There isn't nothing you can do about the weather. _____

    _____

11. Thad doesn't know nobody in his algebra class. _____

    _____

12. The bus didn't have no empty seats when we got on. _____

    _____

Eggs? What eggs? Chicken eggs! Down through the ages, eggs have been eaten around the world. In America, the most popular eggs to eat are chicken eggs. Chicken eggs are classified primarily by their weight. Small eggs weigh approximately 18 ounces a dozen. Medium eggs weigh 21 ounces a dozen. Large eggs weigh 24 ounces a dozen. Extra large eggs weigh a hefty 27 ounces a dozen. Jumbo eggs, which are classified as the largest sellable eggs, weigh 30 ounces a dozen.

1. 6 dozen _____ eggs weigh a total of 180 ounces.

2. How many eggs are in 6 dozen? _____

3. How many eggs are in 12 dozen? _____ What are two different ways you can use to find the answer to this question? _____, _____

4. Which weighs more—3 dozen jumbo eggs or 5 dozen small eggs? _____

5. If 5 dozen eggs weigh a total of 150 ounces, which eggs would they be? _____

6. If you wanted to boil a total of 120 eggs for an Easter egg hunt and you wanted an equal number of each size of egg, how many of each size would you boil? _____

7. What is the minimum weight you can have if you have 4 dozen eggs? _____ ounces of _____ eggs.

8. If you bought a dozen of each size of egg, what should be the total weight in ounces? _____

9. Jan gathered 4 dozen medium-sized eggs, 3 dozen small eggs, 1 dozen large eggs, 2 dozen extra-large eggs, and 1/2 dozen jumbo eggs. How many eggs did she gather? _____ How many ounces did she have altogether? _____

10. Mother bought 3 dozen eggs, but some broke on the way home. When she got home, she tried to divide them evenly between 2 bowls, but she had 1 left over. With 3 and 4 bowls she again had 1 left over. When she divided them into 5 bowls, they came out exactly even! How many eggs did she have? _____

The Skin. Go to the store or look in a magazine for products used to keep your skin healthy. On the chart below, write the name of the product and its purpose. Then ask yourself if this product is necessary to help keep your skin healthy. If the answer is yes, put a star by the product. If you find that the product will not really help keep your skin healthy, put a moon by the product.

Name	Purpose	Star or Moon

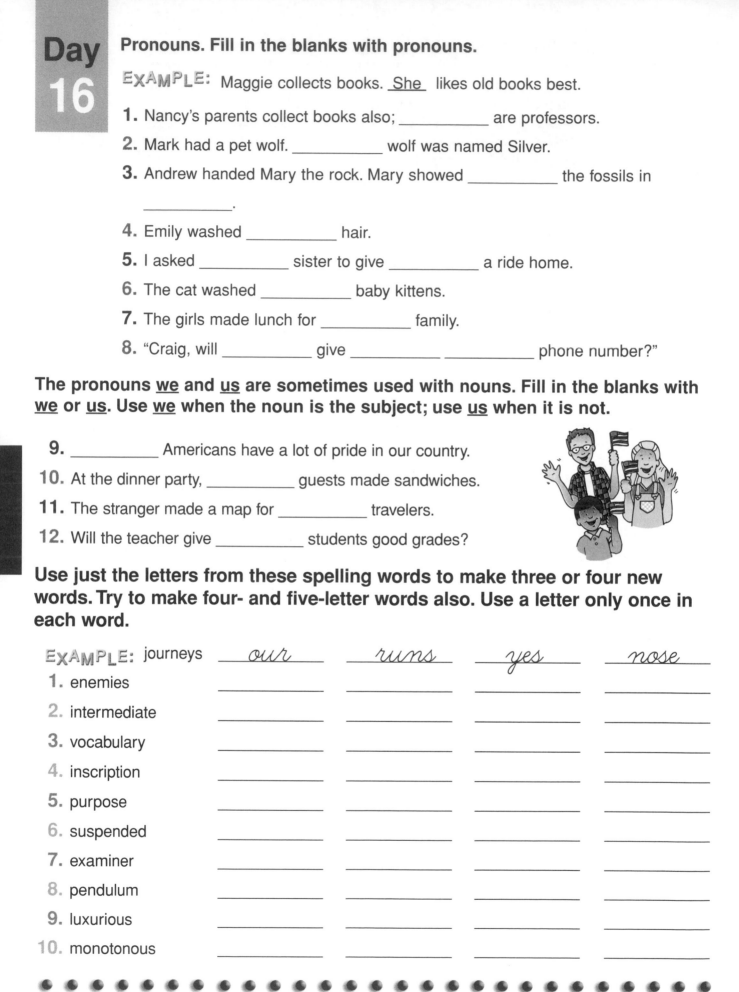

Day 16

Pronouns. Fill in the blanks with pronouns.

EXAMPLE: Maggie collects books. _She_ likes old books best.

1. Nancy's parents collect books also; _____ are professors.

2. Mark had a pet wolf. _____ wolf was named Silver.

3. Andrew handed Mary the rock. Mary showed _____ the fossils in _____.

4. Emily washed _____ hair.

5. I asked _____ sister to give _____ a ride home.

6. The cat washed _____ baby kittens.

7. The girls made lunch for _____ family.

8. "Craig, will _____ give _____ _____ phone number?"

The pronouns <u>we</u> and <u>us</u> are sometimes used with nouns. Fill in the blanks with <u>we</u> or <u>us</u>. Use <u>we</u> when the noun is the subject; use <u>us</u> when it is not.

9. _____ Americans have a lot of pride in our country.

10. At the dinner party, _____ guests made sandwiches.

11. The stranger made a map for _____ travelers.

12. Will the teacher give _____ students good grades?

Use just the letters from these spelling words to make three or four new words. Try to make four- and five-letter words also. Use a letter only once in each word.

EXAMPLE: journeys ___*our*___ ___*runs*___ ___*yes*___ ___*nose*___

1. enemies _____ _____ _____ _____

2. intermediate _____ _____ _____ _____

3. vocabulary _____ _____ _____ _____

4. inscription _____ _____ _____ _____

5. purpose _____ _____ _____ _____

6. suspended _____ _____ _____ _____

7. examiner _____ _____ _____ _____

8. pendulum _____ _____ _____ _____

9. luxurious _____ _____ _____ _____

10. monotonous _____ _____ _____ _____

Let's Go with Division.

Choose a place you would like to go that you can drive to in a few days. Find a map and chart your course. Estimate, then check how many miles it is from your house. Decide how fast you can drive and how many hours you are going to travel each day. Using division, figure out how many days it will take. Make a chart using the information you have. Decide how long you can stay. Remember, you have to save some time to drive home. Try a one-week trip, then a three-week trip. Remember, you have to travel by car. Could you chart your results? Can you estimate the cost of your trip? Involve your parents in this plan to help you!

More Pronouns. Use **I** or **me** in these sentences. When **I** is part of a compound subject, use it last.

EXAMPLE: She and **I** made a cake.

1. Mom and _____ went to the store.

2. When will you come to see Kent and _____?

3. Karen asked _____ to answer the door.

4. Ann Marie and _____ ate our lunch outside.

5. Snakes scare _____ to death.

6. The gift was sent by Aunt Jean and _____.

7. Carla and _____ were both born in May.

Possessive pronouns show ownership. Use possessive pronouns in these sentences.

8. Did you see _____ faces when they saw Santa?

9. _____ handwriting is very neat.

10. The prize is _____ for the asking.

11. The book you gave to Leza was _____.

12. _____ uncle, Clint, is coming for a visit.

13. The prints on the mirror are _____.

14. The elephant stood on _____ drum.

Volcanoes. Answer T for true or F for false to the following statements. If false, correct the sentence so it will be true.

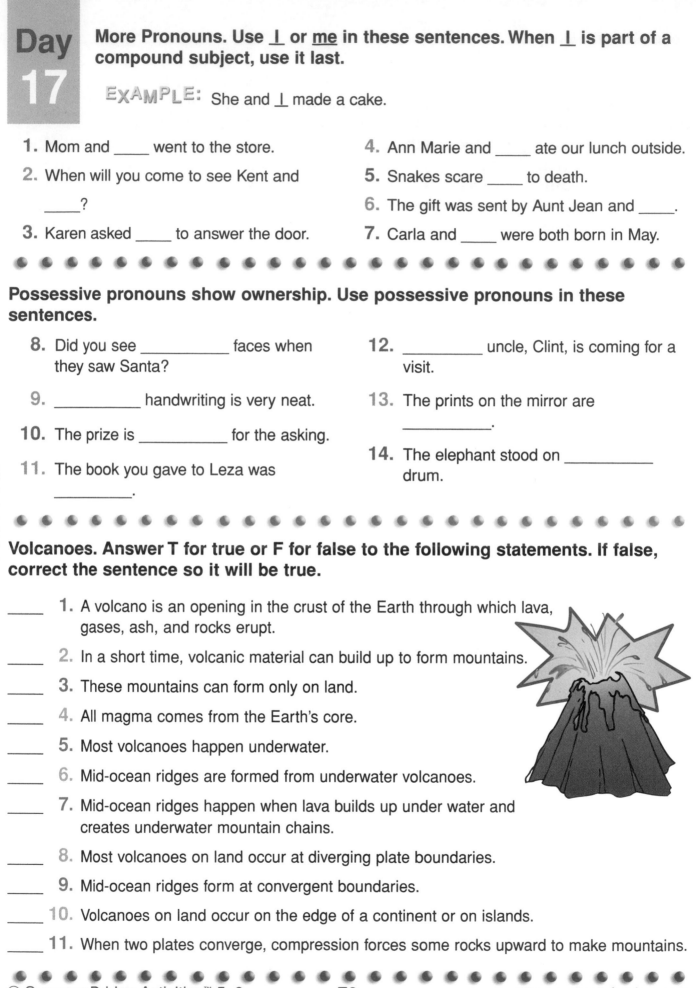

_____ 1. A volcano is an opening in the crust of the Earth through which lava, gases, ash, and rocks erupt.

_____ 2. In a short time, volcanic material can build up to form mountains.

_____ 3. These mountains can form only on land.

_____ 4. All magma comes from the Earth's core.

_____ 5. Most volcanoes happen underwater.

_____ 6. Mid-ocean ridges are formed from underwater volcanoes.

_____ 7. Mid-ocean ridges happen when lava builds up under water and creates underwater mountain chains.

_____ 8. Most volcanoes on land occur at diverging plate boundaries.

_____ 9. Mid-ocean ridges form at convergent boundaries.

_____ 10. Volcanoes on land occur on the edge of a continent or on islands.

_____ 11. When two plates converge, compression forces some rocks upward to make mountains.

Sharpen your skills with this timed multiplication test! Estimate how much time you think it will take you to do these problems. _____
Now do the actual test. How long did it take you to do it? _____
What's the difference between the two times? _____

1. 6 x 7 = ____
2. 12 x 2 = ____
3. 5 x 10 = ____
4. 9 x 6 = ____
5. 7 x 8 = ____
6. 11 x 12 = ____
7. 7 x 5 = ____
8. 11 x 2 = ____
9. 10 x 3 = ____
10. 5 x 6 = ____
11. 9 x 5 = ____
12. 8 x 4 = ____
13. 8 x 0 = ____
14. 6 x 12 = ____
15. 8 x 3 = ____
16. 10 x 2 = ____
17. 6 x 6 = ____
18. 8 x 9 = ____
19. 7 x 2 = ____
20. 8 x 7 = ____
21. 11 x 7 = ____
22. 5 x 2 = ____
23. 10 x 6 = ____
24. 9 x 4 = ____
25. 6 x 3 = ____

26. 8 x 9 = ____
27. 6 x 9 = ____
28. 11 x 10 = ____
29. 10 x 9 = ____
30. 9 x 11 = ____
31. 7 x 3 = ____
32. 12 x 10 = ____
33. 9 x 9 = ____
34. 8 x 8 = ____
35. 7 x 7 = ____
36. 10 x 10 = ____
37. 11 x 3 = ____
38. 6 x 5 = ____
39. 5 x 3 = ____
40. 9 x 2 = ____
41. 12 x 5 = ____
42. 10 x 0 = ____
43. 9 x 10 = ____
44. 8 x 2 = ____
45. 11 x 5 = ____
46. 8 x 8 = ____
47. 7 x 6 = ____
48. 7 x 7 = ____
49. 11 x 9 = ____
50. 5 x 12 = ____

51. 5 x 5 = ____
52. 9 x 0 = ____
53. 9 x 3 = ____
54. 7 x 4 = ____
55. 12 x 4 = ____
56. 9 x 9 = ____
57. 7 x 9 = ____
58. 8 x 5 = ____
59. 10 x 4 = ____
60. 9 x 8 = ____
61. 7 x 6 = ____
62. 10 x 5 = ____
63. 11 x 4 = ____
64. 7 x 8 = ____
65. 12 x 12 = ____
66. 9 x 7 = ____
67. 7 x 11 = ____
68. 5 x 4 = ____
69. 9 x 7 = ____
70. 10 x 8 = ____
71. 9 x 11 = ____
72. 8 x 12 = ____
73. 8 x 6 = ____
74. 12 x 3 = ____
75. 5 x 7 = ____

76. 11 x 5 = ____
77. 9 x 6 = ____
78. 9 x 12 = ____
79. 6 x 8 = ____
80. 7 x 10 = ____
81. 5 x 11 = ____
82. 10 x 10 = ____
83. 6 x 11 = ____
84. 12 x 11 = ____
85. 12 x 9 = ____
86. 8 x 7 = ____
87. 5 x 8 = ____
88. 0 x 8 = ____
89. 8 x 6 = ____
90. 11 x 8 = ____
91. 11 x 12 = ____
92. 10 x 7 = ____
93. 8 x 11 = ____
94. 11 x 6 = ____
95. 6 x 10 = ____
96. 6 x 4 = ____
97. 11 x 8 = ____
98. 12 x 6 = ____
99. 8 x 10 = ____
100. 12 x 12 = ____

101. 8 x 10 = ____
102. 0 x 10 = ____
103. 7 x 9 = ____
104. 10 x 11 = ____
105. 7 x 12 = ____
106. 12 x 12 = ____
107. 11 x 9 = ____
108. 12 x 7 = ____
109. 11 x 6 = ____
110. 9 x 5 = ____
111. 9 x 3 = ____
112. 12 x 9 = ____
113. 11 x 7 = ____
114. 5 x 9 = ____
115. 9 x 10 = ____
116. 9 x 8 = ____
117. 9 x 4 = ____
118. 10 x 12 = ____
119. 8 x 12 = ____
120. 11 x 11 = ____
121. 7 x 12 = ____
122. 8 x 11 = ____
123. 11 x 11 = ____
124. 0 x 9 = ____
125. 12 x 8 = ____

Cover up the answers with another sheet of paper and try it again!

Day 18

Subject Pronouns and Object Pronouns. If the pronoun is not part of the subject it is an object pronoun. Write SP if the pronoun is a subject pronoun. Write OP if it is an object pronoun.

_____ 1. The funny story made <u>us</u> laugh.

_____ 2. McCall held the dance trophy in front of <u>her</u> and Ted.

_____ 3. Will <u>we</u> see any sharks at Sea Life Park?

_____ 4. Denise and <u>I</u> went ice skating with <u>her</u> family.

_____ 5. Don't give <u>her</u> the present until noon.

_____ 6. Did <u>they</u> fly or take the train home?

_____ 7. <u>We</u> are going to Washington D.C. this summer.

_____ 8. Are <u>you</u> a cousin to Hal Tomlyn?

_____ 9. <u>I</u> bought blue gym shoes this year because I like <u>them</u>.

_____ 10. The dog got <u>its</u> paw caught in the bear trap.

Verbs. Regular verbs show action that happened in the past by adding -<u>ed</u> to the base word. But to show past tense for irregular verbs, you have to change the spelling.

EXAMPLE: sit - sat

In the square there are some irregular verbs. Write them under the correct heading below.

<u>Remember</u>: The past participle is used with a helping word when in a sentence.

flown seen do began torn swim am
sang blew drink rang done
been sing did
gone eaten swum fly rung
eat begin ate
go tore blown tear
went blow
bitten bite drunk
ring sung drank was
begun see flew swam bit
saw

Present	Past	Past Participle

Choices. Clayton's mother bought him some new clothes to go to camp. She bought him 4 pairs of shorts—red, blue, green, and white. She also bought him 8 T-shirts—2 red, 2 blue, 2 green, and 2 white. She bought him 4 long-sleeved sweatshirts—2 white and 2 blue.

Use a tree diagram to organize the data to find out how many different choices of shorts and shirts Clayton can wear. _____ total choices

shorts   **shirts**

red

blue

green

white

Our Government. Our government is divided into three branches. Each branch is given different, but equal, powers. In the circle below, write down the branch, the power it has, and draw a picture that could represent each branch.

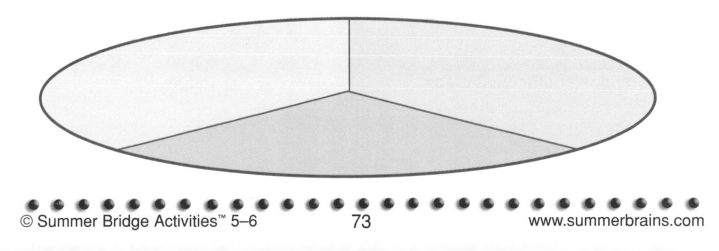

Day 19

Cause and Effect. Below are some parts of sentences that give the cause. Finish the sentence by writing what the effect might be. Look for clue words.

EXAMPLE:

(cause) The old house had not been painted for years, (effect) so the first thing we did was paint it. (The clue word is "so.")

1. Our Thanksgiving turkey was burned because _____.

2. _____ because my new shoes were too tight.

3. The wind was blowing hard, so _____.

4. Because I didn't get up early enough this morning, _____.

5. Some children were playing with matches; as a result, _____.

Now it's your turn to write the cause to the effects.

6. The plane crashed due to _____.

7. _____, my stomach hurt.

8. _____, so we decided to celebrate.

9. The drinks were very sweet because _____.

10. _____, there was no fruit on the trees this summer.

Electricity. In the table below, make a list of all the things you enjoy that use electricity. Now ask a parent, adult, or grandparent to list all the things that use electricity that they did not have when they were your age.

Compare the differences and similarities on your table. Next, create a list of things children in 30 years may have that use electricity that we do not have today. Be creative!

You	Parent/Adult
Grandparent/Elderly Person	**Future**

Broken Line Graphs, "Using Leisure Time."

Keep track of how much television you watch daily in a two-week period, then graph the results. Do the same with how much time you play computer games or TV games, then graph the results. Now do the same with how much time you spend with your friends, then graph the results. You can use the same graph for all three if you use different colored pens or pencils.

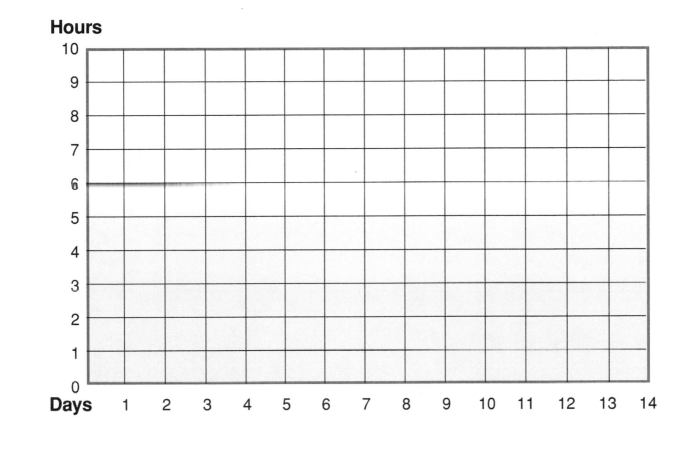

Hours

Days 1 2 3 4 5 6 7 8 9 10 11 12 13 14

Powers of the Government. Decide which branch of government (legislative, executive, or judicial) that each statement describes.

_____ 1. Can impeach the president of the United States.

_____ 2. Approves treaties.

_____ 3. Approves or vetoes bills.

_____ 4. Interprets and examines laws and treaties.

_____ 5. Appoints justices.

Adjectives make reading more interesting. **Remember:** Adjectives modify or describe nouns and pronouns. Read the clues to help you do the crossword puzzle. The answers are adjectives that are listed in the word box below. Dark lines mark the end of words. Use the dictionary for help with definitions.

Across

1. satisfied
4. dignified, lofty, noble
8. filled with fear
11. critical, immediate
12. rough voice
13. courageous, valiant, gallant
14. headstrong, inflexible

Down

1. skilled, competent
2. commanding
3. unbelievable, amazing
5. unable to put up with others' beliefs
6. lively, playful
7. childish, foolish
9. ill-disposed, hateful
10. made of wood

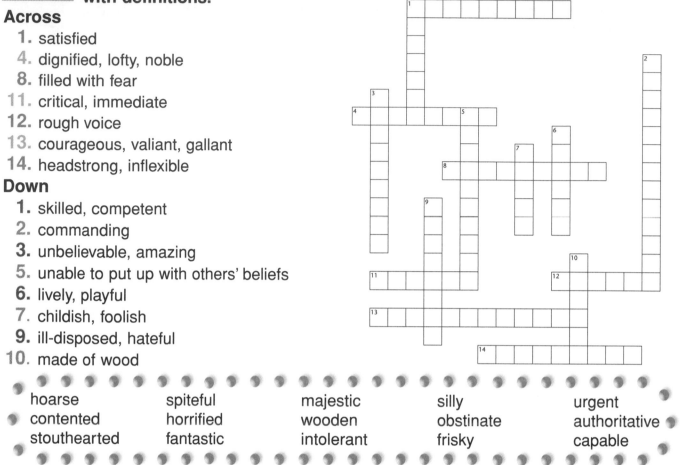

hoarse	spiteful	majestic	silly	urgent
contented	horrified	wooden	obstinate	authoritative
stouthearted	fantastic	intolerant	frisky	capable

Quotation marks go before and after exactly what a person is saying and the titles of stories, poems, and songs. Tell why quotation marks are used in these sentences.

1. Robert asked, "What are the rules for this game?"

_____

2. Mother was fixing lunch when David came home. "Please set the table," she said.

_____

3. Jim gave Lance a copy of "Solving Math Puzzles" to take on his trip.

_____

4. "What's that terrible noise?" cried Carla.

_____

5. Cindy was playing "Tennessee Waltz" on her guitar when Pete came in.

_____

Your turn. Put quotation marks in these sentences.

6. I don't think I can do this by myself, Marge sighed.
7. Hillary is singing America the Beautiful to her sister.
8. Do you like baseball or football best? Debra asked. I like baseball best.
9. Not me, answered Eleanor. I like basketball best.

Words to Sound, Read, and Spell

about	benefited	dining	heard
absence	birthday	disastrous	height
acceptable	bought	discipline	hear
accommodate	breathe	disease	here
accustom	built	dissatisfied	heroes
ache	bury	doctor	hospital
achievement	business	does	hour
acquire	calendar	early	hypocrite
across	category	easy	incredible
address	cemetery	effect	instead
adolescent	certainly	embarrass	interest
advantageous	children	endeavor	interrupt
advertisement	chocolate	enough	irrelevant
advice	choose	environment	jealousy
advise	cite	especially	know
again	close	every	laid
against	color	exaggerate	latter
aisle	coming	exceed	leisurely
all right	comparative	except	lessons
along	concede	exercise	letter
already	conceive	exhausted	license
although	condemn	existence	lieutenant
always	conscientious	experience	listener
amateur	conscious	explanation	little
among	controversial	fascinate	loose
analyze	controversy	favorite	lose
annually	cough	fierce	luxury
anticipated	could	formerly	magnificent
apparent	council	forty	making
appreciate	country	fourth	maneuver
arctic	cousin	friend	many
arguing	criticize	fuel	marriage
argument	cupboard	gaiety	mathematics
arithmetic	dairy	gauge	maybe
arrangement	dear	getting	medicine
athlete	decorate	goes	miniature
aunt	definitely	grammar	minute
awhile	definition	guarantee	miscellaneous
balloon	descendant	guard	mischief
bargain	describe	guess	moral
because	description	guidance	morning
before	desert	half	muscle
belief	dilemma	handkerchief	mysterious
beneficial	diligence	having	necessary

Words to Sound, Read, and Spell

neither	possession	right	tired
nice	possible	rough	tomorrow
niece	practical	route	tragedy
none	practice	said	transferred
noticeable	preferred	says	traveling
numerous	prepare	school	tremendous
occasion	prescription	several	trouble
occurred	pretty	since	truly
occurrence	principal	skiing	unnecessary
occurring	principle	skis	until
often	privilege	some	vacation
once	probably	store	vacuum
opinion	proceed	straight	valuable
opportunity	profession	studying	vegetable
paid	professor	subtle	very
parallel	pursue	succeed	villain
paralyzed	quarter	succession	visible
particular	quiet	surprise	waive
party	quit	teacher	weather
peace	quite	tear	weigh
people	raise	technique	whole
performance	receipt	terrible	woman
personal	receive	their	women
personnel	recommend	there	would
piece	referring	they	wrench
pleasant	remember	thorough	writing
please	repetition	though	yacht
poison	restaurant	thought	you're
politician	rhythm	through	your

Summer Bridge Activities™
Incentive Contract Calendar

Month _____

My parents and I decided that if I complete 15 days of
Summer Bridge Activities™ and read _____ minutes a day,
my incentive/reward will be:

_____

Child's Signature _____
Parent's Signature _____

Day 1   📖 ☆ ____   Day 8   📖 ☆ ____

Day 2   📖 ☆ ____   Day 9   📖 ☆ ____

Day 3   📖 ☆ ____   Day 10 📖 ☆ ____

Day 4   📖 ☆ ____   Day 11 📖 ☆ ____

Day 5   📖 ☆ ____   Day 12 📖 ☆ ____

Day 6   📖 ☆ ____   Day 13 📖 ☆ ____

Day 7   📖 ☆ ____   Day 14 📖 ☆ ____

                             Day 15 📖 ☆ ____

Child: Color the ☆ for daily activities completed.
         Color the 📖 for daily reading completed.

Parent: Initial the _____ for daily activities and reading
         your child completes.

Discover Something New!

Fun Activity Ideas to Go Along with the Third Section!

1. Draw a picture of your favorite friend, toy, or teacher during your favorite time of the year.

2. Put together a collection of leaves from your neighborhood and label as many as you can.

3. Write five questions that you would like to ask the president of the United States.

4. Invent a new ice cream flavor. How is it made? What will you call it?

5. Play football with a Frisbee.

6. Find out how to recycle in your town, then make and deliver flyers to inform all your neighbors.

7. Using a book on astronomy, look for stars and constellations.

8. Write your answer to the following question: How would the world be different without Alexander Graham Bell?

9. Surprise your parents and weed a flower bed or garden, rake the leaves, do the dishes, etc.

10. Play flashlight tag, tonight!

11. Design a comic strip and draw it.

12. Paint a mural on butcher paper.

13. Pretend you live in the year 2028. How will life be different? How will you look? What will you eat? How will you get around? Write it down and draw it.

14. Set up your own miniature golf course in your backyard.

15. Play hockey using a broom.

Division Outcomes. Complete this table to see which of these numbers can be divided by 2, 3, 5, 9, and 10 without having remainders. After you have finished the chart, see if you can come up with some hypotheses to form some divisibility rules.

Day 1

y = yes and n = no

Hypotheses of 2, 3, 5, 9, and 10

Divisible by	2	3	5	9	10
3,825	n	y	y	y	n
930					
792					
856					
1,440					
6,825					
1,854					
41,004					
85,010					
314,402					
4,277,133					
10,009,407					
9,617,590					
9,591,314					

2 Hypothesis
_____
_____
_____
_____

3 Hypothesis
_____
_____
_____
_____

5 Hypothesis
_____
_____
_____
_____

9 Hypothesis
_____
_____
_____

10 Hypothesis
_____
_____
_____

Try out your hypotheses on number combinations of your own to see if they really work.

The Expansion West. Write a dialogue that might have happened between the following people during the expansion west: an Indian, a settler, and a soldier. Remember to keep an open mind about their different points of view. Have your parents, brothers, sisters, or friends read the parts in costume!

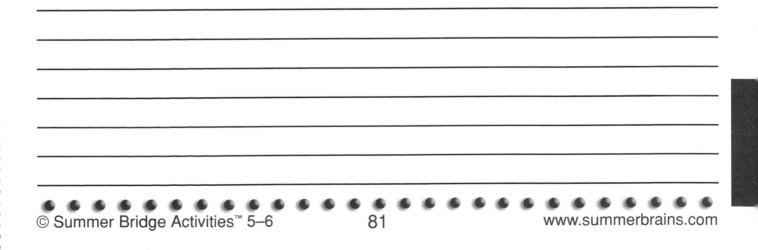

Day 1

Fill in the blank in each sentence with a synonym of the word in the box. Look in the dictionary if you need help.

EXAMPLE: I had to finish _complete_ my work before I could go with my friends.

1. Sarah and Angie go for a walk _____ every day except Sunday.

2. It's fun to watch the little colts play _____ in the green pastures.

3. The electricians have done enough _____ work for this week.

4. I cannot find _____ the information I need _____ for my report.

5. You will have to write _____ all the important events of your trip _____.

6. The lost couple had not had any food _____ for six days.

7. Will you please show _____ how your new invention works?

8. They will try _____ to climb Mount Everest again next summer.

9. Tourists might _____ be able to travel to the moon by the year 2010.

10. The value of this coin will grow _____ over the years.

11. The applicant must reply _____ within three weeks.

12. I think your story _____ was a little far-fetched!

Electric Current. Read each passage on electricity. One sentence in each passage is false. Cross out the false sentence and try to correct it. Then answer the questions after each passage.

1. An electrical current is moving energy. You can see electricity at work in lights, motors, computers, and some toys. Any material that allows an electric current to pass through is called a battery.

   Question: How many things can you think of in 1–2 minutes that need electricity? Have a race with someone to see who can think of the most ideas.

2. Material that does not allow an electric current to pass through it is called a circuit. This material covers conducting materials. It stops electricity from escaping and causing harm.

   Question: What are 5 things you can do to ensure safety in your home with electricity?

   1. _____   2. _____   3. _____

   4. _____   5. _____

Round the Clock Multiplication. Choose numbers between 10 and 100 and put them in the outer circle. Next, put numbers between 1 and 12 in the following circle. Then multiply the outer circle's number by the second circle's number.

EXAMPLE:

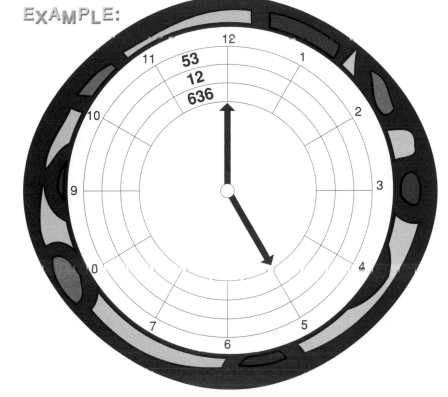

53
12
636

Moving West. Hunters, trappers, and pioneers moved west in the 1800s. Take 5 minutes to brainstorm all the things you would need for a trip west. List as many things as you can! Now take this list and think of different categories in which these items would fit. For example, one category might be food.

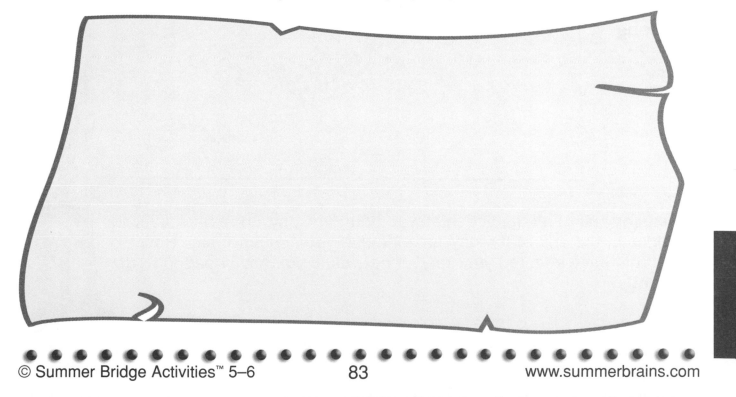

Spelling. What double consonants go in these spelling words?

1. i __ __ ediately
2. su __ __ ort
3. i __ __ egular
4. a __ __ ribute
5. di __ __ erence
6. a __ __ e __ __ ment
7. i __ __ emovable
8. a __ __ reviation
9. exce __ __ ence
10. a __ __ ual

11. su __ __ osed
12. po __ __ ible
13. inte __ __ igence
14. a __ __ egiance
15. bu __ __ ernut
16. i __ __ ocent
17. di __ __ atisfied
18. a __ __ e __ __ ible
19. scri __ __ le
20. permi __ __ ing

Health—Eyes. Label the parts of the eye below using the following words:

retina
cornea
lens
iris
pupil
vitreous humor
optic nerve

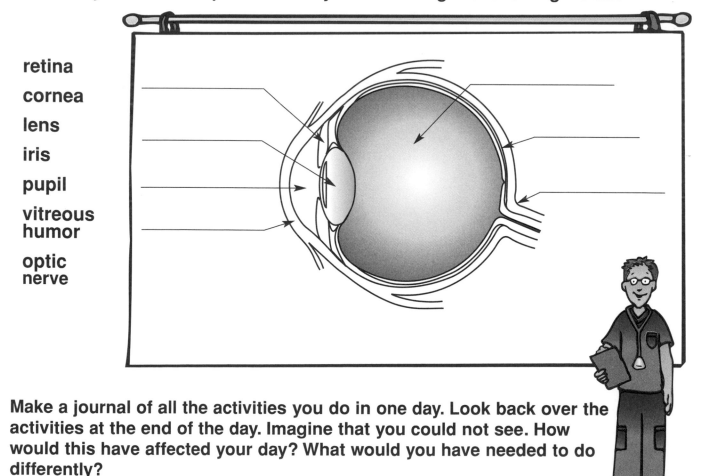

Make a journal of all the activities you do in one day. Look back over the activities at the end of the day. Imagine that you could not see. How would this have affected your day? What would you have needed to do differently?

Polyominoes.

1. These are all polyominoes.

   Why? _____

2. These are not polyominoes.

   Why not? _____

3. Draw some polyominoes of your own using 5 squares.

4. Chart the course by following lines according to the instructions below. How many polyominoes did you chart? _____

   east 1, north 3, east 5, north 3,
   east 1, south 5, east 1, north 3,
   west 5, south 4, west 1, north 6,
   west 1, north 3, east 1, south 2,
   east 5, north 1, west 3, north 1,
   east 4, south 1, east 1, south 6,
   west 1, south 2, west 8, and you
   should be back where you started from.

Start Here

How a Law Is Made. Put into sequence the following steps on how a bill can become a law. Then come up with a bill you think should become a law. Draw a comic strip that shows characters putting these steps into action.

_____ Get the president to approve.

_____ Write a bill.

_____ Get a majority vote in Congress.

_____ If the president vetoes the bill, then it may become a law by 2/3 vote in Congress.

Your own bill: _____

"The <u>Eagle</u> has landed."

American astronauts Neil Armstrong and Buzz Aldrin became the first men on the moon on July 20, 1969. The giant Apollo moon rocket was 363 feet high and weighed six and a half million pounds.

The Lunar Module (LM) left the Apollo at 1:45 P.M. "The Eagle has wings," Armstrong stated. At 3:46 the LM emerged from behind the moon. "The burn was on time," reported Armstrong matter-of-factly. At that time, they were at an altitude of about 20 miles, descending toward 50,000 feet. The astronauts had to make the all-important and final decision whether to remain in orbit or to descend to the lunar surface to make the landing.

At approximately 4:07 P.M., Armstrong pressed the button marked "Proceed." Aldrin and Armstrong realized in horror that the computer-controlled guidance system was taking them right down into a football-field-sized crater with a large number of big boulders and rocks. With only precious seconds to spare, Armstrong took manual control of the spacecraft. He searched for and found a clear area amid the menacing rock field below. "Houston," Armstrong radioed, "Tranquility base here. The Eagle has landed."

It was the first time men from earth had touched down on the moon. Armstrong was the first human being to set foot on the lunar surface. As his left foot touched the moon to take the first step, he spoke the now famous words, "That's one small step for man, one giant leap for mankind."

1. What was Armstrong referring to when he said "The Eagle has landed"?

2. The word "lunar" is used several times. What is another word for lunar?

3. What did "all-important and final decision" really mean to the astronauts?

4. What was the real significance of this mission to humankind?

5. What does this report tell you about what type of men Armstrong and Aldrin are?

6. What does this event say to you personally?

Electricity. Two electrical pathways are series circuits and two are parallel circuits. Label the pictures as either a series circuit or parallel circuit.

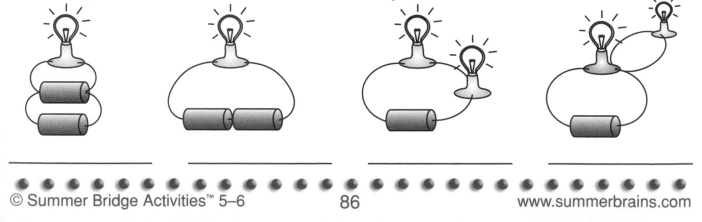

_____   _____   _____   _____

Relationship between Missing Numbers. Find the missing numbers and then write the rule.

1.

M	N
15	20
40	45
90	__
35	__

Rule: $M + 5 = N$

2.

M	N
25	36
19	30
57	__
__	84

Rule: $M + 11 = N$

3.

M	N
54	45
89	80
73	__
__	61

Rule: $M -$ ___

4.

M	N
9	72
11	88
7	__
5	__

Rule: $M \times$ ___

5.

M	N
8	48
4	24
10	__
6	__

Rule: ___

6.

M	N
21	7
30	10
18	__
12	__

Rule: $M \div$ ___

7.

M	N
48	8
12	2
__	7
24	__

Rule: ___

8.

M	N
36	24
57	45
63	__
__	78

Rule: ___

9.

M	N
7	63
__	81
__	54
3	27

Rule: ___

10.

M	N
10	120
__	144
9	108
__	132

Rule: ___

11.

M	N
3.2	5.5
7.1	__
__	7.3
4.4	__

Rule: ___

12.

M	N
35	50
73	__
__	42
100	__

Rule: ___

13.

M	N
24	3
56	__
72	__
__	8

Rule: ___

14.

M	N
4.2	8.4
__	18.6
8.1	16.2
__	15.0

Rule: ___

15.

M	N
0.09	0.14
0.13	0.18
__	0.10
3.21	__

Rule: ___

Trail of Tears. Do research on the Trail of Tears. Write a poem about this event using the letters of Trail of Tears at the beginning of each line. Be sure to include the emotions felt at this time. Make a border around the poem with colors and objects you feel would best describe the mood of your poem.

T ___
R ___
A ___
I ___
L ___
O ___
F ___
T ___
E ___
A ___
R ___
S ___

Contents and Index. Read this fictitious contents and index from a history book. Then answer the questions below.

1. What is the difference between the contents and the index in books?

   _____

   _____

2. If you wanted to know if this book had a section on the War of 1812, where would you look?

   _____

3. If you wanted to see if there was a picture of Andrew Jackson in the book, where would you look?

   _____

4. Where would you look to find out who fought in the Civil War?

   _____

5. How many chapters does this book have? _____

6. How many sections are in chapter one? _____

7. On what page would you look to find out about Native Americans?

   _____

8. On what page could you look to learn who Massasoit was?

   _____

9. How many sections are there about the Civil War?

   _____

10. What information is in the glossary of books?

   _____

Unscramble the syllables to make words. There might be one or two extra syllables in each word. Cross them out. All the words have something to do with transportation. EXAMPLE: ing merg ~~mer~~ _merging_

1. fic duc traf _____

2. bred ough thor fare _____

3. pave ved ment pa _____

4. ped tri pe an des _____

5. y per py slip par _____

6. in en state tar ter _____

7. tude struc tion con _____

8. ed ri strict strik re _____

9. jen mer tus e cy gen _____

10. toe a tow way u _____

11. ger dan dap ous dler _____

12. tion sek ter sti sec in _____

13. ex way te pro press _____

14. mum min i ion _____

Match the term to the mathematical definition dealing with fractions.

1. fraction
2. improper fraction
3. quotient
4. mixed number
5. denominator
6. numerator

a. The answer you get by dividing one number by another number

b. The number found below the line in a fraction

c. A number that names a part of a set or part of a whole

d. The number found above the line in a fraction

e. A number that has a whole number and a fraction

f. A fraction whose numerator is greater than its denominator or can be equal to its denominator

Show your understanding.

7. Show $15 \div 7$ as an improper fraction. _____

8. Show $2 \div 9$ as a fraction. _____

9. Show $11 \div 7$ as an improper fraction.

_____

10. $82 \div 7$ can be written $\frac{82}{7}$ or $7\overline{)82}$.

What is the divisor? _____

What is the remainder? _____

Write it as a mixed number. _____

11. What kind of fractions are these: $\frac{28}{5}$ $\frac{17}{12}$ $\frac{59}{7}$?

_____

Write a mixed fraction for each. _____

_____ _____

12. Write a mixed fraction for the following:

$7\overline{)29}$ $8\overline{)143}$ $25\overline{)90}$ $10\overline{)433}$

_____ _____ _____ _____

A Trailblazer. On his expeditions, Meriwether Lewis kept an illustrated journal on things he discovered. Imagine that you are also an explorer. Go outside and study natural objects or look at photographs of plants, animals, and physical features in your area. Write a journal entry on one of the objects you have found. Look at it as though you have never seen it before. Describe the structure of the object and hypothesize its function. After writing the description, draw and label the object.

Date: _____

Location: _____

Observations: _____

_____

_____

_____

_____

_____

Conclusions Versus Facts. People, young and old, often jump to conclusions. They frequently make up their mind without looking for facts or reasons behind a situation. Write a conclusion for each situation given and then think of facts you need to verify your conclusion.

1. There is a large package with your name on it at your doorstep without a note saying who it's from. It's not your birthday.

   Conclusion:

   Facts needed:

2. Your teacher sends a note home with you addressed directly to your parents. He/she tells you to make sure your parents get it.

   Conclusion:

   Facts needed:

3. When you go to the game, no one will speak to you or play with you.

   Conclusion:

   Facts needed:

4. The house is dark and the doors are locked when you get home.

   Conclusion:

   Facts needed:

5. You have looked all through the house and all over the yard, and you cannot find your pet turtle.

   Conclusion:

   Facts needed:

Natural Resources. Create a poster that reminds us of the importance of the 3 Rs: Reduce, Reuse, and Recycle!

Fraction Frames. Add to find the fraction. The sum of each is found in the center.

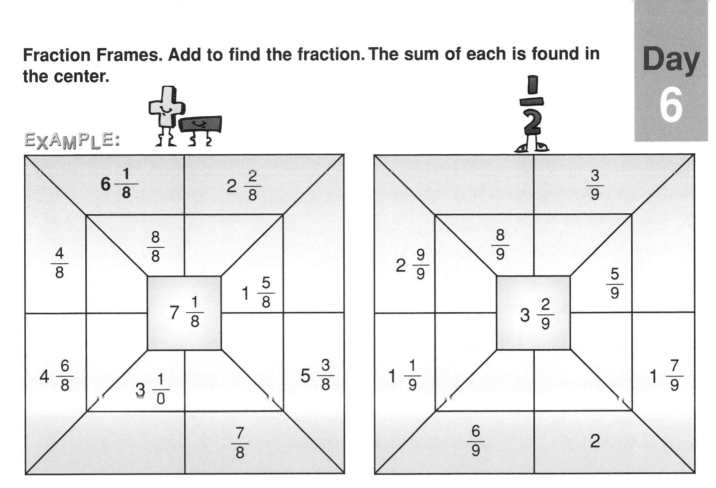

EXAMPLE:

Left frame:
$6\frac{1}{8}$ $2\frac{2}{8}$ $\frac{8}{8}$ $\frac{4}{8}$ $1\frac{5}{8}$ $7\frac{1}{8}$ $4\frac{6}{8}$ $3\frac{1}{0}$ $5\frac{3}{8}$ $\frac{7}{8}$

Right frame:
$\frac{3}{9}$ $\frac{8}{9}$ $2\frac{9}{9}$ $\frac{5}{9}$ $3\frac{2}{9}$ $1\frac{1}{9}$ $1\frac{7}{9}$ $\frac{6}{9}$ 2

Ears. Label the drawing and fill in the outline below with the terms in the proper sequential order; then explain how sound waves reach the brain through the ears.

cochlea   stirrup   pinna   auditory canal   hammer   anvil   eardrum

I. Outer Ear

  A.

II. Middle Ear

  A.

  B.

  C.

  D.

  E.

III. Inner Ear

  A.

Create a commercial that shows the importance of ear safety. Present it to your family.

Adverbs. Underline the adverb in each sentence. At the end of the sentence, write the word it modifies.

1. Brent's broken arm hurts badly. _____

2. The train moved rapidly down the tracks. _____

3. That chorus sang well. _____

4. Our three bulldogs waited eagerly for their walk. _____

5. The monkeys chattered noisily in the trees. _____

6. Yesterday Todd and Travis flew to London. _____

Fill in the blanks with adverbs.

7. The children ran _____ down the stairs.

8. Delicate white snowflakes were falling _____ to the ground.

9. Kirk spoke _____ to his father on the phone.

10. April drove her new car _____ through the middle of town.

11. The old windmill worked _____ after he oiled it.

12. Seven baby possums clung _____ to their mother's back

Categories. Find the word that does not belong in the category. Draw a line through it and write a sentence using the word you drew a line through to tell why it doesn't belong.

EXAMPLE: street - road - turnpike - ~~railroad~~ - freeway - highway   <u>Cars do not travel on a railroad.</u>

1. software - mouse - depth - program - disk _____

2. dawn - daytime - twilight - sunrise - hyphen _____

3. spaghetti - meatballs - menu - rhubarb - lasagna _____

4. cyclone - generator - tornado - hurricane - monsoon _____

5. mythology - petrology - geology - biology - zoology _____

6. almond - chocolate - caramel - butterscotch _____

7. exception - export - impolite - examiner - excavate _____

8. proverb - pronoun - adjective - noun - preposition - verb _____

9. period - comma - apostrophe - colon - clause _____

10. export - portable - support - importance - medieval _____

Watching for Zeros with Decimals. Remember the extra zeros when necessary.

1. $\begin{array}{r} 41.5 \\ \times\,0.17 \\ \hline \end{array}$	2. $\begin{array}{r} 1.09 \\ \times\,0.68 \\ \hline \end{array}$	3. $\begin{array}{r} 3.05 \\ \times\,85.2 \\ \hline \end{array}$

4. $\begin{array}{r} 0.003 \\ \times\,3.9 \\ \hline \end{array}$	5. $\begin{array}{r} 0.07 \\ \times\,1.06 \\ \hline \end{array}$

6. $\begin{array}{r} 0.025 \\ \times\,0.04 \\ \hline \end{array}$ 7. $\begin{array}{r} 0.59 \\ \times\,100 \\ \hline \end{array}$ 8. $\begin{array}{r} 347 \\ \times\,0.06 \\ \hline \end{array}$ 9. $\begin{array}{r} 78.6 \\ \times\,1{,}000 \\ \hline \end{array}$ 10. $\begin{array}{r} 7.029 \\ \times\,0.04 \\ \hline \end{array}$

11. $\begin{array}{r} 7.4 \\ \times\,0.07 \\ \hline \end{array}$ 12. $\begin{array}{r} 0.09 \\ \times\,2.3 \\ \hline \end{array}$ 13. $\begin{array}{r} 0.035 \\ \times\,0.02 \\ \hline \end{array}$ 14. $\begin{array}{r} 0.005 \\ \times\,55 \\ \hline \end{array}$ 15. $\begin{array}{r} 3.72 \\ \times\,0.07 \\ \hline \end{array}$

16. $\begin{array}{r} 27.5 \\ \times\,0.91 \\ \hline \end{array}$ 17. $\begin{array}{r} 60 \\ \times\,0.005 \\ \hline \end{array}$ 18. $\begin{array}{r} 0.92 \\ \times\,12.5 \\ \hline \end{array}$ 19. $\begin{array}{r} 1.08 \\ \times\,2.03 \\ \hline \end{array}$ 20. $\begin{array}{r} 0.06 \\ \times\,0.12 \\ \hline \end{array}$

First Aid. Read the following scenarios. After reading each sentence, determine whether proper first aid procedures were being followed. Make a smiley face if they were done correctly. Make an X if they were not done correctly.

Scenario 1: Dallin fell off his bike and could see a big bruise forming on his leg.
_____ He immediately put ice on it.
_____ Next, he used compression by applying pressure with a cloth on the bruise.
_____ Dallin then elevated his leg.

Scenario 2: While Jana and Adam were playing, a dog bit Adam.
_____ Jana chased the dog for two blocks trying to capture it.
_____ When she came back, Jana called her mom to help Adam.
_____ Jana thought they should put butter on the wound.
_____ Jana's mom washed the bite with soap and water.
_____ They took Adam to the doctor's office.
_____ Jana's mom called animal control.

Scenario 3: Linda felt dizzy and fainted.
_____ Stephen quickly caught her from falling.
_____ He gently put her to the floor and raised her feet.
_____ He turned Linda's face to the side in case she vomited.
_____ Mac suggested they slap or throw water on Linda to wake her up.
_____ Stephen said, "No, let's get an adult to help us."

*As a child, an important thing to remember with first aid is to get emergency help. Make a card of phone numbers you can call in case of an emergency. Put it by your phone.

Answer T for true or F for false to the following statements about a discussion group. Tell why you think the false statements are false.

_____ 1. You talk with others about an idea.

_____ 2. The leader of the group should do most of the talking.

_____ 3. The leader's only job is to keep things moving.

_____ 4. It is important to listen to what is being said.

_____ 5. Everyone should have a turn to talk.

_____ 6. The people in the group should not ask questions.

_____ 7. Questions should be asked by just the leader.

_____ 8. Disagreeing is okay in a discussion group.

_____ 9. One of the leader's duties is to keep order.

_____ 10. All participants should be polite to one another.

_____ 11. Anyone in the group can state the problem.

_____ 12. The discussion leader should sum up what has been decided or discussed at the end of the session.

Natural Resources. Pollution is a problem that affects all people on the Earth. Match the definition with the correct word. Put a smiley face in the column if this term helps with pollution problems. Put a sad face if it does not help our environment. If it is a sad face, come up with an idea of how we can improve in this area!

1. a tanker runs aground and leaks oil

2. energy generated from falling water

3. food for gardens from leaves and clippings

4. exhaust from cars and pollution from factories that create a layer of pollution; heat rays from sun cannot go back into the atmosphere

5. energy generated from the inside of the Earth

6. poisonous materials like paint thinner

7. saving

8. smoke and exhaust that mix with water vapor

9. waste taken to a dump that is eventually covered with earth

_____ greenhouse effect

_____ hazardous waste

_____ acid rain

_____ compost

_____ conservation

_____ geothermal energy

_____ hydroelectric energy

_____ landfill

_____ oil spill

Smiley or Sad	Idea

Finding the Circumference.

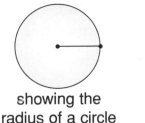

showing the
radius of a circle

showing the
diameter of a
circle

circumference is
the distance
around a circle

<u>**Remember:**</u> **To find the circumference of a circle, you must multiply the diameter by 3.14. With this information, complete the missing data in the table below.**

	Radius of the Circle	Diameter of the Circle	Circumference of the Circle
1.	12 mm	24 mm	75.36 mm
2.	11 inches	22 inches	
3.		18 cm	
4.	10 meters		
5.	13 yards		
6.			150.72 feet
7.		42 inches	
8.	17 cm		
9.			282.60 mm
10.			314 inches
11.		108 yards	
12.			621.72 cm

Women's Rights. Because of women such as Lucy Stone, Susan B. Anthony, Lucretia Mott, Elizabeth Cady Stanton, and Sarah and Angelina Grimke, women have many rights today that they didn't have in earlier times. Research one of these women and write of the trials she had to go through because of what she believed.

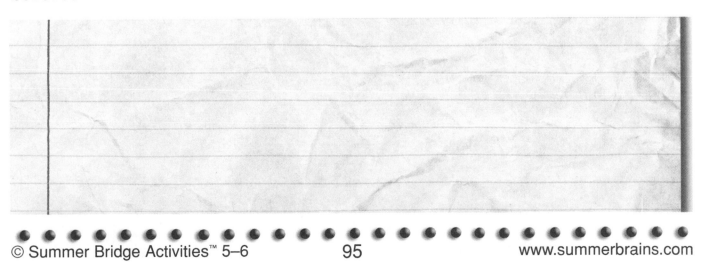

Adjectives tell how many, what kind, or which one about the nouns or pronouns they modify. Fill in the blanks with these kinds of adjectives. Use two adjectives telling how many, two telling what kind, and one telling which ones. At the end of the sentence, tell which kind you used.

1. _____ cars got stuck in the traffic jam. _____

2. _____ adventure was the most exciting I've ever had. _____

3. The _____ teddy bear cost twenty-five dollars. _____

4. There were _____ camels than lions at the zoo. _____

5. The _____ lizard that came after us was huge. _____

Articles: Special Adjectives (a, an, the). Circle the correct word.

6. Was that (a, an, the) alligator or (a, an) crocodile we saw back there?

7. The student gave her teacher (a, an) crisp, red apple.

8. (A, An, The) excited child was playing with (a, an) fluffy kitten.

9. After (a, an) rainstorm (a, an, the) sun glistens on (a, an, the) puddles.

10. If March comes in like (a, an, the) lion, it should go out like (a, an, the) lamb.

Compound Words. Take a word from list A and a word from list B to make compound words. Write the compound word in the middle. A word in list B could be the first word in the compound.

A	
weather	blood
craft	guard
loud	clip
ship	moon
vine	mint
anchor	turtle
watch	man
type	frost
print	in
ware	

1. _____
2. _____
3. _____
4. _____
5. _____
6. _____
7. _____
8. _____
9. _____
10. _____
11. _____
12. _____
13. _____
14. _____
15. _____
16. _____
17. _____
18. _____
19. _____

B	
speaker	news
silver	sight
wrist	wreck
man	writer
walk	board
yard	pepper
neck	woman
space	bite
hound	life
watch	

Multiplying Fractions Pictures.

Question: How do you picture what 1/2 of 1/2 is?

Picture ▭ 1/2 of a box as 1/2 of 1. Now picture what 1/2 of 1/2 is. So 1/2 of 1/2 = 1/4, or 1 ÷ 2 ÷ 2 = 1/4.

With the above information, illustrate and answer the following multiplication problems. Reduce to the simplest terms. <u>Remember</u>: When you multiply fractions, the product gets <u>smaller</u>.

1. 1/2 x 3/4 = _____

2. 1/4 x 1/2 = _____

3. 1/2 x 1/3 = _____

4. 1/3 x 2/3 = _____

5. 2/3 x 1/6 = _____

6. 1/3 x 1/4 = _____

7. 2/3 x 4/5 = _____

8. 2/3 x 2/3 = _____

9. 1/4 x 2/3 = _____

10. 3/4 x 2/5 = _____

11. 5/8 x 2/3 = _____

12. 4/5 x 3/5 = _____

Early Inventions in America. Match the inventor with his invention. Then sketch an invention of your own and explain in detail how it would work and why it would be a good idea.

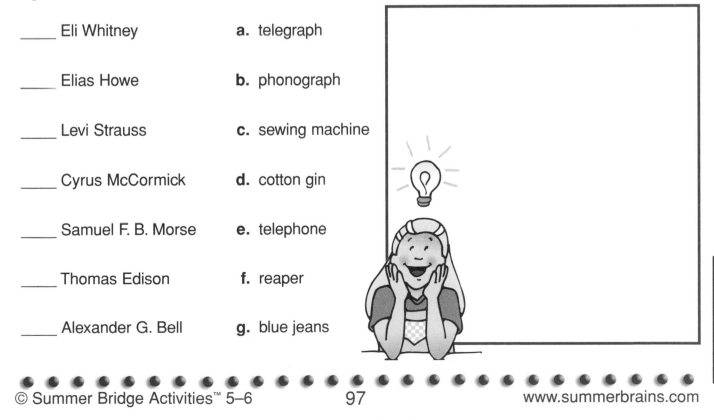

_____ Eli Whitney   **a.** telegraph

_____ Elias Howe   **b.** phonograph

_____ Levi Strauss   **c.** sewing machine

_____ Cyrus McCormick   **d.** cotton gin

_____ Samuel F. B. Morse   **e.** telephone

_____ Thomas Edison   **f.** reaper

_____ Alexander G. Bell   **g.** blue jeans

More than one adjective can be used to modify the same noun. Underline the adjectives in the sentences. Circle the word they modify.

1. The wild, eerie wind frightened the animals.

2. A fuzzy, brown caterpillar was creeping down the sidewalk.

3. Staci splashed some fresh, cool water on her face.

4. The hot, tired explorers swam in a large, clear lake.

5. The spicy aroma of apple cider filled Jason's small, warm tent.

6. I found a wee, puny puppy on my doorstep this morning.

Some adjectives are used to compare. Add -er or -est to these adjectives to complete the sentences.

7. The (rainy) _____ spot in the world is in Hawaii.

8. Our back door is (wide) _____ than our front door.

9. Mozart was one of the world's (young) _____ composers.

10. I think the gorilla is one of the (ugly) _____ of all the apes.

11. New Jersey is one of the (small) _____ states.

12. The swan egg was (large) _____ than the duck egg.

-er

-est

Answer these questions Yes or No. Use the dictionary for help.

1. Is a gizzard a kind of bird? ____

2. Would the boy wear his mukluk? ____

3. Could you work as a gofer? ____

4. Do you wear a goatee on your head? ____

5. Could you play with a googol? ____

6. Would you sit on a cloy? ____

7. Is a truffle a rich chocolate candy? ____

8. Could you plant a vetch? ____

9. Can a little girl wear aarf? ____

10. Does yep mean yes? ____

11. Is a yeti mysterious? ____

12. Could animals be kept in a sedge? ____

13. Is an orlop part of a ship? ____

14. Can you live in a yurt? ____

15. Would you chop wood with an italic? ____

16. Is an albatross a large sea serpent? ____

17. Could you have a huffy on your shirt? ___

18. Would you eat a mango? ____

19. Can you drive an osier? ____

20. Is a lilt a song or tune? ____

Practice Multiplying Fractions. Remember to multiply the numerators, then multiply the denominators.

1. $\dfrac{1}{2} \times \dfrac{3}{4} =$ —

2. $\dfrac{2}{3} \times \dfrac{2}{3} =$ —

3. $\dfrac{3}{4} \times \dfrac{1}{4}$ — —

4. $\dfrac{2}{3} \times \dfrac{5}{7} =$ —

5. $\dfrac{4}{5} \times \dfrac{2}{7} =$ —

6. $\dfrac{1}{6} \times \dfrac{5}{6} =$ —

7. $\dfrac{1}{3} \times \dfrac{2}{3} =$ —

8. $\dfrac{3}{4} \times \dfrac{5}{6} =$ —

9. $\dfrac{5}{9} \times \dfrac{3}{4} =$ —

10. $\dfrac{7}{8} \times \dfrac{2}{5} =$ —

11. $\dfrac{3}{5} \times \dfrac{3}{10} =$ —

12. $\dfrac{6}{7} \times \dfrac{3}{4} =$ —

Multiply. Write each product in its simplest form.

13. $\dfrac{1}{2} \times \dfrac{1}{6} \times \dfrac{2}{3} =$ — or —

14. $\dfrac{2}{3} \times \dfrac{5}{0} \times \dfrac{1}{4} =$ — or —

15. $\dfrac{1}{3} \times \dfrac{5}{7} \times \dfrac{3}{5} =$ — or —

16. $\dfrac{2}{3} \times \dfrac{3}{4} \times \dfrac{1}{2} =$ — or —

17. $\dfrac{8}{9} \times \dfrac{1}{3} \times \dfrac{3}{4} =$ — or —

18. $\dfrac{2}{3} \times \dfrac{1}{2} \times \dfrac{3}{8} =$ — or —

The Underground Railroad. Research the Underground Railroad. In each car there is a word used for a regular railroad. Underneath this word, write what each word would represent in the Underground Railroad. (Example: <u>passenger</u> would represent <u>slave</u>.) In the empty cars, come up with some of your own railroad terms. What would they represent in the Underground Railroad? (Example: <u>fuel</u> could represent <u>food</u>.)

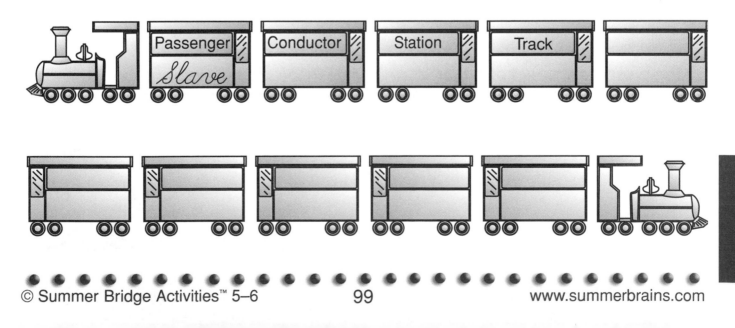

Day 10

Adverbs are words that modify or describe verbs, adjectives, and other adverbs. Adverbs tell how, when, and where. Many end with -ly. Use these adverbs to answer the questions in the chart.

immediately   far   there   nearly   wildly
softly   lately   slowly   carefully   hard
today   often   upstairs   eagerly
closely   soon   never   inside

When ?						
How ?						
Where ?						

Safety. Write down the consequence of each act and how it could have been prevented.

Act	Consequence	How It Could Have Been Prevented
1. Tripping on a toy		
2. Running in halls		
3. Swimming without a lifeguard		
4. Playing with matches		
5. Playing near broken glass		
6. Not wearing a seat belt		
7. Not wearing a helmet when biking		

Using a separate sheet of paper, draw a fire escape plan for your house. Make sure you have a meeting point outside for your family. Share your drawing with your family.

Angles. Fill in the blanks.

When two rays share the same endpoint they form an **(1.)** _____. This endpoint is called the **(2.)** _____ of the angle. The **(3.)** _____ is the unit used for measuring angles. A **(4.)** _____ is used to measure angles. A **(5.)** _____ is marked with **(6.)** _____ degrees. You place the center of the protractor on the vertex of the angle.

The **(7.)** _____ angle looks like a square corner. It measures **(8.)** _____ degrees. An **(9.)** _____ angle is smaller than a right angle or less than 90 degrees. An **(10.)** _____ angle is larger than a right angle or greater than 90 degrees.

Label these three angles.

11. _____   12. _____   13. _____

Use your protractor or the one in the back of the book to measure these angles.

14. _____   15. _____   16. _____   17. _____

Use your protractor to draw an angle for these measures.

18. 75°   19. 60°   20. 15°

Civil War. Look at the list below. Some of the terms have to do with the Civil War. Circle in gray the terms that refer to the Confederate side or a Confederate victory. Circle in blue the terms that refer to the Union side or a Union victory. Circle in red the terms that occurred in other periods of history.

Abraham Lincoln	Fort Duquesne	Valley Forge
Sally Tompkins	General Thomas "Stonewall" Jackson	Frederick Douglass
Saratoga	General Ulysses S. Grant	Bill of Rights
Battle of Bull Run	Andrew Jackson	General Robert E. Lee
1776	Seven Days' Battle	Thomas Jefferson
Paul Revere	John Paul Jones	Jefferson Davis
Antietam	Eli Whitney	General William T. Sherman
Yorktown	Harriet Tubman	

Proofread and circle the mistakes in the following paragraphs. Then rewrite the paragraphs, correcting the mistakes in spelling, punctuation, etc. Write in cursive. Try to find thirty-nine mistakes.

today the term "Native American" is used to descibe those people indigenous to america. however the firt explorers who came to America referred to them as "Indians" unknown to the exploders, most tribes had their own names. for example names used by the deleware indians of eastern north america meant "genuine men".

the Indians' languages way of life, and homes wer all very different. The aztic and maya Indians of central America built large citys The apache and Paiute used brush and mating to make simple huts the plains indians buit coneshaped tepees covered with buffalo skins Cliff dwellers and other Pueblo groups usd sun-dried bricks to make many-storyed houses

_____

_____

_____

_____

_____

_____

_____

_____

_____

_____

Use homophones or homonyms to fill in these blanks. <u>Remember</u>**: They are words that sound or are spelled the same, but mean different things.**

EXAMPLE: _I_ think _I_ have something in my _eye_.

1. Chris will _____ catching a bumble _____ for his insect collection.

2. My _____ Lola had an _____ bite her toe.

3. The _____ was _____ from playing at the concert.

4. _____ visit the _____ of Man in June.

5. Please _____ the door to the _____ closet.

6. Patt _____ me one _____ for good luck.

7. My _____ jeans _____ away in the wind.

8. We went _____ the mall to _____ some cards.

9. My brother _____ _____ pancakes for breakfast.

10. _____, I do not _____ how to play a musical instrument.

Reading Graphs.
Circle graphs compare parts of a whole.

Jake earns $20 a week doing chores for his neighbors. This circle graph shows how he uses his money.

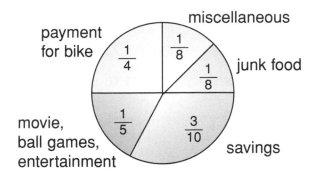

1. How much money does Jake spend on junk food each week? $_____

2. How much on entertainment? $_____

3. How much on debts? $_____

4. How much does he save? $_____

5. Miscellaneous $_____

Bar graphs help you to compare data at a glance.

Valley Fair Music Place recorded the different types of music it sold during the summer months.

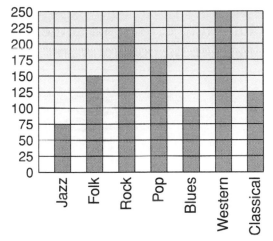

6. Which was the most popular? _____

7. Which sold the least? _____

8. What is the difference between the greatest and the least sold? _____

9. Which type of music came out with the average number sold? _____

10. Which is your favorite kind? _____

A pictograph uses picture symbols to represent data or specific units. Riverton School kept track of how many parents visited their school during Parent Week. They made a pictograph to show the students the results.

Monday	🚶 🚶 🚶 🚶 🚶 🚶 🚶 🚶
Tuesday	🚶 🚶 🚶 🚶 🚶 🚶
Wednesday	🚶 🚶 🚶
Thursday	🚶 🚶 🚶
Friday	🚶 🚶 🚶 🚶 🚶 🚶

Each 🚶 = 10 parents

11. Which day did most parents come? _____

12. What does 🚶 represent? _____

13. How many parents visited the school during Parent Week? _____

14. What other type of graph could you have used to show this data? _____

Day 12

Prepositions are words that show certain relationships between other words. The words below are prepositions.

before	between	after	during	until	to
of	with	behind	near	above	through
for	under	off	across	from	in

Cross out the underlined words, and use one of the prepositions above to show a different relationship between these words.

EXAMPLE:

1. Grayson found his backpack ~~under~~ ____**near**____ his bed.

2. Julie stood <u>beside</u> _____ me at the parade.

3. Did you leave this box <u>on</u> _____ the bench?

4. The children will play <u>after</u> _____ dark.

5. The bats flew <u>into</u> _____ the window.

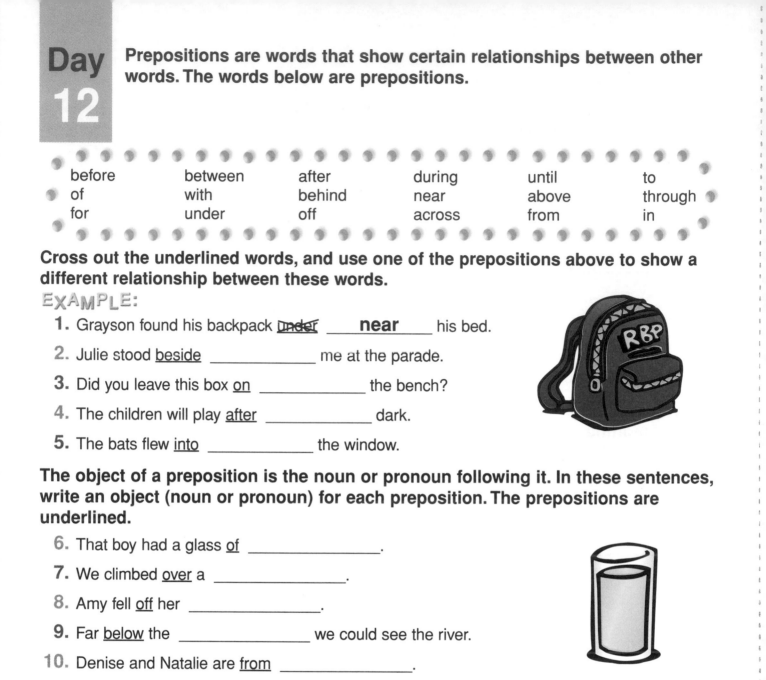

The object of a preposition is the noun or pronoun following it. In these sentences, write an object (noun or pronoun) for each preposition. The prepositions are underlined.

6. That boy had a glass <u>of</u> _____.

7. We climbed <u>over</u> a _____.

8. Amy fell <u>off</u> her _____.

9. Far <u>below</u> the _____ we could see the river.

10. Denise and Natalie are <u>from</u> _____.

Find the word that is spelled wrong. Cross it out and write it correctly above the list.

1. _____
tricycle
bicycle
motorcicle
unicycle
cycler

2. _____
homonym
symphony
synonym
antonym
encyclopidiu

3. _____
opposite
oportunity
opposed
appearance
appointment

4. _____
exhaost
exhibit
exist
example
exceed

5. _____
typing
gypsy
pearamid
paralyze
syllable

6. _____
thoughtful
doughnut
straght
design
twilight

7. _____
unfamilar
unsatisfactory
unusual
united
university

8. _____
cruelty
greedy
luxury
enjoyable
carfree

Percentage is the comparison of a number to 100.

EXAMPLE: 15/100 = 15%   15 to 100 = 15%   15:100 = 15%

Write each ratio as a percent.

1. $\frac{20}{100}$ = ____   2. $\frac{50}{100}$ = ____   3. $\frac{3}{100}$ = ____   4. $\frac{47}{100}$ = ____

5. 9 to 100 = ____   6. 33 to 100 = ____   7. 14 to 100 = ____   8. 1 to 100 = ____

9. 75:100 = ____   10. 69:100 = ____   11. 81:100 = ____   12. 7:100 = ____

Write each percent in the form of a fraction.

13. 19% =   14. 87% =   15. 99% =   16. 24% =

17. 36% =   18. 55% =   19. 8% =   20. 63% =

Write each percentage in the lowest terms of a fraction.

21. 50% = $\frac{50}{100}$ = $\frac{1}{2}$ 22. 20% = ____ = ____   23. 70% = ____ = ____

24. 90% = ____ = ____   25. 45% = ____ = ____   26. 25% = ____ = ____

27. 4% = ____ = ____   28. 2% = ____ = ____   29. 80% = ____ = ____

30. 64% = ____ = ____   31. 15% = ____ = ____   32. 52% = ____ = ____

Progress in the 1800s. Many changes occurred in America with the coming of the railroad, mining, and farming. These events encouraged more and more people to move west. Read and answer the following questions.

1. "Progress cannot be stopped." Do you agree with this statement? Why or why not?

2. Should we stop progress if it is hurting others or their rights are being ignored? Why or why not?

3. How does progress relate to the American Indians being placed on reservations in the 1800s?

4. List some modern examples of progress that hinder the rights of others. Are you in favor of these examples of progress? Why or why not?

The preposition and its object are called a prepositional phrase. Below are some phrases. Underline those that are prepositional phrases. Think about what words are prepositions. Refer to page 104 for help.

EXAMPLE: <u>past</u> <u>him</u>

1. between first and second base
2. near the broken bottle
3. a light hung
4. on your own paper
5. the messy streets
6. animals having four
7. along the trail
8. the circus elephant
9. outside the back door
10. under the house
11. your guide
12. until four o'clock
13. the science experiment
14. are the bridges
15. in the barn
16. how you will be
17. through the bushes
18. from my sister
19. writing her name
20. before our picnic
21. over the hill

Health Problems and Pollution.
Complete each statement with the correct word listed below.

noise pollution
Environmental Protection Agency (EPA)

pollution
toxic waste
carbon monoxide

radon
sewage
landfills

1. _____ is a dangerous gas in polluted air. One source of this gas is cigarette smoke.

2. _____ is a gas that can enter buildings through cracks. It becomes trapped in the building and can cause lung cancer.

3. Any sound that is loud enough to cause harm to your ears and health is called _____.

4. _____, which includes chemical or human waste, can be harmful if dumped into a water supply.

5. Chemical waste that enters the water supply and causes people to be ill is called _____.

6. _____ attract rats, insects, and rodents. These animals spread pathogens to humans.

7. _____ is particulates and products in the environment that can harm health.

8. The _____ is an office of the government that determines rules and laws to control pollution.

Write a newspaper editorial about the importance of decreasing pollution where you live. Include in your editorial at least 3 facts about pollution.

Decimals that name hundreds can easily be written as percents because percent means per hundred.

Write a percent and a decimal for each picture (shaded area).

1. _____ _____   2. _____ _____   3. _____ _____

Write each percentage below as a decimal.

4. 27% = ____	**5.** 35% = ____	**6.** 54% = ____	**7.** 43% = ____
8. 95% = ____	**9.** 7% = ____	**10.** 18% = ____	**11.** 3% = ____

Write each decimal below as a percentage.

12. .15 = ____	**13.** .88 = ____	**14.** .07 = ____	**15.** .91 = ____
16. .05 = ____	**17.** .1 = ____	**18.** .6 = ____	**19.** .4 = ____

Find the number for each percentage below.

20. 8% of 45 = $.08$ x 45 = 3.6	**21.** 7% of 90 = ____ x ____ = ____
22. 40% of 25 = ____ x ____ = ____	**23.** 25% of 67 = ____ x ____ = ____
24. 90% of 185 = ____ x ____ = ____	**25.** 33% of 96 = ____ x ____ = ____

World War I. The casualties in World War I were overwhelming. Study the chart below of the number of estimated combat deaths from the major countries involved. Answer the questions below.

Allied Powers		Central Powers	
Country	**Number of Deaths**	**Country**	**Number of Deaths**
United States	.049 million	Turkey	.7 million
Italy	.5 million	Austria	1.2 million
Great Britain	1 million	Germany	1.8 million
France	1.4 million		
Russia	1.7 million		

1. Did the Allied Powers or Central Powers have more deaths? By how many? _____

2. What was the total number of estimated combat deaths in World War I? _____

3. How many more deaths did Great Britain have than the United States? _____

4. Why do you think Germany lost the most soldiers in World War I? _____

Day 14

Friendly Letter. Rewrite this friendly letter using the correct form, punctuation marks, capital letters, etc. Be sure to indent at the beginning of each paragraph.

1624 bay lane short creek pa 12526 may 10 1996 dear aunt ann and uncle york school will soon be out for the summer i am looking forward to it the year has been good and i have learned a lot but it was a long one mom and dad are going to france in july i don't want to go with them i'm writing this letter to ask if i can stay with you for two weeks it would be july 10 through the 22 i would love to help you take care of the horses and do anything else you want me to do i would also help around the house please let me know if i can come your loving niece julie ann

_____

_____

_____

_____

_____

_____

_____

_____

_____

_____

Now address the envelope for Julie Ann's letter. Be sure to put the addresses on the envelope in the right places. Put in capitals and punctuation marks.

The addresses are
mr and mrs york batty
1010 a and y ranch rt 2
box 10 ely idaho 89621
julie ann fobbs 1624 bay
lane short creek pa 12526

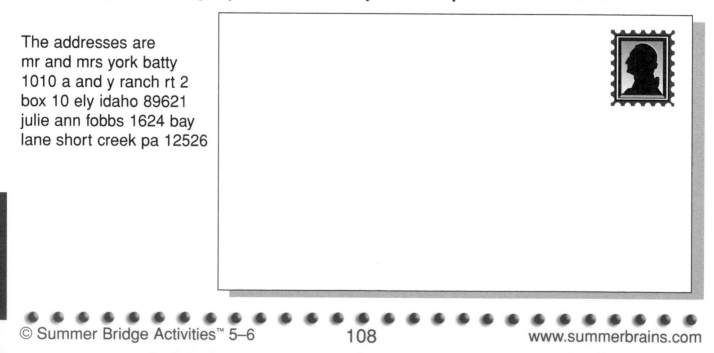

Mixed Practice.

1. $24.98	2. $89.82	3. 86,945	4. 3,921	5. 34,783
14.20	42.47	6,913	1,823	43,927
10.19	8.18	7,428	4,765	50,143
+ 82.27	+ 75.03	+ 5,317	+ 5,283	+ 38,527

6. 674	7. 5,978	8. 95.27	9. 438.5	10. 72,974
x 392	x 703	x 5.93	x 4.86	x .908

11. $74\overline{)95,634}$

12. $82\overline{)809,593}$

13. $69\overline{)593,745}$

14. $93\overline{)729,374}$

15. $6\frac{3}{5} \times 1\frac{2}{8} =$

16. $2\frac{1}{2} \times 4\frac{1}{5} =$

17. $10 \times 4\frac{3}{5} =$

18. $8\frac{1}{3} \times 4\frac{1}{6} =$

19. $2\frac{2}{5} + 6\frac{3}{4} =$

20. $8 - 2\frac{3}{4} =$

Civil Rights Movement. The answers are already given, but you need to come up with the questions. All the questions regard the Civil Rights Movement in the 1950s and 1960s.

1. Answer: The separation of black and white people from each other.

   Question:

2. Answer: An organization that tries to help African-Americans gain their civil rights.

   Question:

3. Answer: In 1955, she refused to give up her seat on the bus to a white passenger.

   Question:

4. Answer: A reverend who believed that African-Americans needed to protest against

   inequality in a nonviolent manner.

   Question:

Day 15

Use these adverbs to fill in the puzzle. Use each word only once. One has been done for you.

yesterday
least
completely
carefully
loudly
slowly

almost
badly
above
yeah
yet
rapidly

impatiently
too
today
better
yonder
quickly

lightly
wildly
hardest
confidentially
lusciously
reluctantly

c o m p l e t e l y

Words to Sound, Read, and Spell

absurdity	autograph	compress	difficult	expelled	historic
acceptable	automatic	conceited	diminutive	exported	honor
accident	automobile	concession	diploma	extend	horror
accidentally	autumn	condition	director	extraordinary	humiliated
accomplish	avail	conduct	disagree	factual	humor
accomplished	available	conductor	disappear	factually	humorous
account	average	confiscated	discourage	famous	hydrant
accuse	aviator	confused	discovery	fashion	hyphen
accuser	avoid	considerate	disposal	fatal	hypnotism
ache	avoidable	constitution	disposition	fatally	ideal
acquit	barometer	consult	disrespectful	figure	ideally
acquitted	beauties	consume	dissatisfied	final	identified
actual	beautiful	consumer	distress	finally	identifies
actually	beige	contain	distrust	finesse	identify
address	bicycle	contradiction	dividing	flaming	imaginary
addresses	bleach	contrary	doubt	flattery	immediately
adhesive	blunder	convenient	dramatize	flexible	immense
adjective	boundary	convertible	duplex	fluently	immune
admirable	brackish	convict	duplexes	forbidden	impending
adorable	bravery	convince	dynamic	foreign	importance
advance	breakable	cost	earthquake	foreigner	impossible
adventure	builder	couch	echo	forfeit	impractical
adventurous	buoyant	couches	ecstatic	forgivable	impression
advertise	burglar	counterfeit	edict	forgiveness	improvement
advertisement	business	counterfeiting	editor	formation	incapable
advertiser	businesses	courier	either	fortune	inconsiderate
advice	buyer	criminal	emigrating	forty-two	inconvenient
advisable	calculators	criminally	emission	fragile	independent
aisle	calendar	cruelty	emits	freight	indignantly
alley	campus	crystal	emitted	furious	individual
alleys	campuses	cue	emphatically	further	individually
allowable	capitalize	cyclone	employ	fury	induction
alphabetically	captivity	dangerous	employing	gallery	infernal
although	causes	debt	enemies	gardener	inject
amazement	celery	deceitful	enemy	gauge	injection
ambition	cemetery	deceive	engrossed	generally	injured
amuse	center	decode	enjoy	giant	injuries
anchor	chaos	deduction	enjoyable	gigantic	injurious
angel	chemical	deflate	enjoyed	gilded	injury
angle	chlorine	defrost	equal	glamorous	inscribe
anniversary	choir	degrees	equally	glamour	inscription
announce	chord	dehydrate	equator	glimpse	inspection
announcer	chorus	delay	equip	glorious	intelligence
annual	circular	delayed	equipped	glossary	interjection
annually	citation	delaying	error	gnash	intermediate
anxious	clatter	delivery	escort	gnat	introduce
apologies	climax	denounce	exaggerate	gorgeous	inventor
apologize	climaxes	dependable	examine	gossip	invest
apology	clothes	dependent	examiner	governor	invite
apparently	coaxed	depending	example	gratitude	janitor
appearance	code	deposit	exasperated	greedy	journey
applauded	collar	depress	exceed	grief	journeys
appointment	column	depression	excellence	grocery	joyous
appreciation	combine	describe	except	group	judge
arches	command	design	exception	guard	khaki
architecture	comment	desirable	excess	guesses	knuckles
arrange	commentaries	destroy	excitable	guest	labor
arrival	commercial	destroyed	excite	guitar	laborer
assembly	commitment	destroying	exclaim	gypsy	laughable
assignment	committee	determined	exclamation	handling	leashes
assortment	community	determines	excuse	hardly	legally
astonished	compare	determining	exertion	haunches	leisure
astounded	complete	diaries	exhaust	hazard	library
attractive	complexion	diary	exhibit	hazardous	lifeguard
author	complimentary	dictator	expand	heir	loafer
autobiography	composition	dictionary	expel	heiress	locally

luggage	nimble	position	regular	similar	tolerance
lunar	normal	postpone	regulate	simplify	tormentor
luxuries	normally	powerless	reign	sinus	totally
luxurious	notice	practices	relaxed	sinuses	traitor
luxuriously	nuclear	practicing	relied	slavery	traitorous
luxury	nursery	precise	relies	sleigh	transfer
lyric	objectionable	prediction	rely	slogan	transmit
machinery	occur	prefix	relying	solemn	transmitting
magazine	occurred	prefixes	reminder	solid	transportation
magic	omit	preheat	remittance	sorrowful	traveler
magnified	omitted	prehistoric	remnant	spaghetti	truthful
mailboxes	operator	prejudice	replacement	speaker	typhoon
manage	opinion	preposition	reporter	spectacle	typical
manager	opponent	prescribe	requirement	spectacular	tyrant
manufacture	opportunity	pressure	requiring	spectator	undaunted
manufacturer	opposed	preview	respect	speeches	unfamiliar
margin	opposite	problem	respectable	sponsor	unidentified
marvel	opposition	process	respectful	starved	unites
marvelous	optician	produce	respond	statement	unnamed
mayor	optimist	profitable	resume	stating	unnecessary
measurement	orbit	propaganda	retirement	stationary	unretractable
measuring	orchestra	propel	retrieve	stationery	unsatisfactory
mechanic	ordinary	propeller	reverse	stomach	unsuccessful
mediator	organize	propelling	review	strolled	unveiling
meditating	organizer	prosperous	revise	studios	urgent
medley	original	protein	revolutionary	submission	usable
megaphone	originally	publish	rhinestone	submit	use
melodious	outstanding	publisher	rhinoceros	submitting	vanish
melodiously	owing	punctual	rhubarb	subscribe	various
members	paralyze	punctually	rhythm	subscription	vein
mental	paralyzed	punish	ridicule	subtract	venture
mentally	parents	punishable	ridiculous	subvert	verdict
merchandise	particular	purchase	robbery	successful	version
microphone	passenger	purchaser	role	suffix	victorious
microscope	patrol	purpose	roommate	suffixes	victory
microscopic	patrolling	pyramid	routine	suggestion	vigor
military	peculiar	python	rumba	suitable	vigorous
mirror	penalty	quiver	rumor	supplement	villain
misery	pendant	raise	salary	supplied	vinegar
misfortune	pendulum	raises	salmon	supposed	visitor
misplaced	penetrate	raising	sandwich	surface	visual
modern	perceive	reachable	sandwiched	surgery	visualized
monarch	perception	readable	satisfied	suspect	vocabulary
monastery	performance	rearrange	satisfies	suspended	walrus
monotone	perishable	reasonable	satisfy	syllable	walruses
monotonous	permit	reasonableness	satisfying	sympathy	waltz
motto	permitted	receipt	scenery	symphony	waltzes
movable	perpendicular	receptacle	schedule	symptom	washable
muscular	perpetually	receptive	scholastic	system	wearable
mused	personal	recesses	search	talent	weight
mystery	personally	recital	searches	taxes	weird
myth	phonograph	rectangular	secede	telegraph	weirdly
mythology	photograph	reenter	secretary	telepathy	well-balanced
national	pillars	reexamine	seized	telephone	wholesale
naturally	placed	refinery	self-addressed	temporary	worse
nature	planet	reformation	senator	terrified	wrench
navigate	pledge	refrigerator	separate	terrifies	wrenches
navigator	plumber	refugees	separating	terrify	wrist
necessary	poison	regiment	sighed	terrifying	wristwatch
neither	poisonous	register	sightseers	territory	yacht
nervous	popular	regret	silent	terror	
nighttime	porches	regretted	silhouette	threat	

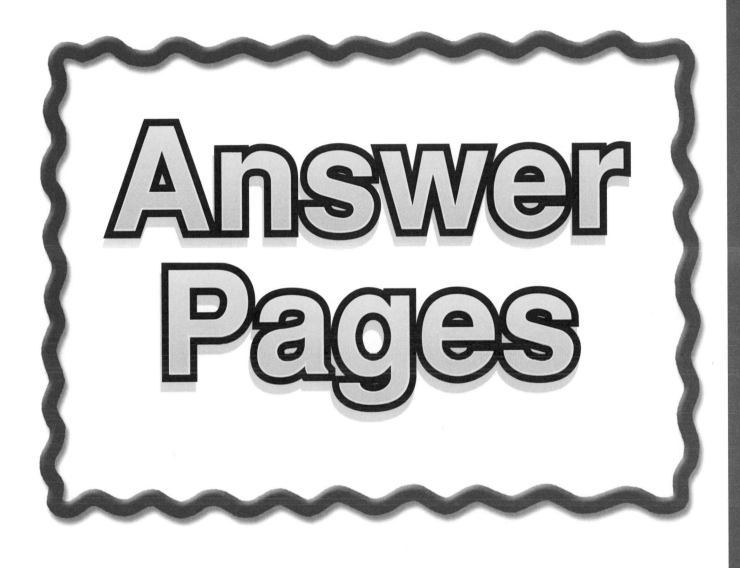

Answer Pages

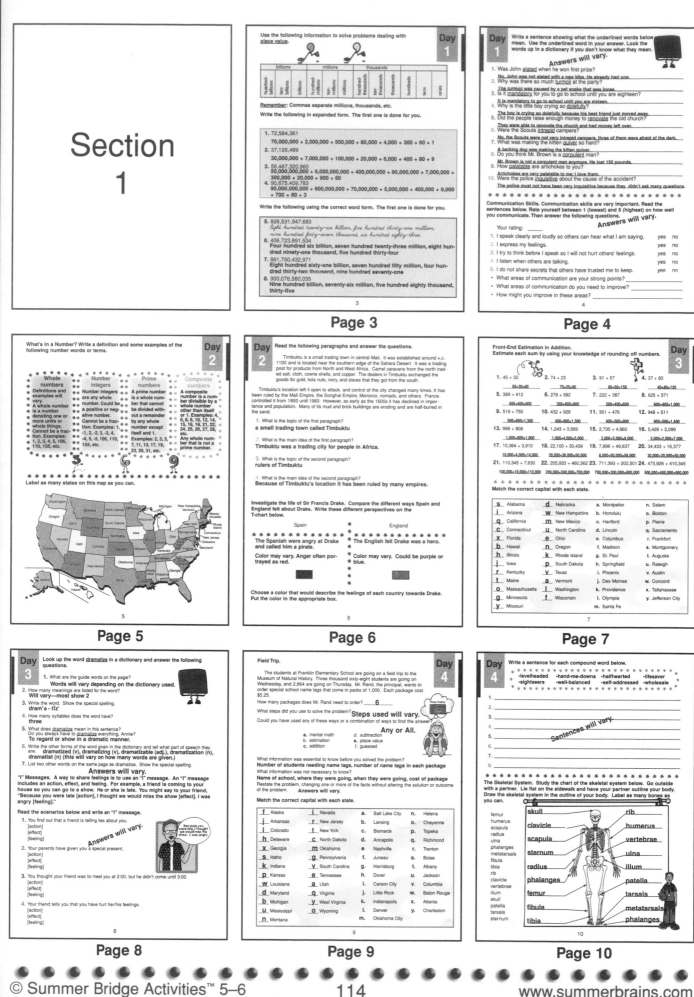

Section 1

Page 3

Page 4

Page 5

Page 6

Page 7

Page 8

Page 9

Page 10

Page 11

Day 5

Estimation with Sums and Differences.
Estimate the sum or difference first; then find the actual sum or difference.

1. 8,666 +9,346 estimate 18,000 actual 18,012	2. 7,543 +2,396 estimate 10,000 actual 9,939	3. 3,693 +1,690 estimate 6,000 actual 5,383	4. 54,561 +36,287 estimate 90,000 actual 90,848
5. 34,865 +62,444 estimate 90,000 actual 97,309	6. 47,267 +55,085 estimate 110,000 actual 102,352	7. 65,639 +53,263 estimate 120,000 actual 118,902	8. 28,790 +83,964 estimate 110,000 actual 112,754
9. 5,394 -2,587 estimate 2,000 actual 2,807	10. 3,368 -2,139 estimate 1,000 actual 1,229	11. 69,293 -22,887 estimate 50,000 actual 46,406	12. 125,394 -69,831 estimate 60,000 actual 55,563
13. 25,689 -13,798 estimate 20,000 actual 11,891	14. 417,937 -409,986 estimate 10,000 actual 7,951	15. 709,723 -337,251 estimate 400,000 actual 372,472	16. 876,259 -395,828 estimate 500,000 actual 480,431

Below are the stressed syllables of some spelling words. Write the other syllables, and then write the words in cursive. Each blank stands for a letter. The first one is done for you.

practice, measure, improvement, amazement, purchaser, refund, magazine, chosen, glamorous, ~~January~~, diamond, attention, trillion, appearance, manager, causing

1. Jan´u a r y — *January*
2. a t ten´t i o n — *attention*
3. pur´c h a s e r — *purchaser*
4. re´f u n d — *refund*
5. tril´l i o n — *trillion*
6. mea´s u r e — *measure*
7. a p pear´a n c e — *appearance*
8. cho´s e n — *chosen*
9. di´a m o n d — *diamond*
10. mag´a z i n e — *magazine*
11. man´a g e r — *manager*
12. caus´i n g — *causing*
13. a maze´m e n t — *amazement*
14. glam´o r o u s — *glamorous*
15. prac´t i c e — *practice*
16. i m prove´v e n t — *improvement*

11

Page 12

Day 5

Cause and Effect.
Some sentences have a clue word to help show the cause-effect relationship. Fill in the blanks with clue words. Then write the cause and effect.

Our school was closed today because of the bad snowstorm we had last night.
Cause: *Bad snow storm.*
Effect: *School was closed.*

1. It snowed all day, **so** the ground was white.
Cause: **it snowed all day**
Effect: **the ground was white**
2. Our electricity went off last night, **as a result or so** we went out to dinner.
Cause: **electricity went off**
Effect: **we went out to dinner**
3. **Because** Joe left the gate unlatched, all the cattle were out in the road.
Cause: **Joe left the gate unlatched**
Effect: **the cattle were out in the road**
4. Scott woke up with the flu today; **therefore or so**, he had to miss school.
Cause: **Scott woke up with the flu**
Effect: **he had to miss school**
5. **Since** I know how much Judy loves to read, I got her a set of books for her birthday.
Cause: **Judy loves to read**
Effect: **I got her books for her birthday**

Science—Structure of the Earth.
Label the different layers of the earth with the terms below. Use the same terms to complete the sentences below.

center of the earth, mantle, crust, lithosphere, inner core, outer core

1. The core of the earth has two parts. The **outer core** is liquid. The **inner core** is solid.
2. One reason the crust and **lithosphere** are brittle is because they are the outermost and coldest layers of the earth.
3. The top layer of the earth is the **crust**
4. The **mantle** is extremely hot and is the thickest layer.
5. As the **center of earth** is approached, pressure and temperature increase.

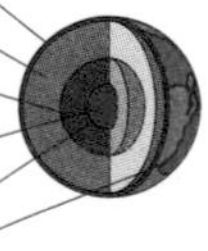

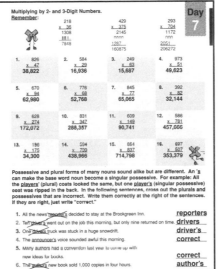

12

Page 13

Day 6

Mental Math for Multiples of 10, 100, and 1,000. Remember to use mental math!

1. 7 x 10 = 70
2. 16 x 10 = 160
3. 10 x 92 = 920
4. 100 x 8 = 800
5. 50 x 50 = 2,500
6. 7 x 600 = 4,200
7. 500 x 200 = 100,000
8. 5 x 900 = 4,500
9. 70 x 60 = 4,200
10. 30 x 400 = 12,000
11. 200 x 300 = 60,000
12. 400 x 600 = 240,000
13. 8 x 1,000 = 8,000
14. 9 x 3,000 = 27,000
15. 30 x 5,000 = 150,000
16. 900 x 200 = 180,000
17. 800 x 600 = 480,000
18. 10 x 1,800 = 18,000
19. 9,000 x 700 = 6,300,000
20. 7,000 x 50 = 350,000
21. 60 x 8,000 = 480,000
22. 700 x 800 = 560,000
23. 900 x 900 = 810,000
24. 1,000 x 19 = 19,000
25. 52 x 2,000 = 104,000
26. 400 x 300 = 120,000
27. 5,000 x 50 = 250,000
28. 250 x 200 = 50,000
29. 15,000 x 30 = 450,000
30. 200,000 x 40 = 8,000,000

Healthy Lifestyles.
Fill in the chart of acts and consequences. Using the last two lines, fill in two acts that you may do in a day and what consequences follow.

Acts	Consequences
1. Do not eat breakfast	
2. Cheat on test	
3.	Get an A in spelling
4. Comfort a friend	
5.	Feel good about yourself
6.	You have a lot of energy
7. Take a shower every day	
8. Adult catches your friend smoking	
9.	Get sick
10. Visit the elderly	
11. Say NO to drugs	
12.	
13.	

Answers will vary. **Answers will vary.**

13

Page 14

Day 6

Syllables. Show the syllables by leaving a space between them. Then write long, short, schwa, or silent for the vowel sound in each syllable. Remember, the schwa sound is usually heard in the unstressed syllable. Use a dictionary if you need help.

Example: terrific *ter ri fic* *schwa short short*

1. jackal — **jack al** — **short schwa**
2. liable — **li a ble** — **long schwa silent**
3. volcano — **vol ca no** — **short long long**
4. that — **that** — **short**
5. attraction — **at trac tion** — **schwa short schwa**
6. billow — **bil low** — **short long**
7. paralysis — **pa ral y sis** — **schwa short schwa short**
8. identify — **i den ti fy** — **long short short long**
9. mold — **mold** — **long**
10. victory — **vic to ry** — **short schwa long**
11. lesson — **les son** — **short silent**
12. referee — **ref er ee** — **short schwa long**

The Muscular System and Nervous System. Fill in the blanks with the correct word.

cerebrum, nervous system, contracts, involuntary muscles, voluntary muscles, spinal cord, medulla, cerebellum

1. Muscles you can control are called **voluntary muscles**.
2. When one muscle in a pair **contracts**, or shortens, the other muscle relaxes.
3. **Involuntary muscles** are muscles that work automatically, such as the heart.
4. The **nervous system** is the network of cells that receive and send messages to and from the brain and spinal cord to every part of your body.
5. The part of your brain that controls your learning and memory is the **cerebrum**.
6. The **cerebellum** controls how your muscles work together.
7. The part of your brain that controls your heart rate and breathing is the **medulla**.
8. The **spinal cord** extends from the base of the brain down your back and is involved with all senses.

14

Page 15

Day 7

Multiplying by 2- and 3-Digit Numbers.
Remember:

218 x 36 = 1308 + 654 = 7848
429 x 375 = 2145 + 3003 + 1287 = 160875
293 x 704 = 1172 + 000 + 2051 = 206272

1. 826 x 47 = **38,822**	2. 584 x 29 = **16,936**	3. 249 x 63 = **15,687**	4. 973 x 51 = **49,623**
5. 670 x 94 = **62,980**	6. 776 x 68 = **52,768**	7. 845 x 77 = **65,065**	8. 392 x 82 = **32,144**
9. 628 x 274 = **172,072**	10. 831 x 347 = **288,357**	11. 609 x 149 = **90,741**	12. 586 x 781 = **457,666**
13. 196 x 175 = **34,300**	14. 594 x 739 = **438,966**	15. 854 x 837 = **714,798**	16. 697 x 507 = **353,379**

Possessive and plural forms of many nouns sound alike but are different. An 's can make the base word noun become a singular possessive. For example: All the players' (plural) coats looked the same, but one player's (singular possessive) coat was ripped in the back. In the following sentences, cross out the plurals and possessives that are incorrect. Write them correctly at the right of the sentences. If they are right, just write "correct."

1. All the news ~~reporter's~~ decided to stay at the Brookgreen Inn. **reporters**
2. Ten ~~driver's~~ went out on the job this morning, but only nine returned on time. **drivers**
3. One ~~drivers~~ truck was stuck in a huge snowdrift. **driver's**
4. The announcer's voice sounded awful this morning. **correct**
5. Many authors had a convention last year to come up with new ideas for books. **correct**
6. The ~~authors~~ new book sold 1,000 copies in four hours. **author's**
7. The ~~organizer's~~ of this party can be proud of themselves. **organizers**

15

Page 16

Day 7

Sequence.
Read this paragraph; then write the main points in the correct order. The third one is done for you.

Traveling Spiders

The baby wolf spider rides on its mother's back. Jumping spiders travel by ballooning. They raise their abdomens so the wind can pull silk threads from their spinnerets. The wind then lifts the little spiders into the air like balloons on strings. Fisher spiders are very lightweight, so they can travel by walking on water. Crab spiders walk backwards and sidewards. All spiders can make and travel on a dragline (a silk thread).

1. **Baby wolf spiders ride on their mother's back**
2. **Jumping spiders travel by ballooning.**
3. *Fisher spiders can walk on water.*
4. **Crab spiders walk backwards and sidewards.**
5. **All spiders can travel on a dragline.**

Digestive System.

Put the steps of the digestive process in the proper sequence.

4 Food moves to the small intestine.
2 The tongue pushes food down the esophagus.
7 Undigested food passes out of the body through the anus.
5 Villi in the small intestine absorb digested food into the bloodstream.
1 Teeth and saliva start to change food.
6 Undigested food moves to the large intestine, or colon.
3 Food goes to the stomach where it is further broken down.

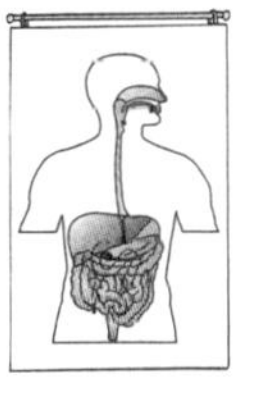

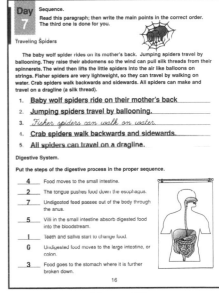

16

Page 17

Day 8

Add, subtract, or multiply. Find the answer to each of the following story problems and tell which operation you used to solve the problem.

1. A person can make 36 single-dipped ice cream cones out of one gallon of ice cream. If you have 12 different flavors of one-gallon ice cream containers, how many cones do you need to use all of the ice cream? **432 cones, multiply**
2. Mrs. Stone hand-dipped 425 chocolates the first of May, 592 the middle of May, and 143 the last part of May. How many chocolates did she make in May? **1,160 chocolates, add**
3. Farmer Tim sold 4,987 pounds of potatoes last year and 12,709 pounds this year. Next year he hopes to do even better. How many more pounds of potatoes did he sell this year than last year? **7,722 pounds, subtract**
4. Denim shorts sell for $27.59 a pair at Lornet Department Store. Its regular denim jeans sell for $12.18 more than its denim shorts. How much do the store's regular denim jeans cost? **$39.77 a pair, add**
5. Mirror Park has 73 ducks on its lake. An average of 670 people visit the ducks each day. If each person fed the ducks 3 pieces of bread each day, how many pieces of bread would each duck get each day? **27.534, multiply then divide**
6. If each person in the United States drank 42 gallons of milk a year, and each gallon cost $1.98, how much would each person spend on milk a year? **$83.16, multiply**
7. Vicki planted 136 red tulip bulbs, 734 white bulbs, and 400 yellow bulbs. How many flowers will she have if each bulb blooms? **1,270 tulips, add**
8. Gloria bought 25 pairs of socks at $5.80 a pair. If her mother gave her $500, would she have enough money left to buy 6 pairs of shoes at $30.00 each? **Yes. multiply, subtract**
9. Grayson came home with 12 popsicles that cost him $3.00 a dozen. He sold 2 popsicles to his sister, Denise, at 50¢ each and 4 popsicles to his brother, Tanner, at 50¢ each. How much profit will Grayson make after he sells the rest to his Grandma Dorothy at 50¢ each? **$3.00, multiply, add, subtract, or multiply, subtract**

Look in an atlas. Which states contain the following latitude and longitude?

1. 40° N, 110° W **Utah**
2. 35° N, 110° W **Arizona**
3. 35° N, 120° W **California**
4. 40° N, 83° W **Ohio**
5. 33° N, 87° W **Alabama**
6. What is the latitude and longitude of one corner of your state? **Answer will vary.**
7. What is the latitude and longitude of your city or town? **Answer will vary.**

17

Page 18

Day 8

Context clues help you learn new words and their meanings. Use the context clues in the following sentences to tell what the underlined words mean.

1. Mary feigned surprise when her friends had a birthday party for her.
feigned— **pretended**
2. My colleagues and I work together on many new projects.
colleagues— **people who work together**
3. Maurice looks at his watch often to make sure he is always punctual.
punctual— **on time**
4. Joseph, a philatelist, has a large collection of stamps.
philatelist— **a stamp collector**
5. The pig napping in the mud was hardly able to bestir itself for its dinner.
bestir— **awaken**

Read the following passage and answer the questions below.

Englishman Sir Walter Raleigh wanted to start a colony in the New World (North America). In 1585, Raleigh sent colonists to what is now North Carolina. The colonists did not want to work and almost starved to death. They were taken back to England. Two years later a second group of colonists sailed over to the same place as the previous colonists. They worked very hard to survive.

Because of a war involving England, Raleigh lost track of the colonists. In 1591, a ship from England finally arrived to check on the colonists, but the colonists had disappeared! There was no sign of life. All the sailors found were some empty trunks, rotted maps, and the word CROATOAN carved on the doorpost of the fort. Croatoan was an island 100 miles south of The Lost Colony. No one knows if the colonists were attacked by the Croatoan Indians or if the settlers went to live on Croatoan Island. The Lost Colony has been a great mystery in American history.

1. How many years has it been since the first colony settled in North Carolina?
Subtract 1585 from present year.
2. What year did Raleigh send the second set of colonists to North Carolina?
1587
3. How many years did it take Raleigh to send a ship to check on the second set of colonists?
4 years
4. Why was this colony called The Lost Colony?
No one knows what happened to the settlers. They disappeared.
5. State what you think might have happened to The Lost Colony.
Answer will vary.
6. Think of a title that would be appropriate for this passage.
Answer will vary.

18

Page 19

Day 9

Find the quotient when dividing whole numbers.

EXAMPLE:

9)829 = 92 R 1 (81, 19, 18, 1)

0£0 ÷ 0 = 0£ with the remainder of 1

Use mental math or scratch paper if needed.

1. 8)231 **28 R7**
2. 4)394 **98 R2**
3. 9)894 **99 R3**
4. 5)3,305 **661**
5. 6)56,707 **9,451 R1**
6. 7)6,845 **977 R6**
7. 90)270 **3**
8. 60)480 **8**
9. 20)1,900 **95**
10. 42)336 **8**
11. 75)675 **9**
12. 63)315 **5**
13. 52)4,173 **80 R13**
14. 70)5,844 **83 R34**
15. 83)4,978 **59 R81**
16. 59)4,538 **76 R54**
17. 94)2,980 **31 R66**
18. 41)3,613 **88 R5**
19. 27)6,641 **245 R26**
20. 52)9,385 **180 R25**
21. 44)9,599 **218 R7**
22. 57)92,831 **1,628 R35**
23. 40)73,847 **1,846 R7**
24. 62)79,365 **1,280 R5**
25. 31)62,620 **2,020**

Spelling.

Find the word that is misspelled in each row and spell it correctly. Use a dictionary if you need help.

1.	refund	remodel	decode	previw	**preview**
2.	deposet	pretend	deflate	pace	**deposit**
3.	mold	respond	brutel	revise	**brutal**
4.	fiction	grieff	unsafe	equip	**grief**
5.	transfer	defend	truthful	penlty	**penalty**
6.	prdict	decide	gossip	fragile	**predict**
7.	beware	precice	porches	capital	**precise**
8.	leashes	cipher	volt	climack	**climax**
9.	month	friendly	wrench	businiss	**business**
10.	jiant	angle	guest	greet	**giant**
11.	surgery	magnit	usually	bearish	**magnet**
12.	slogan	gigantck	beast	galley	**gigantic**

19

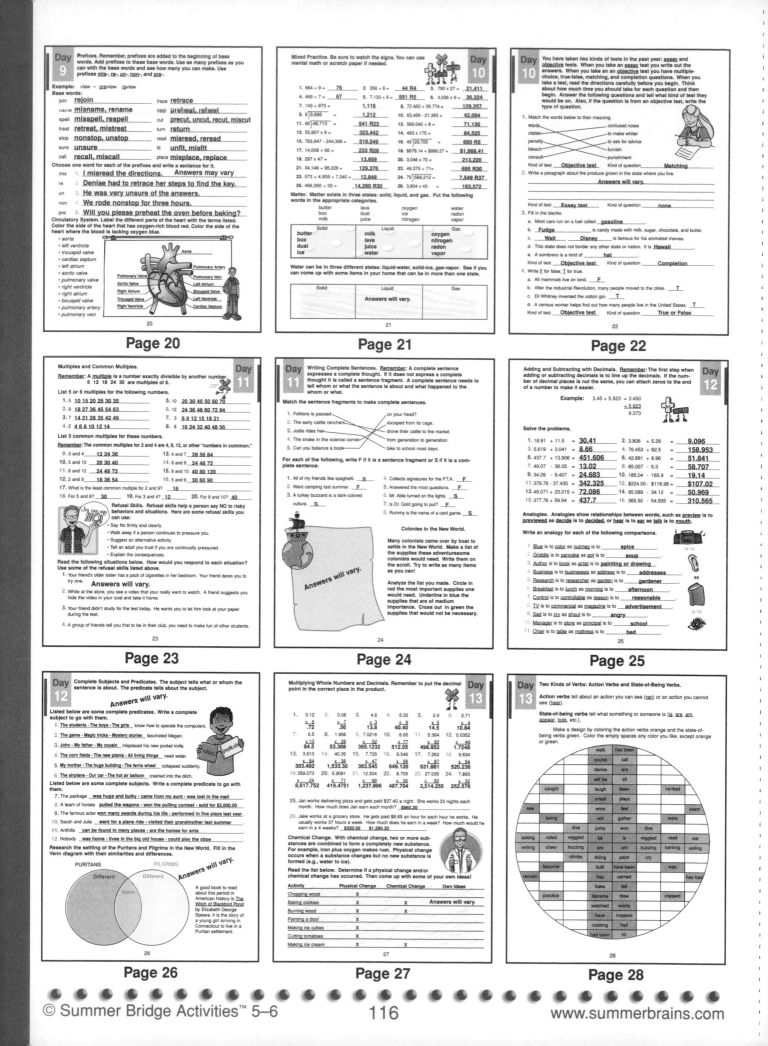

Page 20

Day 9 — Prefixes. Remember, prefixes are added to the beginning of base words. Add prefixes to these base words. Use as many prefixes as you can with the base words and see how many you can make. Use prefixes mis-, re-, un-, non-, and pre-.

Example: view – preview review

Base words:
- join **rejoin**   trace **retrace**
- name **misname, rename**   neat **preheat, reheat**
- spell **misspell, respell**   cut **precut, uncut, recut, miscut**
- treat **retreat, mistreat**   turn **return**
- stop **nonstop, unstop**   read **misread, reread**
- sure **unsure**   fit **unfit, misfit**
- call **recall, miscall**   place **misplace, replace**

Choose one word for each of the prefixes and write a sentence for it.

mis 1. **I misread the directions.** Answers may vary.
re   2. **Denise had to retrace her steps to find the key.**
un   3. **He was very unsure of the answers.**
non 4. **We rode nonstop for three hours.**
pre 5. **Will you please preheat the oven before baking?**

Circulatory System. Label the different parts of the heart with the terms listed. Color the side of the heart that has oxygen-rich blood red. Color the side of the heart where the blood is lacking oxygen blue.

- aorta
- left ventricle
- tricuspid valve
- cardiac septum
- left atrium
- aortic valve
- pulmonary valve
- right ventricle
- right atrium
- bicuspid valve
- pulmonary artery
- pulmonary vein

20

Page 21

Day 10 — Mixed Practice. Be sure to watch the signs. You can use mental math or scratch paper if needed.

1. 684 ÷ 9 = **76**
2. 356 ÷ 8 = **44 R4**
3. 793 x 27 = **21,411**
4. 469 ÷ 7 = **67**
5. 7,133 ÷ 8 = **891 R5**
6. 4,036 x 9 = **36,324**
7. 143 ÷ 973 = **1,116**
8. 72.483 + 56.774 = **129.257**
9. 8)9,696 = **1,212**
10. 63,459 - 21,365 = **42,094**
11. 90)48,713 = **541 R23**
12. 569,040 + 8 = **71,130**
13. 53,907 x 6 = **323,442**
14. 483 x 175 = **84,525**
15. 763,940 - 244,398 = **519,549**
16. 45)29,705 = **660 R5**
17. 14,008 ÷ 60 = **233 R28**
18. $678.14 + $990.27 = **$1,668.41**
19. 297 x 47 = **13,959**
20. 3,046 x 70 = **213,220**
21. 34,148 + 95,228 = **129,376**
22. 49,375 + 71 = **695 R30**
23. 573 + 4,935 + 7,340 = **12,848**
24. 75)566,212 = **7,549 R37**
25. 456,350 ÷ 32 = **14,260 R30**
26. 3,804 x 43 = **163,572**

Matter. Matter exists in three states: solid, liquid, and gas. Put the following words in the appropriate categories.

butter box milk lava dust juice oxygen ice nitrogen water radon vapor

Solid	Liquid	Gas
butter box dust ice	milk lava juice water	oxygen nitrogen radon vapor

Water can be in three different states: liquid-water, solid-ice, gas-vapor. See if you can come up with some items in your home that can be in more than one state.

Solid	Liquid	Gas
	Answers will vary.	

21

Page 22

Day 10 — You have taken two kinds of tests in the past year: essay and objective tests. When you take an essay test you write out the answers. When you take an objective test you have multiple-choice, true-false, matching, and completion questions. When you take a test, read the directions carefully before you begin. Think about how much time you should take for each question and then begin. Answer the following questions and tell what kind of test they would be on. Also, if the question is from an objective test, write the type of question.

1. Match the words below to their meaning.
- equip — furnish
- clatter — confused noise
- penalty — punishment
- bleach — to make whiter
- consult — to ask for advice

Kind of test **Objective test** Kind of question **Matching**

2. Write a paragraph about the produce grown in the state where you live.
Answers will vary.

Kind of test **Essay test** Kind of question **none**

3. Fill in the blanks.
a. Most cars run on a fuel called **gasoline**.
b. **Fudge** is candy made with milk, sugar, chocolate, and butter.
c. **Walt**   **Disney** is famous for his animated movies.
d. This state does not border any other state or nation. It is **Hawaii**.
e. A sombrero is a kind of **hat**.

Kind of test **Objective test** Kind of question **Completion**

4. Write F for false, T for true.
a. All mammals live on land. **F**
b. After the Industrial Revolution, many people moved to the cities. **T**
c. Eli Whitney invented the cotton gin. **T**
d. A census worker helps find out how many people live in the United States. **T**

Kind of test **Objective test** Kind of question **True or False**

22

Page 23

Day 11 — Multiples and Common Multiples.

Remember: A multiple is a number exactly divisible by another number. 6 12 18 24 30 are multiples of 6.

List 5 or 6 multiples for the following numbers.
1. 5 **10 15 20 25 30 35**   5. 10 **20 30 40 50 60 70**
2. 9 **18 27 36 45 54 63**   6. 12 **24 36 48 60 72 84**
3. 7 **14 21 28 35 42 49**   7. 3 **6 9 12 15 18 21**
4. 2 **4 6 8 10 12 14**   8. 8 **16 24 32 40 48 56**

List 3 common multiples for these numbers.
Remember: The common multiples for 2 and 4 are 4, 8, 12, or other "numbers in common."
9. 3 and 4 **12 24 36**   13. 4 and 7 **28 56 84**
10. 5 and 10 **20 30 40**   14. 6 and 8 **24 48 72**
11. 8 and 12 **24 48 72**   15. 8 and 10 **40 80 120**
12. 2 and 9 **18 36 54**   16. 5 and 6 **30 60 90**
17. What is the least common multiple for 2 and 9? **18**
18. For 5 and 6? **30** 19. For 3 and 4? **12** 20. For 8 and 10? **40**

Refusal Skills. Refusal skills help a person say NO to risky behaviors and situations. Here are some refusal skills you can use:
- Say No firmly and clearly.
- Walk away if a person continues to pressure you.
- Suggest an alternative activity.
- Tell an adult you trust if you are continually pressured.
- Explain the consequences.

Read the following situations below. How would you respond to each situation? Use some of the refusal skills listed above.
1. Your friend's older sister has a pack of cigarettes in her bedroom. Your friend dares you to try one. **Answers will vary.**
2. While at the store, you see a video that you really want to watch. A friend suggests you hide the video in your coat and take it home.
3. Your friend didn't study for the test today. He wants you to let him look at your paper during the test.
4. A group of friends tell you that to be in their club, you need to make fun of other students.

23

Page 24

Day 11 — Writing Complete Sentences. Remember: A complete sentence expresses a complete thought. If it does not express a complete thought it is called a sentence fragment. A complete sentence needs to tell whom or what the sentence is about and what happened to the whom or what.

Match the sentence fragments to make complete sentences.
1. Folklore is passed — from generation to generation.
2. The early cattle ranchers — drove their cattle to the market.
3. Jodie rides her — bike to school most days.
4. The snake in the science corner — escaped from its cage.
5. Can you balance a book — on your head?

For each of the following, write F if it is a sentence fragment or S if it is a complete sentence.
1. All of my friends like spaghetti. **S**   4. Collects signatures for the P.T.A. **F**
2. Went camping last summer. **F**   5. Answered the most questions. **F**
3. A turkey buzzard is a dark-colored vulture. **S**   6. Mr. Able turned on the lights. **S**
                          7. Is Dr. Gold going to put? **F**
                          8. Rummy is the name of a card game. **S**

Colonies in the New World.

Many colonists came over by boat to settle in the New World. Make a list of the supplies these adventuresome colonists would need. Write them on the scroll. Try to write as many items as you can!

Analyze the list you made. Circle in red the most important supplies one would need. Underline in blue the supplies that are of medium importance. Cross out in green the supplies that would not be necessary.

Answers will vary.

24

Page 25

Day 12 — Adding and Subtracting with Decimals. Remember: The first step when adding or subtracting decimals is to line up the decimals. If the number of decimal places is not the same, you can attach zeros to the end of a number to make it easier.

Example: 3.45 + 5.923 = 3.450
                + 5.923
                  9.373

Solve the problems.
1. 18.91 + 11.5 = **30.41**   2. 3.806 + 5.29 = **9.096**
3. 5.619 + 3.041 = **8.66**   4. 76.453 + 82.5 = **158.953**
5. 437.7 + 13.906 = **451.606**   6. 42.881 + 8.96 = **51.841**
7. 49.07 - 36.05 = **13.02**   8. 65.007 - 6.3 = **58.707**
9. 34.09 - 9.407 = **24.683**   10. 185.04 - 165.9 = **19.14**
11. 379.76 - 37.435 = **342.325** 12. $224.00 - $116.98 = **$107.02**
13. 49.071 + 23.015 = **72.086** 14. 85.089 - 34.12 = **50.969**
15. 377.76 + 59.94 = **437.7**   16. 365.50 - 54.935 = **310.565**

Analogies. Analogies show relationships between words, such as preview is to previewed as decide is to decided, or hear is to ear as talk is to mouth.

Write an analogy for each of the following comparisons.
1. Blue is to color as nutmeg is to **spice**
2. Griddle is to pancake as pot is to **soup**
3. Author is to book as artist is to **painting or drawing**
4. Business is to businesses as address is to **addresses**
5. Research is to researcher as garden is to **gardener**
6. Breakfast is to lunch as morning is to **afternoon**
7. Control is to controllable as reason is to **reasonable**
8. TV is to commercial as magazine is to **advertisement**
9. Sad is to cry as shout is to **angry**
10. Manager is to store as principal is to **school**
11. Chair is to table as mattress is to **bed**

25

Page 26

Day 12 — Complete Subjects and Predicates. The subject tells what or whom the sentence is about. The predicate tells about the subject.

Answers will vary.

Listed below are some complete predicates. Write a complete subject to go with them.
1. The students - The boys - The girls know how to operate the computers.
2. The game - Magic tricks - Mystery stories fascinated Megan.
3. John - My father - My cousin misplaced his new pocket knife.
4. The corn fields - The new plants - All living things need water.
5. My mother - The huge building - The ferris wheel collapsed suddenly.
6. The airplane - Our car - The hot air balloon crashed into the ditch.

Listed below are some complete subjects. Write a complete predicate to go with them.
7. The package was huge and bulky - came from my aunt - was lost in the mail
8. A team of horses pulled the wagons - won the pulling contest - sold for $2,000.00
9. The famous actor won many awards during his life - performed in three plays last year
10. Sarah and Julie went for a plane ride - visited their grandmother last summer
11. Anthills can be found in many places - are the homes for ants
12. Nobody was home - lives in the big old house - could play the oboe

Research the settling of the Puritans and Pilgrims in the New World. Fill in the Venn diagram with their similarities and differences.

PURITANS   PILGRIMS
Different Same Different

Answers will vary.

A good book to read about this period in American history is The Witch of Blackbird Pond by Elizabeth George Speare. It is the story of a young girl arriving in Connecticut to live in a Puritan settlement.

26

Page 27

Day 13 — Multiplying Whole Numbers and Decimals. Remember to put the decimal point in the correct place in the product.

1. 0.12 x .6 = **.072**
2. 0.08 x 7 = **.56**
3. 4.6 x 3 = **13.8**
4. 5.05 x 8 = **40.40**
5. 2.9 x 5 = **14.5**
6. 2.71 x 4 = **10.84**
7. 6.5 x 13 = **84.5**
8. 1.906 x 28 = **53.368**
9. 7.0216 x 52 = **365.1232**
10. 6.65 x 77 = **512.05**
11. 5.364 x 93 = **498.852**
12. 0.0352 x 49 = **1.7248**
13. 3.613 x 84 = **303.492**
14. 40.35 x 38 = **1,533.30**
15. 7.735 x 47 = **363.545**
16. 9.546 x 68 = **649.128**
17. 7.263 x 87 = **631.881**
18. 9.634 x 54 = **520.236**
19. 359.073 x 24 = **8,617.752**
20. 5.9081 x 71 = **419.4751**
21. 12.504 x 99 = **1,237.896**
22. 8.709 x 56 = **487.704**
23. 27.035 x 93 = **2,514.255**
24. 7.893 x 32 = **252.576**

25. Jan works delivering pizza and gets paid $37.40 a night. She works 23 nights each month. How much does Jan earn each month? **$860.20**

26. Jake works at a grocery store. He gets paid $8.65 an hour for each hour he works. He usually works 37 hours a week. How much does he earn in a week? How much would he earn in 4 weeks? **$320.05 $1,280.20**

Chemical Change. With chemical change, two or more substances are combined to form a completely new substance. For example, iron plus oxygen makes rust. Physical change occurs when a substance changes but no new substance is formed (e.g., water to ice).

Read the list below. Determine if a physical change and/or chemical change has occurred. Then come up with some of your own ideas!

Activity	Physical Change	Chemical Change	Own Ideas
Chopping wood	X		
Baking cookies	X	X	Answers will vary.
Burning wood	X	X	
Painting a door	X		
Making ice cubes	X		
Cutting tomatoes	X		
Making ice cream	X	X	

27

Page 28

Day 13 — Two Kinds of Verbs: Action Verbs and State-of-Being Verbs.

Action verbs tell about an action you can see (ran) or an action you cannot see (hear).

State-of-being verbs tell what something or someone is (is, are, am, appear, look, etc.).

Make a design by coloring the action verbs orange and the state-of-being verbs green. Color the empty spaces any color you like, except orange or green.

walk	has been
sound	call
dance	are
will be	sit
caught	laugh	been	honked
smell	plays
see	wore	feel	seem
being	will	gather
jump	won	dive
asking	rolled	wiggled	be	is	wiggled	read	eat
writing	cheer	buzzing	are	am	buzzing	barking	selling
climbs	skiing	paint	cry
become	built	have been	was
remain	has	carried	has been
bake	felt
practice	became	blew	clapped
watched	wants
have	mopped
cooking	had
had been	hit

28

Page 29

Measuring with Metrics.

Day 14

1 centimeter = 10 millimeters	1 meter = 10 decimeters
1 decimeter = 10 centimeters	1 meter = 100 centimeters
1 decimeter = 100 millimeters	1 meter = 1,000 millimeters

1 kilometer = 1,000 meters

Estimate and then measure the following using the metric system. If you need a metric ruler, there is one in the back of this book.

	Estimation	Measurement (Use more than one term of measurement.)
a book		
toaster		
width of a drawer		Measurements will vary.
your little finger		
a can of soup		
a necklace		
a spatula		
an eraser		
bathroom floor		
garbage can		
flashlight		

Choose things that you would like to measure.

Answers will vary.

29

Page 30

Day 14

Pronunciation and Spelling.

Do you remember that g and c both have a hard and soft sound? G as in sugar (hard) and g as in giant (soft), c as in camel (hard) and c as in city (soft). In the first column of blanks, put **S** or **H** after each word to tell if the c or g is soft or hard. In the second column, match the hard or soft c and g words to the word or words that mean about the same.

EXAMPLE:

1. geyser	H	attracting	10
2. music	H	writing instrument	7
3. cyclone	S/H	produce	4
4. generate	S	schedule	19
5. slogan	H	operation	15
6. calico	H/H	melody, harmony	2
7. pencil	S	violent contact	17
8. regulate	H	grain	22
9. picture	H	refusal, not positive	23
10. magnet	H	painting	9
11. country	H	hot spring	1
12. gelatin	S	motto	5
13. pillage	S	without pretense	20
14. process	S	recommendation	24
15. surgery	S	messenger	18
16. against	S/H	jelly-like substance	12
17. collide	H	territory/land	11
18. angel	S	hurricane	3
19. calendar	H	adjust	8
20. sincere	S	illusions	21
21. magic	S/H	cloth	6
22. cereal	S	transform	14
23. negative	H	in contact with	16
24. advice	S	looting	13

30

Page 31

Day 15

Equal Metric Measures. Use the metric measure information on page 29 if you need help to do this activity.

Change each measurement to millimeters.

1. 25 cm	2. 3 m	3. 9 dm	4. 10 dm	5. 12 m	6. 17 cm
250 mm	**3,000**	**900** mm	**1,000**	**12,000** mm	**170**

Change each measurement to centimeters.

7. 8 m	8. 50 mm	9. 100 m	10. 4 km	11. 400 mm	12. 5 km
800 cm	**5** cm	**10,000** cm	**400,000** cm	**40**	**500,000** cm

Use greater than (>), less than (<), and equal (=) signs.

13. 37 m **>** 370 cm 14. 51 m **>** 5 dm 15. 216 cm **>** 216 mm
16. 40 cm **=** 400 mm 17. 5 m **<** 15 km 18. 80 km **=** 80,000 m

An Experiment with Chemical and Physical Change.

Materials: 5 pennies, 1 nickel, 1 dime, and 1 quarter
salt
vinegar, water, milk
aluminum foil

Directions: Fold foil into a pan with sides turned up.
Place coins in pan.
Pour salt (about 1 tsp.) over coins.
Pour vinegar over each coin.
Observe.

Questions:

1. What happened to each coin? **Only the pennies will become shiny.**
2. Why did this happen? **The discoloration pennies was removed by a chemical reaction.**
3. Predict what would happen if you did this experiment with water or milk.
   Water: **Answer will vary.**
   Milk: **Answer will vary.**
4. Repeat the experiment with the water and milk.
5. Was your prediction right? **Answer will vary.**
6. Which experiment demonstrates chemical change? **salt and vinegar**
   Which experiment demonstrates physical change? **salt and water, salt and milk**
7. Experiment with different liquids to determine if they cause a physical or chemical change.

31

Page 32

Day 15

The six sentences below tell the sequence of events in a story. They are in order. Write a story to go with them. Make sure the events in your story are in this order. Give your story a title. Write in cursive.

1. On Saturday, Mom and I went to a professional basketball game.
2. We rode the crowded subway to the game.
3. The Coliseum was even more crowded than the subway.
4. Mom and I traded seats because I couldn't see very well!
5. We both wanted our home team to win.
6. Because we were so tired after the game, we took a taxi home.

Title:

Answers will vary.

32

Section 2

Page 37

Day 1

Negative and Positive Numbers.

A negative number has a quantity less than zero. A positive number, on the other hand, is a number greater than zero.

Illustrate and/or explain positive and negative numbers using thermometer.

Answers will vary. Here are a few examples:
Seconds before blast off would be negative numbers – 10, 9, 8, 7, 6, 5, 4, 3, 2, 1, 0, Blast off! Afterwards the numbers would be positive.
Write a story problem to go with one of the illustrations and/or explanations you used above.

Answers will vary.

Facts from the Colonies in the 1600s and 1700s.

The Southern Colonies. From the list below, choose the word that means almost the same as the underlined word or phrase in the sentences.

indign   indentured servants   proprietor
slaves   cash crops

proprietor 1. George Calvert was the first owner of a colony.
cash crops 2. A lot of Southern farmers grew crops that they could sell for money.
indigo 3. In the 1740s, Eliza Lucas developed a blue dye made from a plant.
indentured servants 4. Originally, people who agreed to work five or seven years to pay their passage to America labored on Southern farms. These people were eventually replaced by
slaves people captured from Africa who were forced to work for nothing.

The Middle Colonies. Circle all the colonies considered to be the Middle Colonies.

(New Jersey)   Georgia   Rhode Island
(Delaware)   (New York)   (Pennsylvania)

The New England Colonies. Circle the correct answer to complete each statement.

1. A person who wanted to purify the church was called a
   a. Programmer   (b.) Puritan   c. Convert
2. A person whose expertise is shipbuilding is called a
   a. carpenter   b. cartwright   (c.) shipwright
3. Usually in the center of town was a grassy area called a
   a. field   (b.) common   c. meadow

37

Page 38

Day 1

Word Meanings.
Fill in the blanks from the word list below.

inland   suspicious   desert   escorts   conduct
frank   allergy   knead   margin   impression
inlets   stethoscope   appalled   subscribe   owing

1. All the **inlets** around the lake were crowded with boats.
2. Everyone in the class had a chance to listen to my heart through the **stethoscope**.
3. The night watchman became **suspicious** of the two men parked near the back door of the building.
4. We **subscribe** to at least four different newspapers.
5. Did you leave a **margin** on both sides of your paper?
6. Ted spends too much money. He is always **owing** for something.
7. She was **frank** in telling me she did not like my new dress.
8. Use both hands when you **knead** the bread dough.
9. My **allergy** acts up every time I go to the theater because I'm allergic to perfume.
10. Tuly's **conduct** at the party was rude and inexcusable.

Here is a list of words you should know how to spell. Put the words in alphabetical order.

stranger   pottery   individual   journey   rely
toiletry   reunite   robbery   adventure   delay
subscription   alleys   cemetery   identify   unnecessary
announcement   celery   victorious   enemy   grocery
hurried   deciding   toil   misplaced

1. **adventure**	9. **grocery**	17. **reunite**
2. **alleys**	10. **hurried**	18. **robbery**
3. **announcement**	11. **identify**	19. **stranger**
4. **celery**	12. **individual**	20. **subscription**
5. **cemetery**	13. **journey**	21. **toil**
6. **deciding**	14. **misplaced**	22. **toiletry**
7. **delay**	15. **pottery**	23. **unnecessary**
8. **enemy**	16. **rely**	24. **victorious**

38

Page 39

Day 2

Deposits and Deductions.

Amanda opened a checking account on May 15th with $500.25. On May 31st she deposited another $496.80. On June 4th she withdrew $145.00 to buy a bicycle. On June 15th she deposited $435.20. On June 30th she deposited $600.00. On July 1st she withdrew $400.00 to go to Camp Rockland, plus she also needed $63.00 for a sleeping bag. On July 15th she deposited $110.00. On July 24th she withdrew $900.00 to buy a compact TV with a built-in VCR.

Use the chart below to record Amanda's checking account record.

DATE	DEPOSITED	WITHDREW	TOTAL $
May 15	$500.25		$500.25
May 31	$496.80		$997.05
June 4		$145.00	$852.05
June 15	$435.20		$1,287.25
June 30	$600.00		$1,887.25
July 1		$463.00	$1,424.25
July 15	$110.00		$1,534.25
July 24		$900.00	$634.25

Remember, when you deposit money you add, and when you withdraw money you subtract.

Use Amanda's checking account record to graph the total dollar amounts.

$2,000.00	
$1,800.00	
$1,600.00	
$1,400.00	
$1,200.00	
$1,000.00	
$800.00	
$600.00	
$500.00	
$400.00	

May 15 / May 31 / June 4 / June 15 / June 30 / July 1 / July 15 / July 24

39

Page 40

Day 2

Topic Sentences.
Remember: The topic sentence expresses the main idea of the paragraph. Underline the topic sentences of these paragraphs.

1. The beginning of his life was very unusual. He was born in Texas into a large family. He fell out of a covered wagon and was not missed for many days because he had so many brothers and sisters. His parents couldn't find him, so he was raised by coyotes. He thought he was a coyote until he discovered he didn't have four feet and a tail.

2. Nuclear energy is the most awesome power that exists. It produces tremendous heat and light. It has been used to produce hydrogen and atomic bombs. It results from changes in the core of atoms. One important use of nuclear energy is in producing electricity. Scientists believe that if it were fully developed, nuclear energy could produce all the world's electricity for millions of years.

Now it's your turn! Write a topic sentence for these two paragraphs. Try to make it interesting so others will want to read the paragraph.

3. **Sentences will vary.**
   They are among the world's oldest and largest living things. Some are thousands of years old and over 200 feet tall. Some of them are about 100 feet around at the base. You can see them in California and Oregon. They are the giant sequoia and redwood trees.

4. **Sentences will vary.**
   It ranges from great works like Michelangelo's carvings to African masks. A piece of sculpture can be very large, like the Statue of Liberty, or small enough to sit on a table or hold in your hand. It has always played an important part in the history of man. Sculpture is an excellent way to express your own ideas and feelings.

Fill in the vowels for these spelling words. Then write each word three times in cursive.

1. rh i n o c e r o s	rhinoceros	rhinoceros	rhinoceros
2. c h e m i c a l	chemical	chemical	chemical
3. st o m a c h	stomach	stomach	stomach
4. rh u b a r b	rhubarb	rhubarb	rhubarb
5. sc h o l a s t i c	scholastic	scholastic	scholastic
6. rh y t h m	rhythm	rhythm	rhythm
7. l u gg a g e	luggage	luggage	luggage
8. r e m a i n d e r	remainder	remainder	remainder
9. o m i tt e d	omitted	omitted	omitted
10. m i l i t a r y	military	military	military

40

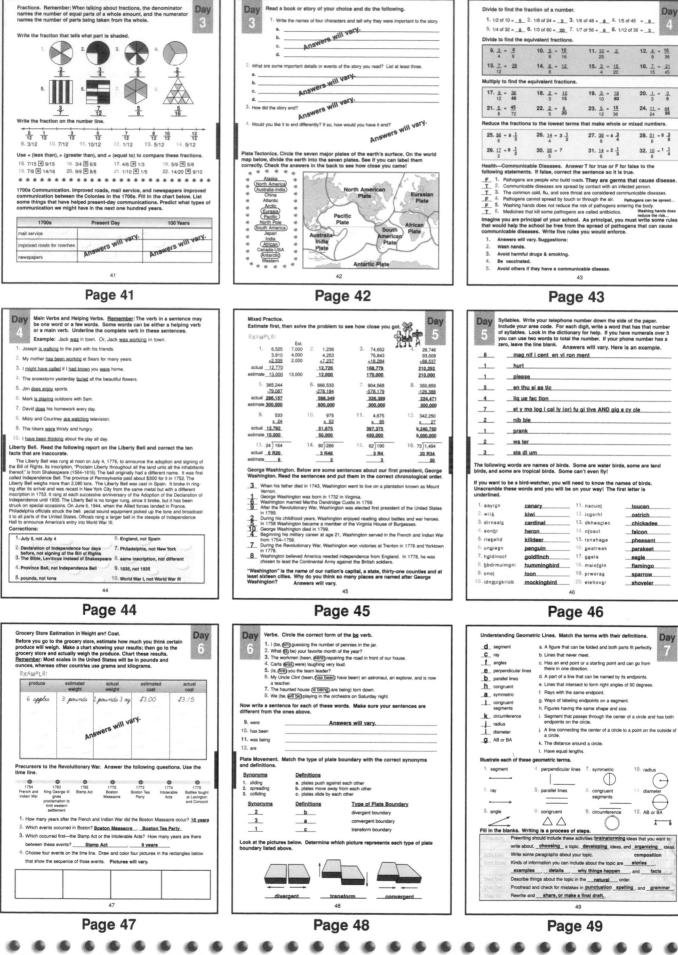

Page 41

Page 42

Page 43

Page 44

Page 45

Page 46

Page 47

Page 48

Page 49

Page 50

Day 7 **Read this part of the Declaration of Independence and answer the questions below.**

We hold these truths to be self-evident, that all men are created equal, that they are endowed by their Creator with certain unalienable Rights, that among these are Life, Liberty and the pursuit of Happiness.
That to secure these rights, Governments are instituted among Men, deriving their just powers from the consent of the governed.
That whenever any Form of Government becomes destructive of these ends, it is the Right of the People to alter or to abolish it, and to institute new Government, laying its foundation on such principles and organizing its powers in such form, as to them shall seem most likely to effect their Safety and Happiness.

1. What are the basic rights of all people in accordance to the Declaration of Independence? **Life, liberty, and the pursuit of happiness.**
2. Why are governments "instituted," or created? **To secure the rights of the people.**
3. If people feel the government is not acting in their best interest, what should they do? **People need to change or abolish the old government and create a new one.**
4. On what principles will the new American government be founded? **Founded on principles that will effect the safety and happiness of people.**
5. Draw and color a flag below that expresses the feelings and beliefs of the Declaration of Independence. **Pictures will vary.**

Earth's Magnetic Field. Read the following passage and answer the questions below.

The earth is like a huge magnet. It has a magnetic field. Its magnetism is the strongest at the North and South Poles. When rock forms, any magnetic particles will align themselves with the earth's magnetic field. They will point towards either the North or South Poles. There are some rocks that do not point to the current North and South poles. Scientists conclude that either the North and South Poles have moved, or the rocks themselves have moved since they were formed. Most feel the rocks and continents have moved. Geologists use this information to determine how the continents have moved over time.

1. Why is the earth compared to a magnet? **It has a magnetic field.**
2. Where are the earth's strongest points of magnetism? **North and South poles**
3. How can geologists study the movements of the continents? **The geologists study rocks that have been formed. They note where the rocks have moved from the current North and South poles.**
4. How might the magnetism of the earth affect a compass? **A compass is made so it will turn toward the North Pole and away from the South Pole.**
5. What would happen to a ship and its compass if the earth's magnetic strong area became the western part of the earth and NOT the North Pole? **The compass would point to the new point of magnetism.**

50

Page 51

Day 8 **Find the Perimeter. Remember: To find the perimeter you have to add the lengths of each side.**

1. **46** inches
2. **24** centimeters
3. **21** yards
4. **110** meters
5. **80** feet
6. **124** decimeters

Find the Area. Remember: Area is measured in square units. Area = length x width.
Remember: 1/2 x base x height for triangles

7. **20** cm² (square centimeters)
8. **64** square yards
9. **432** square inches
10. **12** square inches
11. **104** m²
12. **840** dm²

The Revolutionary War. Answer T for true or F for false to the following statements. If false, correct the statement so it will be true.

F 1. Loyalists supported the colonists. **Loyalists supported King George and Great Britain.**
T 2. Thomas Paine convinced many colonists to break from Great Britain with his pamphlet Common Sense.
F 3. The British had no struggle in taking Breed's Hill, known as the Battle of Bunker Hill. **The British had to attack three times.**
F 4. The Declaration of Independence was written by John Adams on July 4, 1775. **The Declaration of Independence was written by Thomas Jefferson on July 4, 1776.**
T 5. The patriots had support from many American women when fighting their battles.
T 6. Mary Ludwig Hays, known as Molly Pitcher, carried pitchers of water to men who were fighting in battles.

51

Page 52

Day 8 **Earthquakes.**
Many earthquakes occur at the plate boundaries. Study the following map of earthquake epicenters and answer the questions below.

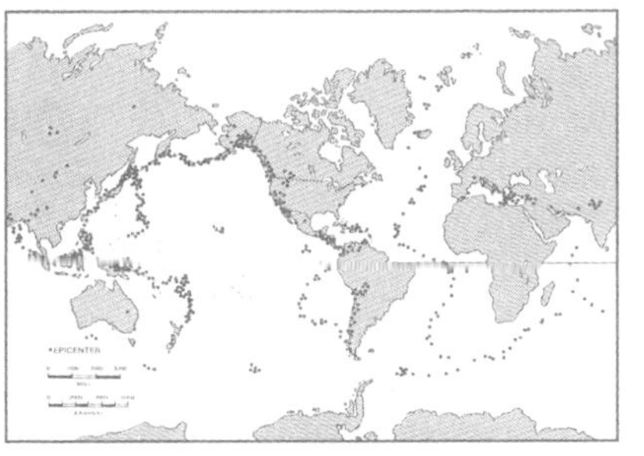

1. Color the areas with the most earthquake activity. What pattern do you see? **Most earthquakes occur in narrow curving zones.**
2. Review the map on plate boundaries on page 42. What is similar about these boundaries and earthquake activity? **Most earthquakes occur where there are plate boundaries.**
3. Explain how you came up with your answer for question 2. **Force acts on the rocks at plate boundaries. This causes a fracture in the rocks.**
4. Observe the earthquakes that occur in the interior of the plates (e.g., China, U.S., and Australia). How is the distribution of these earthquakes different from that of earthquakes along the plate boundaries? **There are fewer and they are more spread out.**

52

Page 53

Day 9 **Write the rest of the number families. The first one is done for you.**

1. 78 x 42 = 3,276; 42 x 78 = 3,276; 3,276 ÷ 42 = 78; 3,276 ÷ 78 = 42
2. 39 x 56 = 2,184; **56 x 39 = 2,184**; **2,184 ÷ 56 = 39**; **2,184 ÷ 39 = 56**
3. 95 x 37 = 3,515; **37 x 95 = 3,515**; **3,515 ÷ 37 = 95**; **3,515 ÷ 95 = 37**
4. 49 x 76 = **3,724**; **76 x 49 = 3,724**; **3,724 ÷ 76 = 49**; **3,724 ÷ 49 = 76**
5. 141 x 27 = **3,807**; **27 x 141 = 3,807**; **3,807 ÷ 27 = 141**; **3,807 ÷ 141 = 27**
6. 3,762 ÷ 38 = **99**; **3,762 ÷ 99 = 38**; **99 x 38 = 3,762**; **38 x 99 = 3,762**
7. 26,320 ÷ 47 = **560**; **26,320 ÷ 560 = 47**; **560 x 47 = 26,320**; **47 x 560 = 26,320**
8. 48,306 ÷ 83 = **582**; **48,306 ÷ 582 = 83**; **582 x 83 = 48,306**; **83 x 582 = 48,306**
9. 194 x 92 = **17,848**; **92 x 194 = 17,848**; **17,848 ÷ 92 = 194**; **17,848 ÷ 194 = 92**
10. 16,019 ÷ 83 = **193**; **16,019 ÷ 193 = 83**; **193 x 83 = 16,019**; **83 x 193 = 16,019**
11. 2,650 x 54 = **143,100**; **54 x 2,650 = 143,100**; **143,100 ÷ 54 = 2,650**; **143,100 ÷ 2,650 = 54**
12. 876,600 ÷ 360 = **2,435**; **876,600 ÷ 2,435 = 360**; **2,435 x 360 = 876,600**; **360 x 2,435 = 876,600**

Respiratory System.

There are a lot of ways you can take care of your respiratory system. Some ways are exercising regularly, not smoking, and not inhaling chemicals produced by products such as paint or glue. Look at some old magazines and ask your parents if you can cut out pictures of people caring for their respiratory system. If you don't have any old magazines, draw and color pictures.

Answers will vary.

53

Page 54

Day 9 **Read these paragraphs. Remember to ask yourself:**
1. **Does the paragraph have one main idea?**
2. **Do all the sentences in the paragraph tell about the main idea?**
3. **Is every sentence in the paragraph a complete sentence?**

Draw a line through the sentence or sentences that do not belong in the paragraph. Tell why.

1. Water in the ocean never stops moving. The most well-known movements are waves. Waves are set in motion by earthquakes, winds, and the gravitational pull of the sun and moon. ~~Ocean water is also very salty.~~ On shore, we see waves caused by the wind. Their size depends on whether they come from far across the ocean or are caused by winds from nearby storms.
It does not tell about the main idea.
2. The beaver is a furry animal with a flat, wide tail that looks like a paddle. There are more beavers in the U.S. and Canada than anywhere else. The beaver's strong front teeth are used for cutting down trees. They use the branches to build dams and homes, but they eat the bark from them first. ~~Beavers almost always seem.~~ We often call people who work hard "eager beavers."
It is not a complete sentence.
3. Write a paragraph. Try to remember the three rules as you write.
Answers will vary.

Earthquakes. Read the paragraph and fill in the blanks with the words listed.

seismologists, epicenter, focus, earthquake, fault, seismic waves, above, energy, fracture, beneath

An **earthquake** is sudden shaking of the ground that happens when **energy** stored in rock is released. A **fault** is a break, or **fracture**, in the Earth's crust. As rock breaks, stored energy moves along the fault. The hypocenter, or **focus**, is where an earthquake begins. This occurs **beneath** the Earth's surface. The point on the Earth's crust which is directly **above** the focus is called the **epicenter**. **Seismic waves**, or shock waves, move out from the focus and cause the ground to shake. **Seismologists** study and record these shock waves and determine the size of the earthquake.

54

Page 55

Day 10 **Multiplying with "Napier's Bones."**
In 1617, John Napier used a method of multiplying with rods marked with numbers. Some people call it "Napier's Bones," or "lattice" multiplication. When placing the appropriate "bones" side by side, you read the product of multiplication.

Use the "lattice" approach by multiplying the digits of the two factors. Write them on the lattice form, then add along the diagonals, carrying the remainder to the next diagonal.

Example:
528 x 347 = 183,216

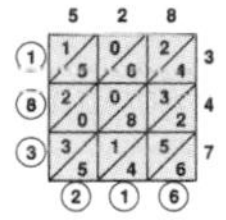

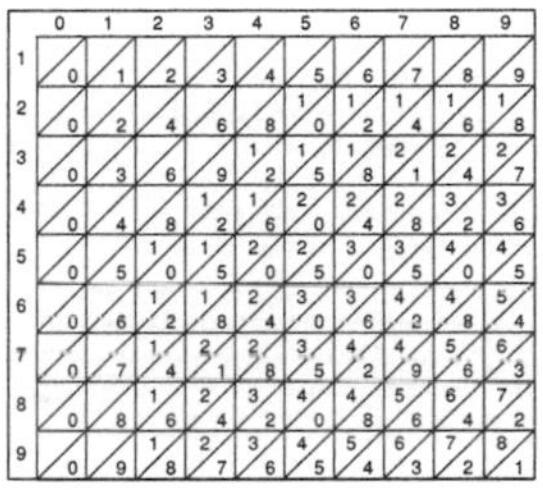

1. 476 x 304 = **144,704**	2. 722 x 436 = **314,792**	3. 821 x 569 = **467,149**
4. 835 x 321 = **268,035**	5. 605 x 843 = **510,015**	6. 349 x 275 = **95,975**
7. 652 x 872 = **568,544**	8. 349 x 731 = **255,119**	9. 644 x 590 = **379,960**
10. 863 x 182 = **157,066**	11. 295 x 452 = **133,340**	12. 524 x 604 = **316,496**
13. 466 x 459 = **213,894**	14. 989 x 329 = **325,381**	15. 916 x 334 = **305,944**
16. 627 x 670 = **308,471**	17. 881 x 705 = **621,105**	18. 518 x 367 = **190,106**
19. 1,073 x 272 = **291,856**	20. 1,855 x 146 = **270,830**	21. 4,312 x 9,403 = **40,545,736**
22. 1,283 x 474 = **608,142**	23. 9,190 x 355 = **3,262,450**	24. 5,963 x 540 = **3,220,020**

55

Page 56

Day 10 **Some key words and punctuation marks signal that an author is giving a context clue. These include dashes, commas, parentheses, and phrases like which is, in other words, for instance, and etc. In these sentences write what the underlined words mean. Then write the key words or punctuation marks that helped you tell the word's meaning.**

Example: The candidate shouted through a megaphone (large funnel-shaped horn) so the crowd could hear him.
megaphone *Large funnel-shaped cone; parentheses*

1. I feel torpid—sluggish and lazy—in the hot summer weather.
torpid **sluggish and lazy; dashes**
2. Paul Bunyan used an adze, which is a flat-bladed ax, to cut down the forest.
adze **flat-bladed ax; which is**
3. The cook made ragout, a highly seasoned stew, every day for the ranch hands.
ragout **highly seasoned stew; commas**
4. Jason mashed his patella, in other words, his kneecap.
patella **kneecap; in other words**
5. The silver jubilee anniversary, that is, the 25th anniversary, was celebrated for ten days.
jubilee **an anniversary; that is**
6. David can play a marimba (a xylophone).
marimba **an insturment with bars like a xylophone; parentheses**

For 7 and 8 use the above words and write your own sentences. Use context clues in each one. Use a dictionary to find the meanings.
7. **Sentences will vary.**
8.

Add a prefix or a suffix to the following base or root words. Then choose six of the words you made and write a sentence with them.

1. **dis**agree	8. **mis**placed	15. **dis**respect**ful**
2. **in**capable	9. avoid**able**	16. **ex**change
3. delay**ed**	10. **un**number**ed**	17. loyal**ty**
4. hazard**ous**	11. care**less**	18. **in**depend**ent**
5. **un**necessary	12. smart**est**	19. thought**ful**
6. marvel**ous**	13. **ad**verb	20. **im**mature
7. **un**comfort**able**	14. **im**plant	21. act**or**

Answers will vary.

56

Page 57

Mixed Practice. Find the missing factors. **Day 11**

1. 67 x **8** = 536	2. 96 x **9** = 864	3. **5** x 77 = 385
4. **11** x 84 = 924	5. 2,210 ÷ **26** = 85	6. 5,518 ÷ **89** = 62
7. 29 x **68** = 1,972	8. 19,347 - **877** = 18,470	9. 23,432 + **657** = 24,089
10. 32 x **200** = 6,400	11. **150** x 75 = 11,250	12. 4,905 ÷ **15** = 327
13. 56,993 - **1,395** = 55,598	14. 4,266 ÷ **6** = 711	15. 33 x **542** = 17,886
16. **5,529** + 34,561 = 40,090	17. 307 x **59** = 18,113	18. 741 x **83** = 61,503
19. 50,000 ÷ **40** = 1,250	20. **286** x 56 = 16,016	21. 40,572 ÷ **322** = 126
22. 19,263 + **47,127** = 66,390	23. 73,477 - **11,172** = 62,305	24. **190,499** - 80,399 = 110,099
25. **1,350** x 48 = 64,800	26. 83,037 ÷ **89** = 933	27. **14,687** ÷ 19 = 773
28. **9,408** ÷ 49 = 192	29. 932 x **381** = 355,092	30. 5,396 + 3,217 + **2,377** = 10,990

Endocrine System. Read the phrases below. Determine whether the pituitary gland or thyroid gland is responsible. Write P for pituitary and T for thyroid.

1. **P** A person's height
2. **P** Influences the reproductive system
3. **T** Rate at which the body uses food
4. **P** Helps control growth rate
5. **T** May affect the weight of a person

57

Page 58

Day 11 **Irregular Verbs. Change the present form of the verb at the first of the sentence to the past form. Write the past form in the blank.**

EXAMPLE: wear I *wore* an old coat to school.

ring 1. The telephone **rang** ten times before she answered it.
build 2. The contractor **built** a new apartment building every year for five years.
feed 3. Aunt Dawn **fed** her cats three times a day.
choose 4. We each **chose** a friend to go with us to Disneyland.
spend 5. My brother **spent** all of his allowance on ice cream.
spin 6. The top **spun** for five minutes.
run 7. Our family **ran** in a marathon two summers ago.
eat 8. The monkey **ate** four bananas.
shake 9. I was so afraid of the dark that I **shook** all over when the lights went out.
hold 10. Kit **held** his breath for one minute.
bleed 11. My nose **bled** for half an hour last night.
draw 12. The class **drew** pictures showing what they did on their field trip.
ride 13. Alexander **rode** his Shetland pony in the rodeo parade last summer.
teach 14. Julie's mother **taught** us how to jump double dutch with our new jump ropes.
fight 15. My sisters and I **fought** a lot when we were children.

Quotes.
Make a list of favorite or frequently used quotes among your family and friends. Have your family and friends help you compile your list.
EXAMPLE: If wishes were fishes we'd all take a swim.

Answers will vary.

58

Page 59

Day 12

Simplifying Fractions. Simplify the fractions down to the lowest term possible.

EXAMPLE:

1. 5/10 = 1/2 2. 8/12 = 2/3 3. 6/9 = 2/3 4. 15/25 = 3/5 5. 9/27 = 1/3
6. 50/75 = 2/3 7. 16/20 = 4/5 8. 9/72 = 1/8 9. 18/45 = 2/5 10. 60/100 = 3/5
11. 24/32 = 3/4 12. 75/100 = 3/4 13. 36/45 = 4/5 14. 16/24 = 2/3 15. 16/72 = 2/9
16. 30/80 = 3/8 17. 8/64 = 1/8 18. 15/40 = 3/8 19. 27/45 = 3/5 20. 18/24 = 3/4
21. 10/35 = 2/7 22. 4/18 = 2/9 23. 9/15 = 3/5 24. 14/21 = 2/3 25. 21/28 = 3/4
26. 8/40 = 1/5 27. 45/120 = 3/8 28. 32/48 = 2/3 29. 144/180 = 4/5 30. 18/144 = 1/8
31. 150/200 = 3/4 32. 32/40 = 4/5 33. 81/135 = 3/5 34. 280/420 = 2/3 35. 72/96 = 3/4

Heroes in America. Match these people with the important contributions they made during America's fight for independence.

d George Washington — a. "Swamp Fox," guerrilla warfare
i Thomas Jefferson — b. commander of American ship *Bonhomme Richard*
g Patrick Henry — c. dressed in men's clothing and joined the army
e Benjamin Franklin — d. crossed the Delaware River on Christmas Eve
h Thomas Paine — e. "Gentlemen, we must all hang together, or most assuredly we shall all hang separately."
b John Paul Jones — f. carried pitchers of water to soldiers
f Mary Ludwig Hays — g. "Give me liberty or give me death!"
a Francis Marion — h. Common Sense
c Deborah Sampson — i. wrote the Declaration of Independence

Choose one of these people and do a small report on him/her. After giving so much of themselves to gain independence for America, how do you think they would feel if they saw America today? What do you think they would say?

59

Page 60

Day 12

Direct objects are nouns or pronouns that complete or receive the action of the verb. They follow action verbs only. Circle the verb and underline the direct objects in these sentences. Use the direct objects to complete the puzzle.

EXAMPLE:

1. John Smith (guided) the colonists in the new world.
2. The robber (threw) the jewels into the bag and ran.
3. Sarah (bought) some groceries at the supermarket.
4. The crowd (begged) the musicians to play more.
5. We (captured) the tarantula in an old glass jar.
6. The sun (melted) the icicles that were on the house.
7. My brother, the quarterback, (made) a touchdown.
8. The movers (loaded) the furniture into the truck.
9. Loryn (watches) movies with her friends.
10. Trenton (sold) fifty tickets for the drawing.
11. Julia (cut) the watermelon into a dozen pieces.
12. The tangled string (ruined) my kite.
13. Allie (borrowed) my new umbrella.

Complete the puzzle.

t o u c h D o w n
k I t e
f u R n i t u r e
w a t e r m E l o n
g r o C e r i e s
t a r a n T u l a
m O v i e s
u m B r e l l a
J e w e l s
t i c k E t s
i C i c l e s
c o l o n i s T s
m u s i c i a n S

60

Page 61

Day 13

Mysterious Division Power. Choose any 2-digit number. Write it 3 times to make a 6-digit number. Divide it by 13; then divide the answer by 21, and divide that answer by 37.

EXAMPLE: 14 141,414 ÷ 13 = 10,878 ÷ 21 = 518 ÷ 37 = 14 MAGIC!

1. 56 565,656 ÷ 13 = 43,512 ÷ 21 = 2,072 ÷ 37 = 56
2. 35 353,535 ÷ 13 = 27,195 ÷ 21 = 1,295 ÷ 37 = 35
3. 73 737,373 ÷ 13 = 56,721 ÷ 21 = 2,701 ÷ 37 = 73
4. 29 292,929 ÷ 13 = 22,533 ÷ 21 = 1,073 ÷ 37 = 29
5. 80 808,080 ÷ 13 = 62,160 ÷ 21 = 2,960 ÷ 37 = 80

Now use your own 2-digit numbers.

6. ___ ______ ÷ 13 = ___ ÷ 21 = ___ ÷ 37 = ___
7. ___ ______ ÷ 13 = ___ ÷ 21 = ___ ÷ 37 = ___
8. ___ ______ ÷ 13 = ___ ÷ 21 = ___ ÷ 37 = ___
9. ___ ______ ÷ 13 = ___ ÷ 21 = ___ ÷ 37 = ___
10. ___ ______ ÷ 13 = ___ ÷ 21 = ___ ÷ 37 = ___
11. ___ ______ ÷ 13 = ___ ÷ 21 = ___ ÷ 37 = ___
12. ___ ______ ÷ 13 = ___ ÷ 21 = ___ ÷ 37 = ___

Answers will vary.

Teeth. Match the appropriate term and definition.

b crown — a. soft tissue that contains nerves and blood vessels in center of tooth
d root — b. part of tooth above the gum
f enamel — c. hard tissue that covers the root
e dentin — d. part of tooth that holds it in the jawbone
a pulp — e. hard tissue that forms body of tooth
c cementum — f. hard tissue that covers the crown of tooth

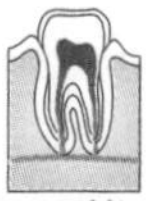

Write a short story titled "The Tale of Tooth City." Have a villain whose name might be "Wicked Wizard Plaque." Be creative with your story. Have a happy ending with healthy teeth.

Stories will vary.

61

Page 62

Day 13

Syllables. Read these sentences; then write the underlined word on the line, leaving a space between the syllables. Use the dictionary if you need help.

1. We used some old wicker chairs on our patio. — wick er
2. Lavender is a shade of the color purple. — lav en der
3. My brother, who is six feet six inches tall, has enormous feet. — e nor mous
4. In the spring, my favorite flowering bush is the lilac. — li lac
5. We use natural gas to heat our house. — nat u ral
6. If you want to be a doctor of dermatology, you would study about skin diseases. — der ma tol o gy
7. I could hear a whispering voice behind me. — whis per ing
8. Have you ever been to San Francisco? — San Fran cis co
9. The coauthor of my new book is Carla Powers. — co au thor
10. We think it's fun to visit cities that have cobblestone streets. — cob ble stone
11. How old were you when you learned the alphabet? — al pha bet
12. Allen acted like a zombie after being up all night. — zom bie
13. The comedian's originality was amusing. — o rig i nal i ty
14. Jay was in misery for a long time after the accident. — mis er y

Analogies. Analogies are similar relationships between two pairs of words. Write an analogy to finish each sentence.

EXAMPLE:

1. Tree is to lumber as wheat is to flour.
2. Page is to book as state is to the United States.
3. Brake is to stop as engine is to go.
4. Mechanic is to motors as plumber is to pipes.
5. Bird is to nest as wolf is to den.
6. Bricks are to a wall as fingers are to hand.
7. Finger is to hand as toe is to foot.
8. Penny is to dime as inch is to foot.
9. Space is to rocket as water is to boat.
10. Stage is to actor as pit is to orchestra.
11. Diamond is to jewel as steel is to metal.
12. Fame is to famous as study is to studious.

62

Page 63

Day 14

Chart the graph point by point. The first number tells how far to go to the right. The second number tells how far to move up. The distance between the grid lines represents 2 units.

1. Place the dot and letter on the point called for. The first one is done for you.

(2, 2) dot A
(12, 16) dot H
(16, 12) dot J
(6, 4) dot P
(14, 10) dot K
(10, 14) dot G
(4, 6) dot B
(8, 12) dot F
(8, 6) dot O
(12, 8) dot L
(8, 10) dot D
(10, 8) dot N
(13, 13) dot I
(6, 8) dot C
(10, 11) dot E
(11, 10) dot M
(16, 4) draw a ☆
(4, 14) draw a ☆
(2, 18) draw a ☆
(16, 8) draw a ●
(2, 10) draw a ●
(10, 18) draw a ●

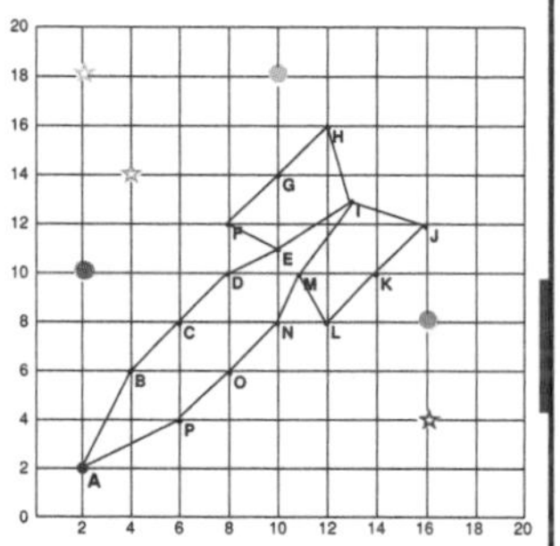

2. Connect dots A through P in alphabetical order.
3. Connect dot P to A.
4. Connect dots E to I and I to M.

Make a "point by point" direction course and have a friend or family member see if they can graph it. You could make a design, picture, or map. Use your imagination and have fun.

63

Page 64

Day 14

Circle the correct noun.

1. The (Farmers', Farmers) Market was only open on Friday. — Farmers'
2. That (mountain, mountains) peak is too hard for me to climb. — mountain
3. (Ed White's, Ed White) was the first astronaut to walk in space. — Ed White
4. We saw a herd of (deer, deers) along the side of the road. — deer
5. Why do (goose, geese) have webbed (foot, feet)? — geese, feet

Write the plural form of each noun to fill in the blanks.

potato, man, trout, party, elf

6. The potatoes on our farm were the best!
7. The nurse took the pulses of the men.
8. My father caught ten rainbow trout that day.
9. The parties we went to were all fun.
10. Many elves worked on the shoes for the queen.

Fill in the blanks with proper nouns. Answers will vary.

11. We live very close to the Rocky Mountains.
12. Halloween comes in the month of October.
13. The Hawaiian Islands are very beautiful.
14. Judge Fisher went on vacation as soon as the trial was over.
15. Robert's favorite basketball team is the Jazz.

Practice writing and spelling these words three times each. Then have someone give you a test on them. Use another piece of paper for the test.

1. practicing — practicing, practicing, practicing
2. guesses — guesses, guesses, guesses
3. manufacture — manufacture, manufacture, manufacture
4. poisonous — poisonous, poisonous, poisonous
5. loafer — loafer, loafer, loafer
6. vigorous — vigorous, vigorous, vigorous
7. boundary — boundary, boundary, boundary
8. prejudice — prejudice, prejudice, prejudice

64

Page 65

Day 15

Exchange and Share $906.00. You have $906.00 to share among 7 family members. Find out if you can share it equally. To begin with, you have nine $100 bills, no $10 bills, and six $1 bills. Share and exchange down.

1. You have nine $100 bills. How many $100 bills does each family member get? 1 How many are left? 2
2. Exchange the $100 bills you have left for 20 $10 bills.
3. Each family member gets 2 $10 bills. How many are left? 6
4. Exchange your $10 bills for 60 $1 bills. How many $1 bills do you have altogether? 66
5. Each family member gets 9 $1 bills. How many are left? 3
6. Each family member gets 1 $100 bills, 2 $10 bills, and 9 $1 bills.
7. How much money does each family member get? $129
8. What could you do with the amount left over? Answers will vary.
9. Is there another way to share the money equally? Show us! Answers will vary.

Make up your own "Exchange and Share" situation or use the following: $504 among 21 people. Use the above method.

The Bill of Rights is the name given to the first ten amendments added to the Constitution. Other amendments also have been added. Read the passages below and determine which situations are constitutional or unconstitutional. Then write down which amendment would support your decision.

1. In the 1960s, a group of black students walked around with signs that said "Down with segregation!" Constitutional–Amendment 1,
2. A city police department would not allow women to join the police force. Unconstitutional–Amendment 14
3. A person accused of a serious crime refuses to give evidence against himself. Constitutional–Amendment 5
4. A town does not like the religious beliefs of a particular group, so it forbids that group to build a place where they can worship. Unconstitutional–Amendment 1
5. A woman accused of a serious crime wants a trial with a jury. The government says she doesn't have enough money for this type of trial. Unconstitutional–Amendment 6
6. A group of students who just turned eighteen want to vote for whom they would like as the president of the United States. Constitutional–Amendment 26
7. The president of the United States wants to run for office again. This would be his/her third term. Unconstitutional–Amendment 22

65

Page 66

Day 15

Contractions. Words like let's (let us), you'll (you will), etc., are contractions. Contractions that have the word not in them are called negatives. The rule is NEVER use double negatives when you write or speak. Other words like nothing, never, and nobody are also negatives. In these sentences, find the double negatives and rewrite the sentence in cursive, using the correct word. Some answers will vary.

EXAMPLE: The fight didn't solve nothing. *The fight didn't solve anything.*

1. The team didn't want no trouble.
The team didn't want any trouble.
2. Haven't you never seen Yellowstone Park?
Haven't you ever seen Yellowstone Park?
3. There weren't no eggs left in the carton.
There were no eggs left in the carton. Or: There weren't any eggs left in the carton.
4. I haven't never been happier to finish a school year.
I have never been happier to finish a school year. Or: I haven't ever been happier...
5. This path doesn't lead nowhere.
This path doesn't lead anywhere.
6. Can't no one in this class solve the puzzle?
Can't anyone in this class solve the puzzle?
7. Richard didn't have nothing to read.
Richard didn't have anything to read.
8. Nanette said that she hadn't never thought of that idea.
Nanette said that she had never thought of that idea.
9. Don't spill none of the juice on the carpet.
Don't spill any of the juice on the carpet.
10. There isn't nothing you can do about the weather.
There isn't anything you can do about the weather.
11. Thad doesn't know nobody in his algebra class.
Thad doesn't know anybody in his algebra class.
12. The bus didn't have no empty seats when we got on.
The bus didn't have any empty seats when we got on.

66

Page 67

Day 16

Eggs? What eggs? Chicken eggs! Down through the ages, eggs have been eaten around the world. In America, the most popular eggs to eat are chicken eggs. Chicken eggs are classified primarily by their weight. Small eggs weigh approximately 18 ounces a dozen. Medium eggs weigh 21 ounces a dozen. Large eggs weigh 24 ounces a dozen. Extra large eggs weigh a hefty 27 ounces a dozen. Jumbo eggs, which are classified as the largest sellable eggs, weigh 30 ounces a dozen.

1. 6 dozen jumbo eggs weigh a total of 180 ounces.
2. How many eggs are in 6 dozen? 72
3. How many eggs are in 12 dozen? 144 What are two different ways you can use to find the answer to this question? 12 x 12 = 144, 72 x 2 = 144
4. Which weighs more—3 dozen jumbo eggs or 5 dozen small eggs? They both total 90 ounces.
5. If 5 dozen eggs weigh a total of 150 ounces, which eggs would they be? jumbo
6. If you wanted to boil a total of 120 eggs for an Easter egg hunt and you wanted an equal number of each size of egg, how many of each size would you boil? 2 dozen
7. What is the minimum weight you can have if you have 4 dozen eggs? 72 ounces of small eggs.
8. If you bought a dozen of each size of egg, what should be the total weight in ounces? 120 ounces
9. Jan gathered 4 dozen medium-sized eggs, 3 dozen small eggs, 1 dozen large eggs, 2 dozen extra-large eggs, and 1/2 dozen jumbo eggs. How many eggs did she gather? 126 How many ounces did she have altogether? 231 ounces
10. Mother bought 3 dozen eggs, but some broke on the way home. When she got home, she tried to divide them evenly between 2 bowls, but she had 1 left over. With 3 and 4 bowls she again had 1 left over. When she divided them into 5 bowls, they came out exactly even! How many eggs did she have? 25 eggs

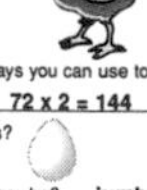

The Skin. Go to the store or look in a magazine for products used to keep your skin healthy. On the chart below, write the name of the product and its purpose. Then ask yourself if this product is necessary to help keep your skin healthy. If the answer is yes, put a star by the product. If you find that the product will not really help keep your skin healthy, put a moon by the product.

Name	Purpose	Star or Moon
	Answers will vary.	

67

Page 68

Day 16

Pronouns. Fill in the blanks with pronouns.

EXAMPLE: Maggie collects books. She likes old books best.

Some answers will vary.

1. Nancy's parents collect books also; **they** are professors.
2. Mark had a pet wolf. **His** wolf was named Silver.
3. Andrew handed Mary the rock. Mary showed **us or him** the fossils in **it**.
4. Emily washed **her** hair.
5. I asked **my** sister to give **me** a ride home.
6. The cat washed **its** baby kittens.
7. The girls made lunch for **their** family.
8. "Craig, will **you** give **them** **your** phone number?"

The pronouns we and us are sometimes used with nouns. Fill in the blanks with we or us. Use we when the noun is the subject; use us when it is not.

9. **We** Americans have a lot of pride in our country.
10. At the dinner party, **we** guests made sandwiches.
11. The stranger made a map for **us** travelers.
12. Will the teacher give **us** students good grades?

Use just the letters from these spelling words to make three or four new words. Try to make four- and five-letter words also. Use a letter only once in each word.

Example: journeys	our	runs	yes	nose
1. enemies	men	is	mine	seem
2. intermediate	ate	term	men	time
3. vocabulary	cab	lay	buy	vocal
4. inscription	ton	script	point	rip
5. purpose	so	purse	rose	us
6. suspended	pen	us	depend	end
7. examiner	exam	near	examine	mine
8. pendulum	pen	mud	plume	plum
9. luxurious	ours	sir	sour	soil
10. monotonous	not	ton	noun	mount

68

Page 69

Day 17

Let's Go with Division.

Choose a place you would like to go that you can drive to in a few days. Find a map and chart your course. Estimate, then check how many miles it is from your house. Decide how fast you can drive and how many hours you are going to travel each day. Using division, figure out how many days it will take. Make a chart using the information you have. Decide how long you can stay. Remember, you have to save some time to drive home. Try a one-week trip, then a three-week trip. Remember, you have to travel by car. Could you chart your results? Can you estimate the cost of your trip? Involve your parents in this plan to help you!

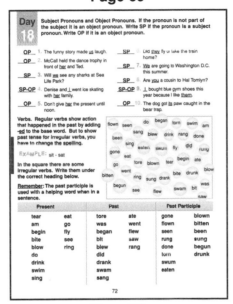

N
W
E
S
Answers will vary.

69

Page 70

Day 17

More Pronouns. Use I or me in these sentences. When I is part of a compound subject, use it last.

EXAMPLE: She and I made a cake.

1. Mom and **I** went to the store.
2. When will you come to see Kent and **me**?
3. Karen asked **me** to answer the door.
4. Ann Marie and **I** ate our lunch outside.
5. Snakes scare **me** to death.
6. The gift was sent by Aunt Jean and **me**.
7. Carla and **I** were both born in May.

Possessive pronouns show ownership. Use possessive pronouns in these sentences. **Some answers will vary.**

8. Did you see **their** faces when they saw Santa?
9. **Your** handwriting is very neat.
10. The prize is **ours** for the asking.
11. The book you gave to Leza was **mine**.
12. **My** uncle, Clint, is coming for a visit.
13. The prints on the mirror are **his or hers or mine.**
14. The elephant stood on **its** drum.

Volcanoes. Answer T for true or F for false to the following statements. If false, correct the sentence so it will be true.

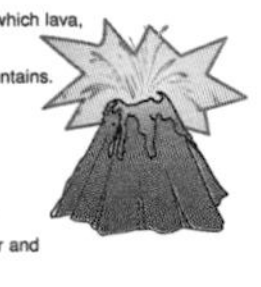

T 1. A volcano is an opening in the crust of the Earth through which lava, gases, ash, and rocks erupt.
F 2. In a short time, volcanic material can build up to form mountains. **It takes a long time.**
F 3. These mountains can form only on land. **They also form on the ocean floor.**
F 4. All magma comes from the Earth's core. **Magma comes from the upper mantle.**
T 5. Most volcanoes happen underwater.
T 6. Mid-ocean ridges are formed from underwater volcanoes.
T 7. Mid-ocean ridges happen when lava builds up under water and creates underwater mountain chains.
F 8. Most volcanoes on land occur at diverging plate boundaries. **They occur at converging plate boundaries.**
F 9. Mid-ocean ridges form at convergent boundaries. **They occur at divergent boundaries.**
T 10. Volcanoes on land occur on the edge of a continent or on islands.
T 11. When two plates converge, compression forces some rocks upward to make mountains.

70

Page 71

Day 18

Sharpen your skills with this timed multiplication test! Estimate how much time you think it will take you to do these problems. ______ Now do the actual test. How long did it take you to do it? ______ What's the difference between the two times? ______

1. 6 x 7 = 42	26. 8 x 9 = 72	51. 5 x 5 = 25	76. 11 x 5 = 55	101. 8 x 10 = 80
2. 12 x 2 = 24	27. 6 x 9 = 54	52. 9 x 0 = 0	77. 9 x 6 = 54	102. 0 x 10 = 0
3. 5 x 10 = 50	28. 11 x 10 = 110	53. 9 x 3 = 27	78. 9 x 12 = 108	103. 7 x 9 = 63
4. 9 x 6 = 54	29. 10 x 9 = 90	54. 7 x 4 = 28	79. 6 x 8 = 48	104. 10 x 11 = 110
5. 7 x 8 = 56	30. 9 x 11 = 99	55. 12 x 4 = 48	80. 7 x 10 = 70	105. 7 x 12 = 84
6. 11 x 12 = 132	31. 7 x 3 = 21	56. 9 x 9 = 81	81. 5 x 11 = 55	106. 12 x 12 = 144
7. 7 x 5 = 35	32. 12 x 10 = 120	57. 7 x 9 = 63	82. 10 x 10 = 100	107. 11 x 9 = 99
8. 11 x 2 = 22	33. 9 x 9 = 81	58. 8 x 5 = 40	83. 6 x 11 = 66	108. 12 x 7 = 84
9. 10 x 3 = 30	34. 8 x 8 = 64	59. 10 x 4 = 40	84. 12 x 11 = 132	109. 11 x 6 = 66
10. 5 x 6 = 30	35. 7 x 7 = 49	60. 9 x 8 = 72	85. 12 x 9 = 108	110. 9 x 5 = 45
11. 9 x 5 = 45	36. 10 x 10 = 100	61. 7 x 6 = 42	86. 8 x 7 = 56	111. 9 x 3 = 27
12. 8 x 4 = 32	37. 11 x 3 = 33	62. 10 x 5 = 50	87. 5 x 8 = 40	112. 12 x 9 = 108
13. 8 x 0 = 0	38. 6 x 5 = 30	63. 11 x 4 = 44	88. 0 x 8 = 0	113. 11 x 7 = 77
14. 6 x 12 = 72	39. 5 x 3 = 15	64. 7 x 8 = 56	89. 8 x 6 = 48	114. 5 x 9 = 45
15. 8 x 3 = 24	40. 9 x 2 = 18	65. 12 x 12 = 144	90. 11 x 8 = 88	115. 9 x 10 = 90
16. 10 x 2 = 20	41. 12 x 5 = 60	66. 9 x 7 = 63	91. 11 x 12 = 132	116. 9 x 8 = 72
17. 6 x 6 = 36	42. 10 x 0 = 0	67. 7 x 11 = 77	92. 10 x 7 = 70	117. 9 x 4 = 36
18. 8 x 9 = 72	43. 9 x 10 = 90	68. 5 x 4 = 20	93. 8 x 11 = 88	118. 10 x 12 = 120
19. 7 x 2 = 14	44. 8 x 2 = 16	69. 9 x 7 = 63	94. 11 x 6 = 66	119. 8 x 12 = 96
20. 8 x 7 = 56	45. 11 x 5 = 55	70. 10 x 8 = 80	95. 6 x 10 = 60	120. 11 x 11 = 121
21. 11 x 7 = 77	46. 8 x 8 = 64	71. 9 x 11 = 99	96. 6 x 4 = 24	121. 7 x 12 = 84
22. 5 x 2 = 10	47. 7 x 6 = 42	72. 0 x 12 = 06	97. 11 x 8 = 88	122. 8 x 11 = 88
23. 10 x 6 = 60	48. 7 x 7 = 49	73. 8 x 6 = 48	98. 12 x 6 = 72	123. 11 x 11 = 121
24. 9 x 4 = 36	49. 11 x 9 = 99	74. 12 x 3 = 36	99. 8 x 10 = 80	124. 0 x 9 = 0
25. 6 x 3 = 18	50. 5 x 12 = 60	75. 5 x 7 = 35	100. 12 x 12 = 144	125. 12 x 8 = 96

Cover up the answers with another sheet of paper and try it again!

71

Page 72

Day 18

Subject Pronouns and Object Pronouns. If the pronoun is not part of the subject it is an object pronoun. Write SP if the pronoun is a subject pronoun. Write OP if it is an object pronoun.

OP 1. The funny story made us laugh.
OP 2. McCall held the dance trophy in front of her and Ted.
SP 3. Will we see any sharks at Sea Life Park?
SP-OP 4. Denise and I went ice skating with her family.
OP 5. Don't give her the present until noon.
SP 6. Did they fly or take the train home?
SP 7. We are going to Washington D.C. this summer.
SP 8. Are you a cousin to Hal Tomlyn?
SP-OP 9. I bought blue gym shoes this year because I like them.
OP 10. The dog got its paw caught in the bear trap.

Verbs. Regular verbs show action that happened in the past by adding -ed to the base word. But to show past tense for irregular verbs, you have to change the spelling.

EXAMPLE: sit - sat

In the square there are some irregular verbs. Write them under the correct heading below.

flown seen do began torn swim am sang blew drink rang done been sing eaten swum fly did rung gone eat tore blown tear begin ate go went bitten ring sung drank bite drunk blow begun see flew swam bit was saw

Remember: The past participle is used with a helping word when in a sentence.

Present		Past		Past Participle	
tear	eat	tore	ate	gone	blown
am	go	was	went	flown	bitten
begin	fly	began	flew	seen	been
bite	see	bit	saw	rung	sung
blow	ring	blew	rang	done	begun
do		did		torn	drunk
drink		drank		swum	
swim		swam		eaten	
sing		sang			

72

Page 73

Day 19

Choices. Clayton's mother bought him some new clothes to go to camp. She bought him 4 pairs of shorts—red, blue, green, and white. She also bought him 8 T-shirts—2 red, 2 blue, 2 green, and 2 white. She bought him 4 long-sleeved sweatshirts—2 white and 2 blue.

Use a tree diagram to organize the data to find out how many different choices of shorts and shirts Clayton can wear. 24 total choices

shorts	shirts
red	red T-shirt, green T-shirt, blue T-shirt, white T-shirt, blue sweatshirt, white sweatshirt
blue	red T-shirt, green T-shirt, blue T-shirt, white T-shirt, blue sweatshirt, white sweatshirt
green	red T-shirt, green T-shirt, blue T-shirt, white T-shirt, blue sweatshirt, white sweatshirt
white	red T-shirt, green T-shirt, blue T-shirt, white T-shirt, blue sweatshirt, white sweatshirt

Our Government. Our government is divided into three branches. Each branch is given different, but equal, powers. In the circle below, write down the branch, the power it has, and draw a picture that could represent each branch.

Legislative Branch- power to make laws.

Executive Branch- power to enforce laws made by Congress.

Judicial Branch- power to settle disagreements about what the laws mean.

73

Page 74

Day 19

Cause and Effect. Below are some parts of sentences that give the cause. Finish the sentence by writing what the effect might be. Look for clue words. **Answers will vary.**

EXAMPLE: (cause) The old house had not been painted for years, (effect) so the first thing we did was paint it. (The clue word is "so.")

1. Our Thanksgiving turkey was burned because **the oven was not working right**.
2. **My feet hurt at the end of the day** because my new shoes were too tight.
3. The wind was blowing hard, so **we decided not to go gliding that day**.
4. Because I didn't get up early enough this morning, **I was late for school**.
5. Some children were playing with matches; as a result, **the house burned down**.

Now it's your turn to write the cause to the effects.

6. The plane crashed due to **the thick fog**.
7. **Because I had eaten so much**, my stomach hurt.
8. **Our class won the prize**, so we decided to celebrate.
9. The drinks were very sweet because **Ronda spilled sugar in the punch bowl**.
10. **Since we had such a cold spell in April**, there was no fruit on the trees this summer.

Electricity. In the table below, make a list of all the things you enjoy that use electricity. Now ask a parent, adult, or grandparent to list all the things that use electricity that they did not have when they were your age.

Compare the differences and similarities on your table. Next, create a list of things children in 30 years may have that use electricity that we do not have today. Be creative!

Answers will vary.

You	Parent/Adult
Grandparent/Elderly Person	**Future**

74

Page 75

Day 20

Broken Line Graphs, "Using Leisure Time."

Keep track of how much television you watch daily in a two-week period, then graph the results. Do the same with how much time you play computer games or TV games, then graph the results. Now do the same with how much time you spend with your friends, then graph the results. You can use the same graph for all three if you use different colored pens or pencils.

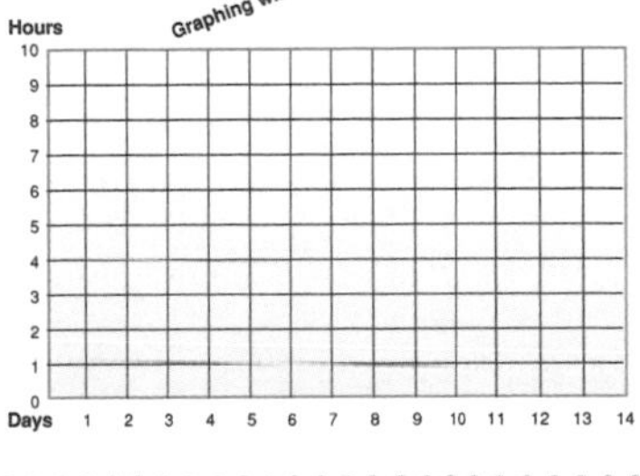

Hours
Graphing will vary.
10
9
8
7
6
5
4
3
2
1
0
Days
1 2 3 4 5 6 7 8 9 10 11 12 13 14

Powers of the Government. Decide which branch of government (legislative, executive, or judicial) that each statement describes.

legislative 1. Can impeach the president of the United States.
legislative 2. Approves treaties.
executive 3. Approves or vetoes bills.
judicial 4. Interprets and examines laws and treaties.
executive 5. Appoints justices.

75

Page 76

Day 20

Adjectives make reading more interesting. Remember: Adjectives modify or describe nouns and pronouns. Read the clues to help you do the crossword puzzle. The answers are adjectives that are listed in the word box below. Dark lines mark the end of words. Use the dictionary for help with definitions.

Across
1. satisfied
4. dignified, lofty, noble
8. filled with fear
11. critical, immediate
12. rough voice
13. courageous, valiant, gallant
14. headstrong, inflexible

Down
1. skilled, competent
2. commanding
3. unbelievable, amazing
5. unable to put up with others' beliefs
6. lively, playful
7. childish, foolish
9. ill-disposed, hateful
10. made of wood

Crossword answers — Across: 1 contented, 4 majestic, 8 horrified, 11 urgent, 12 hoarse, 13 stouthearted, 14 obstinate. Down: 1 capable, 2 authoritative, 3 fantastic, 5 intolerant, 6 frisky, 7 silly, 9 spiteful, 10 wooden.

hoarse	spiteful	majestic	silly	urgent
contented	horrified	wooden	obstinate	authoritative
stouthearted	fantastic	intolerant	frisky	capable

Quotation marks go before and after exactly what a person is saying and the titles of stories, poems, and songs. Tell why quotation marks are used in these sentences.

1. Robert asked, "What are the rules for this game?"
Robert is speaking.
2. Mother was fixing lunch when David came home. "Please set the table," she said.
Mother is talking.
3. Jim gave Lance a copy of "Solving Math Puzzles" to take on his trip.
Name of a book or article.
4. "What's that terrible noise?" cried Carla.
Carla is speaking.
5. Cindy was playing "Tennessee Waltz" on her guitar when Pete came in.
Name of a song.

Your turn. Put quotation marks in these sentences.

6. "I don't think I can do this by myself," Marge sighed.
7. Hillary is singing "America the Beautiful" to her sister.
8. "Do you like baseball or football best?" Debra asked. "I like baseball best."
9. "Not me," answered Eleanor. "I like basketball best."

76

Section 3

Division Outcomes. Complete this table to see which of these numbers can be divided by 2, 3, 5, 9, and 10 without having remainders. After you have finished the chart, see if you can come up with some hypotheses to form some divisibility rules.

Day 1

Hypotheses of 2. 3. 5. 9. and 10

2 Hypothesis The number can be divided equally by 2 if a 0, 2, 4, 6, or 8 is found in the one's place.

3 Hypothesis The number can be divided equally by 3 if the sum of the numbers when added together can be divided by 3.

5 Hypothesis The number can be divided equally by 5 if 0 or 5 is found in the one's place.

9 Hypothesis The number can be divided equally by 9 if the sum of the numbers when added together can be divided by 9.

10 Hypothesis The number can be divided equally by 10 if a 0 is found in the one's place.

y = yes and n = no

Divisible by	2	3	5	9	10
3,825	n	y	y	y	n
930	y	y	y	n	y
792	y	y	n	y	n
856	y	n	n	n	n
1,440	y	y	y	y	y
6,825	n	y	y	n	n
1,854	y	y	n	y	n
41,004	y	y	n	y	n
85,010	y	n	y	n	y
314,402	y	n	n	n	n
4,277,133	n	y	n	y	n
10,009,407	n	y	n	n	n
9,617,590	y	n	y	n	y
9,591,314	y	n	n	n	n

Try out your hypotheses on number combinations of your own to see if they really work.

The Expansion West. Write a dialogue that might have happened between the following people during the expansion west: an Indian, a settler, and a soldier. Remember to keep an open mind about their different points of view. Have your parents, brothers, sisters, or friends read the parts in costume!

Answers will vary.

81

Page 81

Day 1

Fill in the blank in each sentence with a synonym of the word in the box. Look in the dictionary if you need help.

Example: I had to [finish] complete my work before I could go with my friends.

Answers may vary.

1. Sarah and Angie go for a [walk] stroll every day except Sunday.
2. It's fun to watch the little colts [play] frolic or romp in the green pastures.
3. The electricians have done [enough] sufficient work for this week.
4. I cannot [find] locate the information I [need] require for my report.
5. You will have to [write] record all the important events of your [trip] journey.
6. The lost couple had not had any [food] nourishment for six days.
7. Will you please [show] demonstrate how your new invention works?
8. They will [try] attempt/ endeavor to climb Mount Everest again next summer.
9. Tourists [might] may be able to travel to the moon by the year 2010.
10. The value of this coin will [grow] increase over the years.
11. The applicant must [reply] respond within three weeks.
12. I think your [story] tale was a little far-fetched!

Electric Current. Read each passage on electricity. One sentence in each passage is false. Cross out the false sentence and try to correct it. Then answer the questions after each passage.

1. An electrical current is moving energy. You can see electricity at work in lights, motors, computers, and some toys. Any material that allows an electric current to pass through is called a ~~battery~~. **a conductor**

   Question: How many things can you think of in 1–2 minutes that need electricity? Have a race with someone to see who can think of the most ideas.

   Answers will vary.

2. Material that does not allow an electric current to pass through it is called a ~~circuit~~. This material covers conducting materials. It stops electricity from escaping and causing harm. **an insulator**

   Question: What are 5 things you can do to ensure safety in your home with electricity?

   1. ______ 2. Answers will vary. 3. ______ 4. ______ 5. ______

82

Page 82

Round the Clock Multiplication. Choose numbers between 10 and 100 and put them in the outer circle. Next, put numbers between 1 and 12 in the following circle. Then multiply the outer circle's number by the second circle's number.

Day 2

EXAMPLE:

Answers will vary.

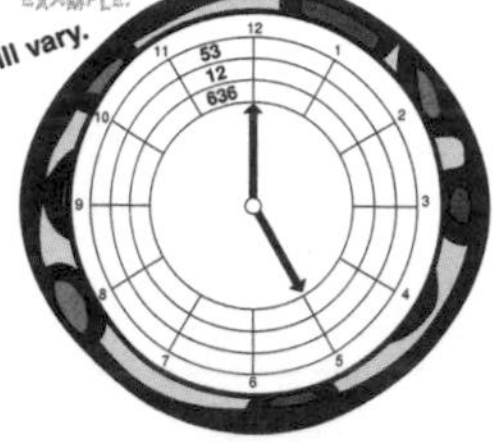

Moving West. Hunters, trappers, and pioneers moved west in the 1800s. Take 5 minutes to brainstorm all the things you would need for a trip west. List as many things as you can! Now take this list and think of different categories in which these items would fit. For example, one category might be food.

Answers will vary.

83

Page 83

Day 2

Spelling. What double consonants go in these spelling words?

1. i m m ediately
2. su p p ort
3. i r r egular
4. a t t ribute
5. di f f erence
6. a s s e s s ment
7. i r r emovable
8. a b b reviation
9. exce l l ence
10. a n n ual
11. su p p osed
12. po s s ible
13. inte l l igence
14. a l l egiance
15. bu t t ernut
16. i n n ocent
17. di s s atisfied
18. a c c e s s ible
19. scri b b le
20. permi t t ing

Health—Eyes. Label the parts of the eye below using the following words:

retina
cornea
lens
iris
pupil
vitreous humor
optic nerve

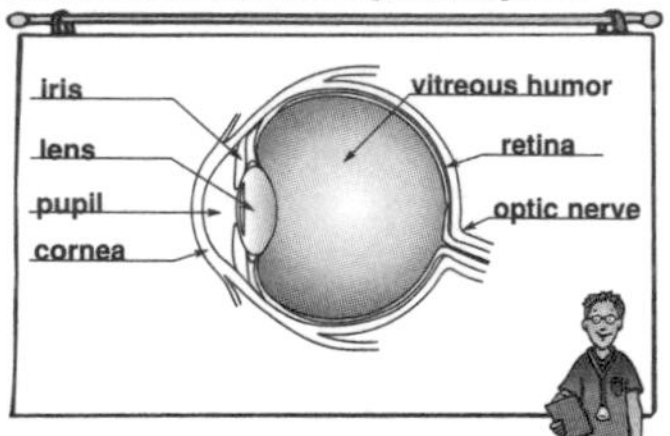

Make a journal of all the activities you do in one day. Look back over the activities at the end of the day. Imagine that you could not see. How would this have affected your day? What would you have needed to do differently?

Answers will vary.

84

Page 84

Polyominoes.

Day 3

1. These are all polyominoes.

   Why? Each square shares at least one of its sides with another square.
2. These are not polyominoes.

   Why not? The squares do not share a common side.
3. Draw some polyominoes of your own using 5 squares.

   Answers will vary
4. Chart the course by following lines according to the instructions below. How many polyominoes did you chart? 4

   east 1, north 3, east 5, north 3, east 1, south 5, east 1, north 3, west 5, south 4, west 1, north 6, west 1, north 3, east 1, south 2, east 5, north 1, west 3, north 1, east 4, south 1, east 1, south 6, west 1, south 2, west 8, and you should be back where you started from.

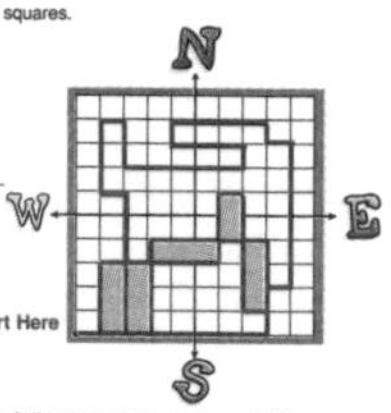

How a Law is Made. Put into sequence the following steps on how a bill can become a law. Then come up with a bill you think should become a law. Draw a comic strip that shows characters putting these steps into action.

3 Get the president to approve.

1 Write a bill.

2 Get a majority vote in Congress.

4 If the president vetoes the bill, then it may become a law by 2/3 vote in Congress.

Your own bill: Answers will vary.

85

Page 85

Day 3

"The Eagle has landed."

American astronauts Neil Armstrong and Buzz Aldrin became the first men on the moon on July 20, 1969. The giant Apollo moon rocket was 363 feet high and weighed six and a half million pounds.

The Lunar Module (LM) left the Apollo at 1:45 P.M. "The Eagle has wings," Armstrong stated. At 3:46 the LM emerged from behind the moon. "The burn was on time," reported Armstrong matter-of-factly. At that time, they were at an altitude of about 20 miles, descending toward 50,000 feet. The astronauts had to make the all-important and final decision whether to remain in orbit or to descend to the lunar surface to make the landing.

At approximately 4:07 P.M., Armstrong pressed the button marked "Proceed." Aldrin and Armstrong realized in horror that the computer-controlled guidance system was taking them right down into a football-field-sized crater with a large number of big boulders and rocks. With only precious seconds to spare, Armstrong took manual control of the spacecraft. He searched for and found a clear area amid the menacing rock field below. "Houston," Armstrong radioed, "Tranquility base here. The Eagle has landed."

It was the first time men from earth had touched down on the moon. Armstrong was the first human being to set foot on the lunar surface. As his left foot touched the moon to take the first step, he spoke the now famous words, "That's one small step for man, one giant leap for mankind."

1. What was Armstrong referring to when he said "The Eagle has landed"? **The Lunar Module landing on the moon.**
2. The word "lunar" is used several times. What is another word for lunar? **moon**
3. What did "all-important and final decision" really mean to the astronauts? **There was no turning back.**
4. What was the real significance of this mission to humankind? **Answers will vary.**
5. What does this report tell you about what type of men Armstrong and Aldrin are? **Answers will vary.**
6. What does this event say to you personally? **Answers will vary.**

Electricity. Two electrical pathways are series circuits and two are parallel circuits. Label the pictures as either a series circuit or parallel circuit.

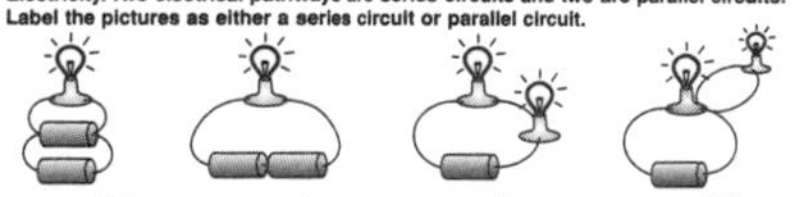

parallel — series — series — parallel

86

Page 86

Relationship between Missing Numbers. Find the missing numbers and then write the rule.

Day 4

1. M	1. N	2. M	2. N	3. M	3. N	4. M	4. N	5. M	5. N
15	20	25	36	54	45	9	72	8	48
40	45	19	30	89	80	11	88	4	24
90	95	57	68	73	64	7	56	10	60
35	40	73	84	70	61	5	40	6	36
Rule: M + 5=N		Rule: M + 11=N		Rule: M - 9=N		Rule: M x 8=N		Rule: M x 6=N	

6. M	6. N	7. M	7. N	8. M	8. N	9. M	9. N	10. M	10. N
21	7	48	8	36	24	7	63	10	120
30	10	12	2	57	45	9	81	12	144
18	6	42	7	63	51	6	54	9	108
12	4	24	4	90	78	3	27	11	132
Rule: M ÷ 3=N		Rule: M ÷ 6=N		Rule: M - 12=N		Rule: M x 9 = N		Rule: M x 12=N	

11. M	11. N	12. M	12. N	13. M	13. N	14. M	14. N	15. M	15. N
3.2	5.5	35	50	24	3	4.2	8.4	0.09	0.14
7.1	9.4	73	88	56	7	9.3	18.6	0.13	0.18
5	7.3	27	42	72	9	8.1	16.2	.05	0.10
4.4	6.7	100	115	64	8	7.5	15.0	3.21	3.26
Rule: M+2.3=N		Rule: M+15=N		Rule: M ÷ 8=N		Rule: M x 2=N		Rule: M+0.05=N	

Trail of Tears. Do research on the Trail of Tears. Write a poem about this event using the letters of Trail of Tears at the beginning of each line. Be sure to include the emotions felt at this time. Make a border around the poem with colors and objects you feel would best describe the mood of your poem.

T
R
A
I
L Poems will vary.
O
F
T
E
A
R
S

87

Page 87

Day 4

Contents and Index. Read this fictitious contents and index from a history book. Then answer the questions below.

Contents

Index

1. What is the difference between the contents and the index in books? **The contents is in front listing things in order of appearance. The index is at the back, alphabetically listing main topics.**
2. If you wanted to know if this book had a section on the War of 1812, where would you look? 2-contents or index
3. If you wanted to see if there was a picture of Andrew Jackson in the book, where would you look? index
4. Where would you look to find out who fought in the Civil War? contents
5. How many chapters does this book have? two
6. How many sections are in chapter one? four
7. On what page would you look to find out about Native Americans? **You would have to look under American Indians.**
8. On what page could you look to learn who Massasoit was? 172
9. How many sections are there about the Civil War? 5
10. What information is in the glossary of books? **It gives definitions of specialized or technical terms used.**

Unscramble the syllables to make words. There might be one or two extra syllables in each word. Cross them out. All the words have something to do with transportation. Example: ing merg ~~mer~~ merging

1. fic ~~dux~~ traf — traffic
2. ~~bed~~ ough thor fare — thoroughfare
3. pave ~~vex~~ ment ~~pe~~ — pavement
4. ped tri ~~pe~~ an des — pedestrian
5. y per ~~pe~~ slip ~~bee~~ — slippery
6. in ~~ex~~ state ~~be~~ ter — interstate
7. ~~bue~~ struc tion con — construction
8. ed ~~x~~ strict ~~stik~~ re — restricted
9. ~~bed~~ mer ~~be~~ e cy gen — emergency
10. ~~be~~ a tow way ~~ix~~ — towaway
11. ger dan ~~deg~~ ous ~~dier~~ — dangerous
12. tion ~~sek~~ ter ~~sk~~ sec in — intersection
13. ex way ~~te~~ ~~pro~~ press — expressway
14. mum min i ~~bex~~ — minimum

88

Page 88

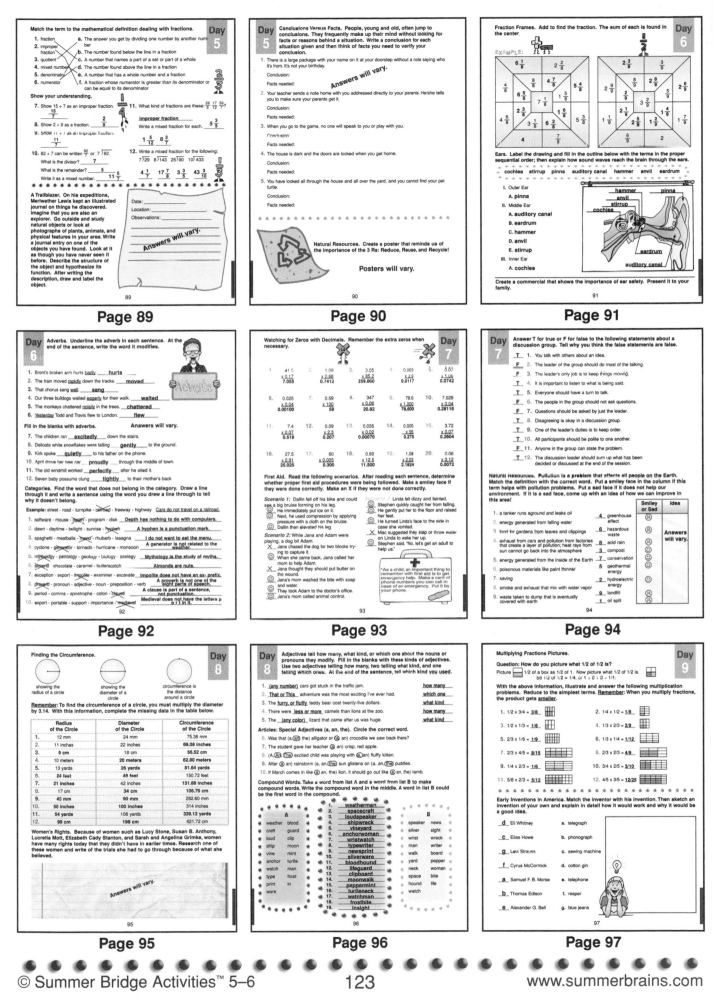

Page 89

Day 5

Match the term to the mathematical definition dealing with fractions.

1. fraction — a. The answer you get by dividing one number by another number
2. improper fraction — b. The number found below the line in a fraction
3. quotient — c. A number that names a part of a set or part of a whole
4. mixed number — d. The number found above the line in a fraction
5. denominator — e. A number that has a whole number and a fraction
6. numerator — f. A fraction whose numerator is greater than its denominator or can be equal to its denominator

Show your understanding.

7. Show 15 ÷ 7 as an improper fraction. **15/7**
8. Show 2 + 9 as a fraction. **2/9**
9. Show 11 ÷ 7 as an improper fraction. **11/7**
10. 82 ÷ 7 can be written 82/7 or 7)82.
    What is the divisor? **7**
    What is the remainder? **11**
    Write it as a mixed number. **11 5/7**
11. What kind of fractions are these: 28/15 17/12 59/7? **improper fraction**
    Write a fraction for each. **5 3/5**
12. Write a mixed fraction for the following:
    7)29 8)143 25)90 10)433
    4 1/7   17 7/8   3 3/5   43 3/10

A Trailblazer. On his expeditions, Meriwether Lewis kept an illustrated journal on things he discovered. Imagine that you are also an explorer. Go outside and study natural objects or look at photographs of plants, animals, and physical features in your area. Write a journal entry on one of the objects you have found. Look at it as though you have never seen it before. Describe the structure of the object and hypothesize its function. After writing the description, draw and label the object.

Date:
Location:
Observations:

Answers will vary.

Page 90

Day 5

Conclusions Versus Facts. People, young and old, often jump to conclusions. They frequently make up their mind without looking for facts or reasons behind a situation. Write a conclusion for each situation given and then think of facts you need to verify your conclusion.

1. There is a large package with your name on it at your doorstep without a note saying who it's from. It's not your birthday.
   Conclusion:
   Facts needed:

2. Your teacher sends a note home with you addressed directly to your parents. He/she tells you to make sure your parents get it.
   Conclusion:
   Facts needed:

3. When you go to the game, no one will speak to you or play with you.
   Conclusion:
   Facts needed:

4. The house is dark and the doors are locked when you get home.
   Conclusion:
   Facts needed:

5. You have looked all through the house and all over the yard, and you cannot find your pet turtle.
   Conclusion:
   Facts needed:

Answers will vary.

Natural Resources. Create a poster that reminds us of the importance of the 3 Rs: Reduce, Reuse, and Recycle!

Posters will vary.

Page 91

Day 6

Fraction Frames. Add to find the fraction. The sum of each is found in the center.

EXAMPLE:

Ears. Label the drawing and fill in the outline below with the terms in the proper sequential order; then explain how sound waves reach the brain through the ears.

cochlea   stirrup   pinna   auditory canal   hammer   anvil   eardrum

I. Outer Ear
   A. pinna
II. Middle Ear
   A. auditory canal
   B. eardrum
   C. hammer
   D. anvil
   E. stirrup
III. Inner Ear
   A. cochlea

Create a commercial that shows the importance of ear safety. Present it to your family.

Page 92

Day 6

Adverbs. Underline the adverb in each sentence. At the end of the sentence, write the word it modifies.

1. Brent's broken arm hurts badly. **hurts**
2. The train moved rapidly down the tracks. **moved**
3. That chorus sang well. **sang**
4. Our three bulldogs waited eagerly for their walk. **waited**
5. The monkeys chattered noisily in the trees. **chattered**
6. Yesterday Todd and Travis flew to London. **flew**

Fill in the blanks with adverbs.   Answers will vary.

7. The children ran **excitedly** down the stairs.
8. Delicate white snowflakes were falling **gently** to the ground.
9. Kirk spoke **quietly** to his father on the phone.
10. April drove her new car **proudly** through the middle of town.
11. The old windmill worked **perfectly** after he oiled it.
12. Seven baby possums clung **tightly** to their mother's back

Categories. Find the word that does not belong in the category. Draw a line through it and write a sentence using the word you drew a line through to tell why it doesn't belong.

Example: street - road - turnpike - railroad - freeway - highway   Cars do not travel on a railroad.

1. software - mouse - depth - program - disk   Depth has nothing to do with computers.
2. dawn - daytime - twilight - sunrise - hyphen   A hyphen is a punctuation mark.
3. spaghetti - meatballs - hand - linguine - lasagna   I do not want to eat the menu.
4. cyclone - generator - tornado - hurricane - monsoon   A generator is not related to the weather.
5. mythology - petrology - geology - biology - zoology   Mythology is the study of myths.
6. almond - chocolate - caramel - butterscotch   Almonds are nuts.
7. exception - export - impolite - examiner - excavate   Impolite does not have an ex- prefix.
8. proverb - pronoun - adjective - noun - preposition - verb   A proverb is not one of the eight parts of speech.
9. period - comma - apostrophe - colon - clause   A clause is part of a sentence, not punctuation.
10. export - portable - support - importance - medieval   Medieval does not have the letters p o r t in it.

Page 93

Day 7

Watching for Zeros with Decimals. Remember the extra zeros when necessary.

1. 41.5 ×0.17 = 7.055	2. 1.09 ×0.68 = 0.7412	3. 3.05 ×85.2 = 259.860	4. 0.003 ×3.9 = 0.0117	5. 0.07 ×1.06 = 0.0742
6. 0.025 ×0.04 = 0.00100	7. 0.59 ×100 = 59	8. 347 ×0.06 = 20.82	9. 78.6 ×1.000 = 78,600	10. 7.029 ×0.04 = 0.28116
11. 7.4 ×0.07 = 0.518	12. 0.09 ×2.3 = 0.207	13. 0.035 ×0.02 = 0.00070	14. 0.005 ×55 = 0.275	15. 3.72 ×0.07 = 0.2604
16. 27.5 ×0.91 = 25.025	17. 60 ×0.005 = 0.300	18. 0.92 ×12.5 = 11.500	19. 1.08 ×2.03 = 2.1924	20. 0.06 ×0.12 = 0.0072

First Aid. Read the following scenarios. After reading each sentence, determine whether proper first aid procedures were being followed. Make a smiley face if they were done correctly. Make an X if they were not done correctly.

Scenario 1: Dallin fell off his bike and could see a big bruise forming on his leg.
☺ He immediately put ice on it.
☺ Next, he used compression by applying pressure with a cloth on the bruise.
☺ Dallin then elevated his leg.

Scenario 2: While Jana and Adam were playing, a dog bit Adam.
X Jana chased the dog for two blocks trying to capture it.
☺ When she came back, Jana called her mom to help Adam.
X Jana thought they should put butter on the wound.
☺ Jana's mom washed the bite with soap and water.
☺ They took Adam to the doctor's office.
☺ Jana's mom called animal control.

Linda felt dizzy and fainted.
☺ Stephen quickly caught her from falling.
☺ He gently put her to the floor and raised her feet.
☺ He turned Linda's face to the side in case she vomited.
X Mac suggested they slap or throw water on Linda to wake her up.
☺ Stephen said, "No, let's get an adult to help us."

*As a child, an important thing to remember with first aid is to get emergency help. Put a card with phone numbers you can call in case of an emergency. Put it by your phone.

Page 94

Day 7

Answer T for true or F for false to the following statements about a discussion group. Tell why you think the false statements are false.

T 1. You talk with others about an idea.
F 2. The leader of the group should do most of the talking.
F 3. The leader's only job is to keep things moving.
T 4. It is important to listen to what is being said.
T 5. Everyone should have a turn to talk.
F 6. The people in the group should not ask questions.
F 7. Questions should be asked by just the leader.
T 8. Disagreeing is okay in a discussion group.
T 9. One of the leader's duties is to keep order.
T 10. All participants should be polite to one another.
T 11. Anyone in the group can state the problem.
T 12. The discussion leader should sum up what has been decided or discussed at the end of the session.

Natural Resources. Pollution is a problem that affects all people on the Earth. Match the definition with the correct word. Put a smiley face in the column if this term helps with pollution problems. Put a sad face if it does not help our environment. If it is a sad face, come up with an idea of how we can improve in this area!

		Smiley or Sad	Idea
1. a tanker runs aground and leaks oil	4 greenhouse effect	☹	
2. energy generated from falling water	8 hazardous waste	☹	
3. food for gardens from leaves and clippings	7 acid rain	☺	Answers will vary.
4. exhaust from cars and pollution from factories that create a layer of pollution; heat rays from sun cannot go back into the atmosphere	3 compost	☹	
5. energy generated from the inside of the Earth	2 conservation	☺	
6. poisonous materials like paint thinner	5 geothermal energy	☹	
7. saving	6 hydroelectric energy	☺	
8. smoke and exhaust that mix with water vapor	9 landfill	☹	
9. waste taken to dump that is eventually covered with earth	1 oil spill	☹	

Page 95

Day 8

Finding the Circumference.

showing the radius of a circle   showing the diameter of a circle   circumference is the distance around a circle

Remember: To find the circumference of a circle, multiply the diameter by 3.14. With this information, complete the missing data in the table below.

	Radius of the Circle	Diameter of the Circle	Circumference of the Circle
1.	12 mm	24 mm	75.36 mm
2.	11 inches	22 inches	69.08 inches
3.	9 cm	18 cm	56.52 cm
4.	10 meters	20 meters	62.80 meters
5.	13 yards	26 yards	81.64 yards
6.	24 feet	48 feet	150.72 feet
7.	21 inches	42 inches	131.88 inches
8.	17 cm	34 cm	106.76 cm
9.	45 mm	90 mm	282.60 mm
10.	50 inches	100 inches	314 inches
11.	54 yards	108 yards	339.12 yards
12.	99 cm	198 cm	621.72 cm

Women's Rights. Because of women such as Lucy Stone, Susan B. Anthony, Lucretia Mott, Elizabeth Cady Stanton, and Sarah and Angelina Grimke, women have many rights today that they didn't have in earlier times. Research one of these women and write of the trials she had to go through because of what she believed.

Answers will vary.

Page 96

Day 8

Adjectives tell how many, what kind, or which one about the nouns or pronouns they modify. Fill in the blanks with these kinds of adjectives. Use two adjectives telling how many, two telling what kind, and one telling which ones. At the end of the sentence, tell which kind you used.

1. (any number) cars got stuck in the traffic jam. **how many**
2. That or This adventure was the most exciting I've ever had. **which one**
3. The furry, or fluffy teddy bear cost twenty-five dollars. **what kind**
4. There were less or more camels than lions at the zoo. **how many**
5. The (any color) lizard that came after us was huge. **what kind**

Articles: Special Adjectives (a, an, the). Circle the correct word.

6. Was that (a, an) the) alligator or (a, an) crocodile we saw back there?
7. The student gave her teacher (a, an) crisp, red apple.
8. (A, An, The) excited child was playing with (a, an) fluffy kitten.
9. After (a, an) rainstorm (a, an, the) sun glistens on (a, an, the) puddles.
10. If March comes in like (a, an) lion, it should go out like (a, an, the) lamb.

Compound Words. Take a word from list A and a word from list B to make compound words. Write the compound word in the middle. A word in list B could be the first word in the compound.

A
weather blood
craft guard
loud clip
ship moon
vine mint
anchor turtle
watch man
type frost
print in
ware

1. weatherman
2. spacecraft
3. loudspeaker
4. shipwreck
5. vineyard
6. anchorwoman
7. wristwatch
8. typewriter
9. newsprint
10. silverware
11. bloodhound
12. lifeguard
13. clipboard
14. moonwalk
15. peppermint
16. turtleneck
17. watchman
18. frostbite
19. insight

B
speaker news
silver sight
wrist wreck
man writer
walk board
yard pepper
neck woman
space bite
hound life
watch

Page 97

Day 9

Multiplying Fractions Pictures.

Question: How do you picture what 1/2 of 1/2 is?
Picture 1/2 of a box as 1/2 of 1. Now picture what 1/2 of 1/2 is.
So 1/2 of 1/2 = 1/4, or 1 × 1 = 1, 2 × 2 = 4.

With the above information, illustrate and answer the following multiplication problems. Reduce to the simplest terms. Remember: When you multiply fractions, the product gets smaller.

1. 1/2 × 3/4 = **3/8**
2. 1/4 × 1/2 = **1/8**
3. 1/2 × 1/3 = **1/6**
4. 1/3 × 2/3 = **2/9**
5. 2/3 × 1/6 = **1/9**
6. 1/3 × 1/4 = **1/12**
7. 2/3 × 4/5 = **8/15**
8. 2/3 × 2/3 = **4/9**
9. 1/4 × 2/3 = **1/6**
10. 3/4 × 2/5 = **3/10**
11. 5/8 × 2/3 = **5/12**
12. 4/5 × 3/5 = **12/25**

Early Inventions in America. Match the inventor with his invention. Then sketch an invention of your own and explain in detail how it would work and why it would be a good idea.

d Eli Whitney — a. telegraph
c Elias Howe — b. phonograph
g Levi Strauss — c. sewing machine
f Cyrus McCormick — d. cotton gin
a Samuel F. B. Morse — e. telephone
b Thomas Edison — f. reaper
e Alexander G. Bell — g. blue jeans

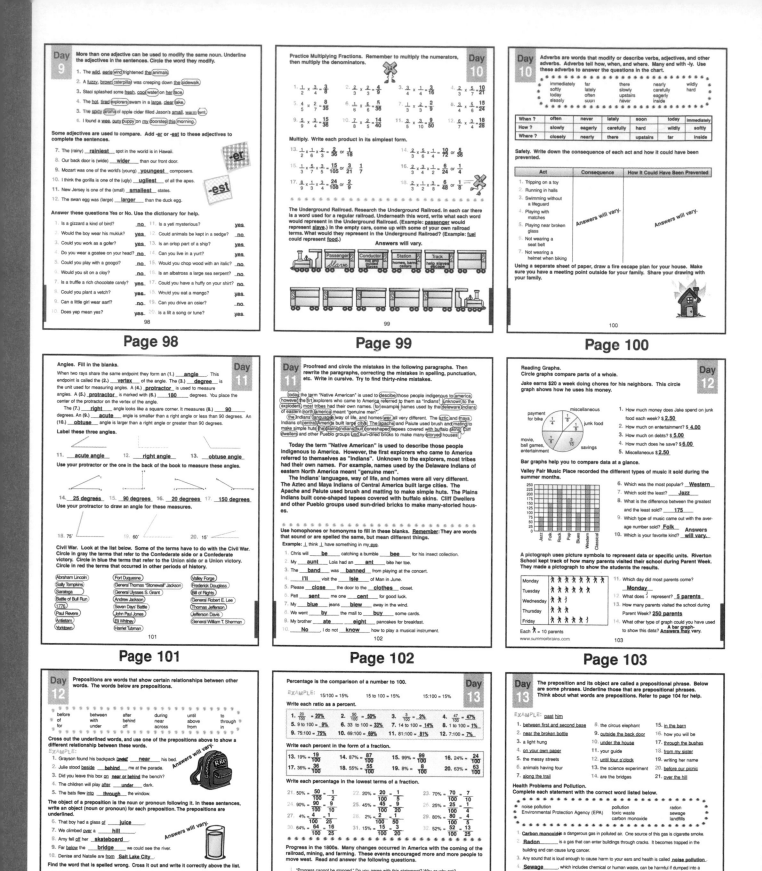

Page 98

Page 99

Page 100

Page 101

Page 102

Page 103

Page 104

Page 105

Page 106

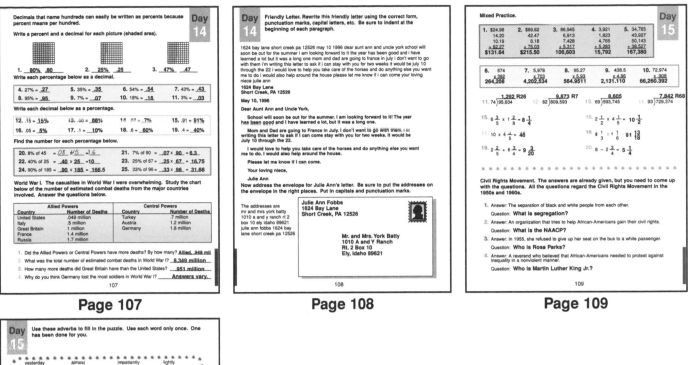

Page 107

Decimals that name hundreds can easily be written as percents because percent means per hundred.

Write a percent and a decimal for each picture (shaded area).

1. __80%__ .80   2. __25%__ .25   3. __47%__ .47

Write each percentage below as a decimal.

4. 27% = __.27__   5. 35% = __.35__   6. 54% = __.54__   7. 43% = __.43__
8. 95% = __.95__   9. 7% = __.07__   10. 18% = __.18__   11. 3% = __.03__

Write each decimal below as a percentage.

12. .15 = __15%__   13. .00 = __.00%__   14. .07 = __7%__   15. .91 = __91%__
16. .05 = __5%__   17. .1 = __10%__   18. .6 = __60%__   19. .4 = __40%__

Find the number for each percentage below.

20. 8% of 45 = .08 #5 3.6   21. 7% of 90 = .07 × 90 = 6.3
22. 40% of 25 = .40 × 25 = 10   23. 25% of 67 = .25 × 67 = 16.75
24. 90% of 185 = .90 × 185 = 166.5   25. 33% of 96 = .33 × 96 = 31.68

World War I. The casualties in World War I were overwhelming. Study the chart below of the number of estimated combat deaths from the major countries involved. Answer the questions below.

Allied Powers		Central Powers	
Country	Number of Deaths	Country	Number of Deaths
United States	.049 million	Turkey	.7 million
Italy	.5 million	Austria	1.2 million
Great Britain	1 million	Germany	1.8 million
France	1.4 million		
Russia	1.7 million		

1. Did the Allied Powers or Central Powers have more deaths? By how many? __Allied, .949 mil__
2. What was the total number of estimated combat deaths in World War I? __8.349 million__
3. How many more deaths did Great Britain have than the United States? __.951 million__
4. Why do you think Germany lost the most soldiers in World War I? __Answers vary.__

107

Page 108

Friendly Letter. Rewrite this friendly letter using the correct form, punctuation marks, capital letters, etc. Be sure to indent at the beginning of each paragraph.

1624 bay lane short creek pa 12526 may 10 1996 dear aunt ann and uncle york school will soon be out for the summer i am looking forward to it the year has been good and i have learned a lot but it was a long one mom and dad are going to france in july i don't want to go with them i'm writing this letter to ask if i can stay with you for two weeks it would be july 10 through the 22 i would love to help you take care of the horses and do anything else you want me to do i would also help around the house please let me know if i can come your loving niece julie ann

1624 Bay Lane
Short Creek, PA 12526

May 10, 1996

Dear Aunt Ann and Uncle York,

School will soon be out for the summer. I am looking forward to it! The year has been good and I have learned a lot, but it was a long one.

Mom and Dad are going to France in July. I don't want to go with them. I'm writing this letter to ask if I can stay with you for two weeks. It would be July 10 through the 22.

I would love to help you take care of the horses and do anything else you want me to do. I would also help around the house.

Please let me know if I can come.

Your loving niece,

Julie Ann

Now address the envelope for Julie Ann's letter. Be sure to put the addresses on the envelope in the right places. Put in capitals and punctuation marks.

The addresses are mr and mrs york batty 1010 a and y ranch rt 2 box 10 ely idaho 89621 julie ann fobbs 1624 bay lane short creek pa 12526

Julie Ann Fobbs
1624 Bay Lane
Short Creek, PA 12526

Mr. and Mrs. York Batty
1010 A and Y Ranch
Rt. 2 Box 10
Ely, Idaho 89621

108

Page 109

Mixed Practice.

1.	2.	3.	4.	5.
$24.98	$89.82	86,945	3,921	34,783
14.20	42.47	6,913	1,823	43,927
10.19	8.18	7,428	4,765	50,143
+ 82.27	+ 75.03	+ 5,317	+ 5,283	+ 38,527
$131.64	$215.50	106,603	15,792	167,380

6.	7.	8.	9.	10.
674	5,978	95.27	438.5	72,974
× 392	× 703	× 5.93	× 4.86	× 908
264,208	4,202,534	564.9511	2,131.110	66,260.392

11. 74)95,634 __1,292 R26__
12. 82)809,593 __9,873 R7__
13. 69)593,745 __8,605__
14. 93)729,374 __7,842 R68__

15. $6\frac{3}{5} \times 1\frac{2}{8} = 8\frac{1}{4}$
16. $2\frac{1}{2} \times 4\frac{1}{5} = 10\frac{1}{2}$
17. $10 \times 4\frac{4}{5} = 46$
18. $3\frac{1}{3} + 1\frac{1}{6} = 91\frac{13}{18}$
19. $2\frac{2}{5} + 6\frac{3}{4} = 9\frac{3}{20}$
20. $8 - 2\frac{3}{4} = 5\frac{1}{4}$

Civil Rights Movement. The answers are already given, but you need to come up with the questions. All the questions regard the Civil Rights Movement in the 1950s and 1960s.

1. Answer: The separation of black and white people from each other.
   Question: **What is segregation?**
2. Answer: An organization that tries to help African-Americans gain their civil rights.
   Question: **What is the NAACP?**
3. Answer: In 1955, she refused to give up her seat on the bus to a white passenger.
   Question: **Who is Rosa Parks?**
4. Answer: A reverend who believed that African-Americans needed to protest against inequality in a nonviolent manner.
   Question: **Who is Martin Luther King Jr.?**

109

Page 110

Use these adverbs to fill in the puzzle. Use each word only once. One has been done for you.

yesterday, least, completely, carefully, loudly, slowly, almost, badly, above, yeah, yet, rapidly, impatiently, too, today, better, yonder, quickly, lightly, wildly, hardest, confidentially, lusciously, reluctantly

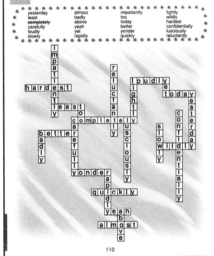

110

Notes

_____
_____
_____
_____
_____
_____
_____
_____
_____
_____
_____
_____
_____
_____
_____
_____
_____
_____
_____
_____
_____

5 Five things I'm thankful for:

1. _____
2. _____
3. _____
4. _____
5. _____

Better Bodies · Better Behavior

Up until now, Summer Bridge Activities has been all about your mind…

But the other parts of you—who you are, how you act, and how you feel—are important too. That's why this year we are introducing a whole new section in Summer Bridge Activities: Building Better Bodies and Behavior. These new pages are all about helping build a better you this summer.

Keeping your body strong and healthy helps you live better, learn better, and feel better. To keep your body healthy, you need to do things like eat right, get enough sleep, and exercise. The Physical Fitness pages of Building Better Bodies will teach you about good eating habits and the importance of proper exercise. You can even train for a Presidential Fitness Award over the summer.

The Character pages are all about building a better you on the inside. They've got fun activities for you and your family to do together. The activities will help you develop important values and habits you'll need as you grow up.

After a summer of Building Better Bodies and Behavior and Summer Bridge Activities, there may be a whole new you ready for school in the fall!

● ●

For Parents: Introduction to Character Education

Character education is simply giving your child clear messages about the values you and your family consider important. Many studies have shown that a basic core of values is universal. You will find certain values reflected in the laws of every country and incorporated in the teachings of religious, ethical, and other belief systems throughout the world.

The character activities included here are designed to span the entire summer. Each week your child will be introduced to a new value, with a quote and two activities that illustrate it. Research has shown that character education is most effective when parents reinforce the values in their child's daily routine; therefore, we encourage parents to be involved as their child completes the lessons.

Here are some suggestions on how to maximize these lessons.
- Read through the lesson yourself. Then set aside a block of time when you and your child discuss the value.
- Plan a block of time to work on the suggested activities.
- Discuss the meaning of the quote with your child. Ask, "What do you think the quote means?" Have your child ask other members of the family the same question. If possible, include grandparents, aunts, uncles, and cousins.
- Use the quote as often as you can during the week. You'll be pleasantly surprised to learn that both you and your child will have it memorized.
- For extra motivation, you can set a reward for completing each week's activities.
- Point out to your child other people who are actively displaying a value. Example: "See how John is helping Mrs. Olsen by raking her leaves."
- Be sure to praise your child each time he or she practices a value: "Mary, it was very courteous of you to wait until I finished speaking."
- Find time in your day to talk about values. Turn off the radio in the car and chat with your children; take a walk in the evening as a family; read a story about the weekly value at bedtime; or give a back rub while you talk about what makes your child happy or sad.
- Finally, model the values you want your child to acquire. Remember, children will do as you do, not as you say.

Name _____ Date _____

How I Measure Up!

You will be filling out this page twice—once now and once at the end of the summer to see how you have grown. Have someone help you measure yourself to fill in the blanks below. Write your answers in inches.

First figure (boy):

- around the neck _____ / _____
- neck to belly button _____ / _____
- around the wrist _____ / _____
- waist to ankle _____ / _____
- foot length _____ / _____
- smile _____ / _____
- shoulder to elbow _____ / _____
- elbow to wrist _____ / _____
- around the waist _____ / _____
- length of longest finger _____ / _____
- around the knee _____ / _____
- around the ankle _____ / _____

Second figure:

- length of longest finger _____ / _____
- around the wrist _____ / _____
- around the neck _____ / _____
- neck to belly button _____ / _____
- around the waist _____ / _____
- waist to ankle _____ / _____
- foot length _____ / _____
- smile _____ / _____
- shoulder to elbow _____ / _____
- elbow to wrist _____ / _____
- around the knee _____ / _____
- around the ankle _____ / _____

Nutrition

The food you eat helps your body grow and gives you energy to work and play. Some foods give you protein or fats. Other foods provide vitamins, minerals, or carbohydrates. These are all things your body needs. Eating lots of different foods from the five major food groups every day can help you stay healthy.

Each day your body needs several servings of food from each group:

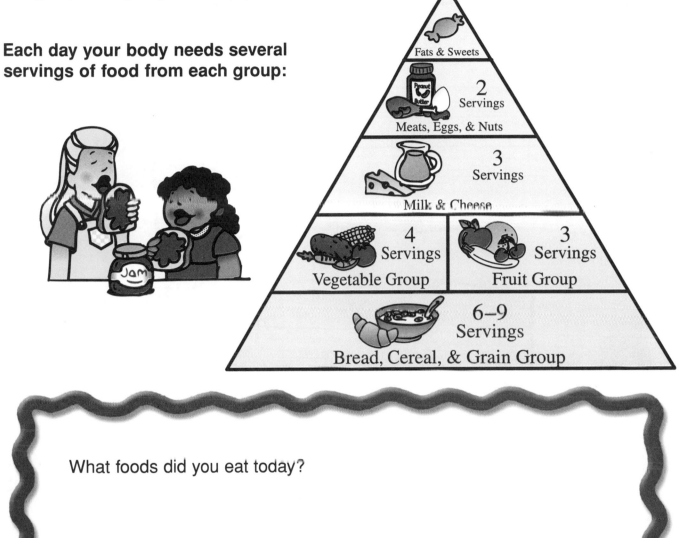

What foods did you eat today?

Which food group did you eat the most foods from today?

From which food group did you eat the least?

Which meal included the most food groups?

Meal Planning

Plan out three balanced meals for one day. Arrange your meals so that by the end of the day, you will have had all the recommended servings of the food groups listed on the Food Pyramid.

Breakfast

Lunch

Dinner

Meal Tracker

Use these charts to record the servings from each food group you eat for one or two weeks. Have another family member keep track, too, and compare.

	Breads / Cereals	Milk	Meat	Fruits	Vegetables	Fats/Sweets
Monday						
Tuesday						
Wednesday						
Thursday						
Friday						
Saturday						
Sunday						

	Breads / Cereals	Milk	Meat	Fruits	Vegetables	Fats/Sweets
Monday						
Tuesday						
Wednesday						
Thursday						
Friday						
Saturday						
Sunday						

	Breads / Cereals	Milk	Meat	Fruits	Vegetables	Fats/Sweets
Monday						
Tuesday						
Wednesday						
Thursday						
Friday						
Saturday						
Sunday						

	Breads / Cereals	Milk	Meat	Fruits	Vegetables	Fats/Sweets
Monday						
Tuesday						
Wednesday						
Thursday						
Friday						
Saturday						
Sunday						

Get Moving!

**Did you know that getting no exercise can be almost as bad for you as smoking?!
So get moving this summer!**

Summer is the perfect time to get out and get in shape. Your fitness program should include three parts:

- Get 30 minutes of aerobic exercise per day, three to five days a week.

- Exercise your muscles to improve strength and flexibility.

- Make it FUN! Do things that you like to do. Include your friends and family.

● ●

Couch Potato Quiz

1. Name three things you do each day that get you moving.

2. Name three things you do a few times a week that are good exercise.

3. How many hours do you spend each week playing outside or exercising?

4. How much TV do you watch each day?

5. How much time do you spend playing computer or video games?

If the time you spend on activities 4 and 5 adds up to more than you spend on 1–3, you could be headed for a spud's life!

Activity Pyramid

The Activity Pyramid works like the Food Pyramid. You can use the Activity Pyramid to help plan your summer exercise program. Fill in the blanks below.

List 1 thing that isn't good exercise that you could do less of this summer.

1._____

List 3 fun activities you enjoy that get you moving and are good exercise.

1._____

2._____

3._____

List 3 activities you would like to do for aerobic exercise this summer.

1._____

2._____

3._____

List 3 exercises you could do to build strength and flexibility this summer.

1._____

2._____

3._____

List 2 sports you would like to participate in this summer.

1._____

2._____

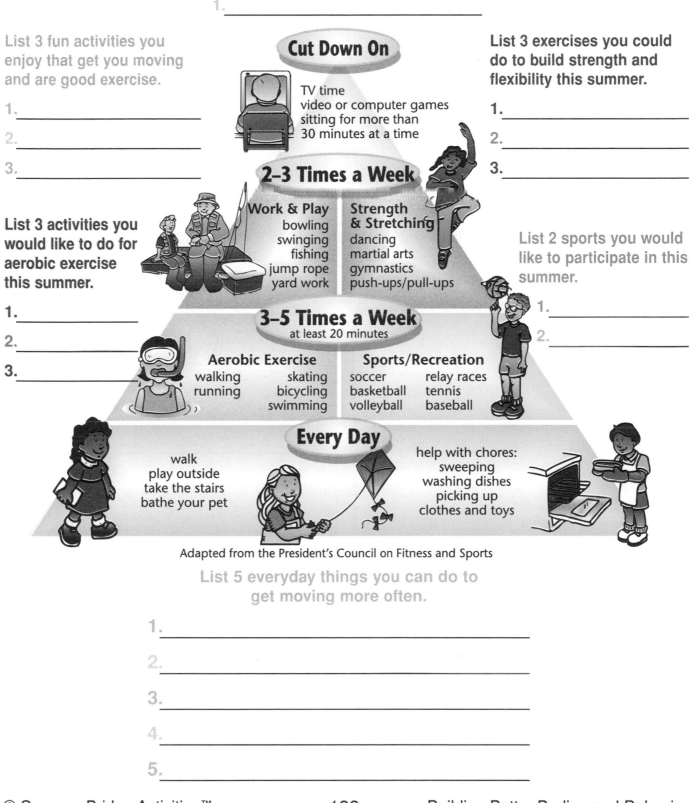

Cut Down On

TV time
video or computer games
sitting for more than
30 minutes at a time

2–3 Times a Week

Work & Play
bowling
swinging
fishing
jump rope
yard work

Strength & Stretching
dancing
martial arts
gymnastics
push-ups/pull-ups

3–5 Times a Week
at least 20 minutes

Aerobic Exercise
walking   skating
running   bicycling
swimming

Sports/Recreation
soccer   relay races
basketball   tennis
volleyball   baseball

Every Day

walk
play outside
take the stairs
bathe your pet

help with chores:
sweeping
washing dishes
picking up
clothes and toys

Adapted from the President's Council on Fitness and Sports

List 5 everyday things you can do to get moving more often.

1._____

2._____

3._____

4._____

5._____

Fitness Fundamentals

Basic physical fitness includes several things:

Cardiovascular Endurance. Your cardiovascular system includes your heart and blood vessels. You need a strong heart to pump your blood. Your blood delivers oxygen and nutrients to your body.

Muscular Strength. This is how strong your muscles are.

Muscular Endurance. Endurance has to do with how long you can use your muscles before they get tired.

Flexibility. This is your ability to move your joints and to use your muscles through their full range of motion.

Body Composition. Your body is made up of what is called lean mass and fat mass.

Lean mass includes the water, muscles, tissues, and organs in your body.

Fat mass includes the fat your body stores for energy. Exercise helps you burn body fat and maintain good body composition.

The goal of a summer fitness program is to improve in all the areas of physical fitness.

You build cardiovascular endurance through **aerobic** exercise. For **aerobic** exercise, you need to work large muscle groups at a steady pace. This increases your heart rate and breathing. You can jog, walk, hike, swim, dance, do aerobics, ride a bike, go rowing, climb stairs, rollerblade, play golf, backpack…

You should get at least 30 minutes of aerobic exercise per day, three to five days a week.

You build muscular strength and endurance with exercises that work your muscles, like sit-ups, push-ups, pull-ups, and weight lifting.

Flexibility. You can increase flexibility through stretching exercises. These are good for warm-ups too.

Find these fitness words.

Word Bank

aerobic	exercise	fat
muscular	flexible	blood
endurance	strength	oxygen
heart rate	joint	hiking

```
u a e y i d t y a g d x p o b
o l s h s t r e n g t h l r c
e w l o o o z v s d m i h d t
g t z w s j o i n t m n k a o
s q a c h i p s a d e t f f m
k c q r x i q f l e x i b l e
e e j o t v k w t e u r g e g
i e s e d r v i n t n f k x o
k e l i d c a d n n e g e j w
u z e d c y u e i g g x i c i
j c i b o r e a h h y w v s i
a m r a a c e m x x x y d i g
f p v n p n d x u s o x e f k
p o c b l o o d e g z a x m c
l e m u s c u l a r m k g i s
```

Your Summer Fitness Program

Start your summer fitness program by choosing at least one aerobic activity from your Activity Pyramid. You can choose more than one for variety.

_____   _____   _____

 Do this activity three to five times each week. Keep it up for at least 20 minutes each time.
(Exercise hard enough to increase your heart rate and your breathing. But don't exercise so hard that you get dizzy or can't catch your breath.)

● ●

Use this chart to plan when you will exercise or to record your activity after you exercise.

DATE	ACTIVITY	TIME

DATE	ACTIVITY	TIME

Plan a reward for meeting your exercise goals for two weeks.
(You can make copies of this chart to track your fitness all summer long.)

Start Slow!
Remember to start out slow. Exercise is about getting stronger. It's not about being superman—or superwoman—right off the bat.

Are You Up to the Challenge?

The Presidential Physical Fitness Award Program was designed to help kids get into shape and have fun. To earn the award, you take five fitness tests. These are usually given by teachers at school, but you can train for them this summer.

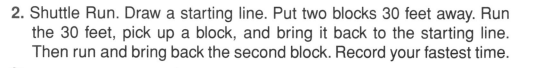

Remember: Start Slow!

1. Curl-ups. Lie on the floor with your knees bent and your feet about 12 inches from your buttocks. Cross your arms over your chest. Raise your trunk up and touch your elbows to your thighs. Do as many as you can in one minute.

2. Shuttle Run. Draw a starting line. Put two blocks 30 feet away. Run the 30 feet, pick up a block, and bring it back to the starting line. Then run and bring back the second block. Record your fastest time.

3. V-sit Reach. Sit on the floor with your legs straight and your feet 8 to 12 inches apart. Put a ruler between your feet, pointing past your toes. Have a partner hold your legs straight, and keep your toes pointed up. Link your thumbs together and reach forward, palms down, as far as you can along the ruler.

4. One-Mile Walk/Run. On a track or some safe area, run one mile. You can walk as often as you need to. Finish as fast as possible. (Ages six to seven may want to run a quarter mile; ages eight to nine, half a mile.)

5. Pull-ups. Grip a bar with an overhand grip (the backs of your hands toward your face). Have someone lift you up if you need help. Hang with your arms and legs straight. Pull your body up until your chin is over the bar; then let yourself back down. Do as many as you can.

Make a chart to track your progress. Keep working all summer to see if you can improve your score.

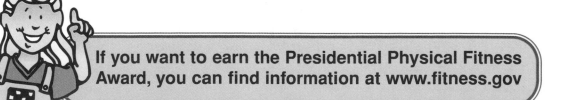

If you want to earn the Presidential Physical Fitness Award, you can find information at www.fitness.gov

Respect

Respect is showing good manners toward all people, not just those you know or who are like you. Respect is treating everyone, no matter what religion, race, or culture, male or female, rich or poor, in a way that you would want to be treated.

The easiest way to do this is to decide to **never** take part in activities and to **never** use words that make fun of people because they are different from you or your friends.

It's not necessary for eagles to be crows. What I am, I am.
~ Sitting Bull

Rob, please pass some cake.

Word Find

Find these words that also mean *respect*.

Word Bank
honor
idolize
admire
worship
recognize
appreciate
venerate
prize

```
m c e t a r e n e v
w j t a h p s e p t
e c a d n n t z i w
z v i m w u k i h r
i e c i h b h n s o
l z e r v b j g r n
o i r e k a u o o o
d r p g m e e c w h
i p p b g c h e r j
q f a b f g u r r z
```

Activity

This week go to the library and check out *The Well: David's Story* by Mildred Taylor (1995). The story is set in Mississippi in the early 1900s and tells about David's family, who shares their well with both black and white neighbors. Be sure to read this book with your parents.

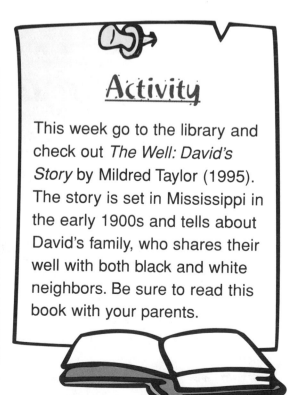

Gratitude

Gratitude is when you thank people for the good things they have given you or done for you. Thinking about people and events in your life that make you feel grateful (thankful) will help you become a happier person.

There are over 465 different ways of saying thank you. Here are a few:

Danke	Toda	Merci	Gracias	Nandri
Spasibo	Arigato	Gadda ge	Paldies	Hvala

Make a list of ten things you are grateful for.

1. _____
2. _____
3. _____
4. _____
5. _____
6. _____
7. _____
8. _____
9. _____
10. _____

A Recipe for Saying Thanks

1. Make a colorful card.
2. On the inside write a thank-you note to someone who has done something nice for you.
3. Address an envelope to that person.
4. Pick out a cool stamp.
5. Drop your note in the nearest mailbox.

Saying thank you creates love.

~ Daphne Rose Kingma

Courtesy

If you were the only person in the world, you wouldn't have to have **good manners** or be **courteous**. However, there are over six billion people on our planet, and good manners help us all get along with each other.

Children with good manners are usually well liked by other children and certainly by adults. Here are some simple rules for good manners:

• When you ask for something, say, "Please."
• When someone gives you something, say, "Thank you."
• When someone says, "Thank you," say, "You're welcome."
• If you walk in front of someone or bump into a person, say, "Excuse me."
• When someone else is talking, wait before speaking.
• Share and take turns.

No kindness, no matter how small, is ever wasted. ~ Aesop's Fables

Word Search. Find these words or phrases that deal with *courtesy*.

Word Bank
etiquette
thank you
welcome
excuse me
please
share
turns
patience
polite
manners

m	u	o	y	k	n	a	h	t
e	m	o	c	l	e	w	e	e
e	s	a	e	l	p	x	f	c
a	m	q	u	f	c	x	r	n
e	t	t	e	u	q	i	t	e
s	r	g	s	n	r	u	t	i
s	r	e	n	n	a	m	g	t
v	m	p	o	l	i	t	e	a
e	i	e	r	a	h	s	h	p

I've Got Manners

Make a colorful poster to display on your bedroom door or on the refrigerator. List five ways you are going to practice your manners. Be creative and decorate with watercolors, poster paints, pictures cut from magazines, clip art, or geometric shapes.

Instead of making a poster, you could make a mobile to hang from your ceiling that shows five different manners to practice.

Consequences

A consequence is what happens after you choose to do something. Some choices lead to good consequences. Other choices lead to bad consequences. An example of this would be choosing whether to eat an apple or a bag of potato chips. The potato chips might seem like a more tasty snack, but eating an apple is better for your body. Or, you may not like to do your homework, but if you choose not to, you won't do well in school, and you may not be able to go out with your friends.

It's hard to look into the future and see how a choice will influence what happens today, tomorrow, or years from now. But whenever we choose to do something, there are consequences that go with our choice. That's why it is important to *think before you choose.*

Remember: The easiest choice does not always lead to the best consequence.

We choose to go to the moon not because it's easy, but because it's hard.
~ John F. Kennedy

Activity

Get a copy of *The Tale of Peter Rabbit* by Beatrix Potter. This simple story is full of choices that lead to bad consequences. Write down three choices Peter made and the consequences that occurred. Who made a good choice, and what was the consequence?

Word Find

Find these words that also mean *consequence*.

Word Bank		
result	outcome	fallout
payoff	effect	reaction
product	aftermath	upshot

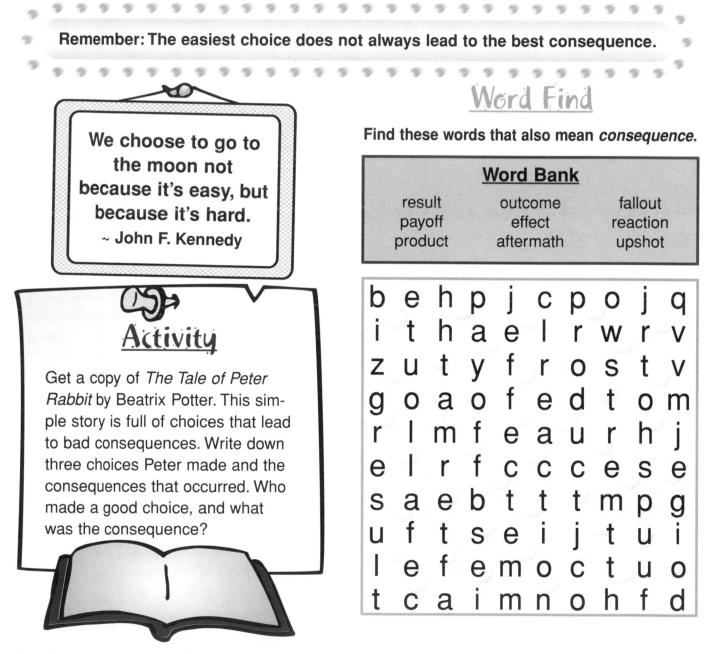

```
b e h p j c p o j q
i t h a e l r w r v
z u t y f r o s t v
g o a o f e d t o m
r l m f e a u r h j
e l r f c c c e s e
s a e b t t t m p g
u f t s e i j t u i
l e f e m o c t u o
t c a i m n o h f d
```

Friendship

Friends come in all sizes, shapes, and ages: brothers, sisters, parents, neighbors, good teachers, and school and sports friends.

There is a saying, "To have a friend you need to be a friend." Can you think of a day when someone might have tried to get you to say or do unkind things to someone else? Sometimes it takes courage to be a real friend.

Recipe for Friendship

1 cup of always listening to ideas and stories
2 pounds of never talking behind a friend's back
1 pound of no mean teasing
2 cups of always helping a friend who needs help

Take these ingredients and mix completely together. Add laughter, kindness, hugs, and even tears. Bake for as long as it takes to make your friendship good and strong.

I get by with a little help from my friends.
~ John Lennon

Family Night at the Movies

Rent *Toy Story* or *Toy Story II*. Each movie is a simple, yet powerful, tale about true friendship. Fix a big bowl of popcorn to share with your family during the show.

Admit One Movies

International Friendship Day

The first Sunday in August is International Friendship Day. This is a perfect day to remember all your friends and how they have helped you during your friendship. Give your friends a call or send them an email or snail-mail card.

Confidence

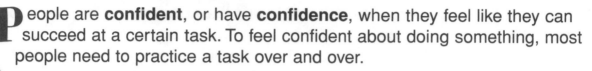

People are **confident**, or have **confidence**, when they feel like they can succeed at a certain task. To feel confident about doing something, most people need to practice a task over and over.

Reading, pitching a baseball, writing in cursive, playing the flute, even mopping a floor are all examples of tasks that need to be practiced before people feel confident they can succeed.

What are five things you feel confident doing?

What is one thing you want to feel more confident doing?

Make a plan for how and when you will practice until you feel confident.

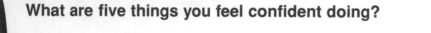

You Crack Me Up!

Materials needed:
1 dozen eggs
a mixing bowl

Cracking eggs without breaking the yolk or getting egg whites all over your hands takes practice.

1. Watch an adult break an egg into the bowl. How did they hold their hands? How did they pull the egg apart?

2. Now you try. Did you do a perfect job the first time? Keep trying until you begin to feel confident about cracking eggs.

3. Use the eggs immediately to make a cheese omelet or custard pie. Refrigerate any unused eggs for up to three days.

Pride

Never bend your head.

Always hold it high.

Look the world

Right in the eye.

~ Helen Keller

Responsibility

You show **responsibility** by doing what you agree or promise to do. It might be a task, such as a homework assignment, or a chore, such as feeding your gerbil.

When you are young, your parents and teachers will give you simple tasks like putting away toys or brushing your teeth without being asked. As you get older, you will be given more responsibility. You might be trusted to come home from a friend's house at a certain time or drive to the store for groceries.

It takes a lot of practice to grow up to be a responsible person. The easiest way to practice is by keeping your promises and doing what you know is right.

A parent is responsible for different things than a child or a teenager. Write three activities you are responsible for every day. Then write three things a parent is responsible for every day.

If you want your eggs hatched, sit on them yourself. ~ Haitian Proverb

Activity

Materials needed:
21 pennies or counters such as beans, rocks, or marbles
2 small containers labeled #1 and #2

Decide on a reward for successfully completing this activity.
Put all the counters in container #1.
Review the three activities you are responsible for every day.
Each night before you go to bed, put one counter for each completed activity into container #2. At the end of seven days count all the counters in container #2.
If you have 16 or more counters in container #2, you are on your way to becoming very responsible. Collect your reward.
My reward is_____.

Service is **helping** another person or group of people without asking for any kind of reward or payment. These are some good things that happen when you do service:

1. You feel closer to the people in your community (neighborhood).
2. You feel pride in yourself when you see that you can help other people in need.
3. Your family feels proud of you.
4. You will make new friends as you help others.

An old saying goes, "Charity begins at home." This means that you don't have to do big, important-sounding things to help people. You can start in your own home and neighborhood.

Activity

Each day this week, do one act of service around your house. Don't ask for or take any kind of payment or reward. Be creative! Possible acts of service are:

1. Carry in the groceries, do the dishes, or fold the laundry.
2. Read aloud to a younger brother or sister.
3. Make breakfast or pack lunches.
4. Recycle newspapers and cans.
5. Clean the refrigerator or your room.

At the end of the week, think of a project to do with your family that will help your community. You could play musical instruments or sing at a nursing home, set up a lemonade stand and give the money you make to the Special Olympics, offer to play board games with children in the hospital, or pick some flowers and take them to a neighbor. The list goes on and on.

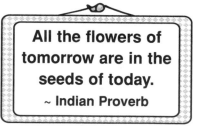

All the flowers of tomorrow are in the seeds of today.
~ **Indian Proverb**

Word Find

Find these words that also mean *service*.

Word Bank		
help	assist	aid
charity	support	boost
benefit	contribute	guide

```
m v l a o d w f d r
c o n t r i b u t e
t b s x c a z v x q
s g p q g w b n y t
i v l y g u v x z i
s n e t e x m n m f
s f h d u d g t e e
a u c h a r i t y n
s u p p o r t u x e
b o o s t g f j g b
```

Honesty and Trust

Being an **honest** person means you don't steal, cheat, or tell lies. **Trust** is when you believe someone will be honest. If you are dishonest, or not truthful, people will not trust you.

You want to tell the truth because it is important to have your family and friends trust you. However, it takes courage to tell the truth, especially if you don't want people to get mad at you or be disappointed in the way you behaved.

How would your parents feel if you lied to them? People almost always find out about lies, and most parents will be more angry about a lie than if you had told them the truth in the first place.

When family or friends ask about something, remember that honesty is telling the truth. Honesty is telling what really happened. Honesty is keeping your promises. *Be proud of being an honest person.*

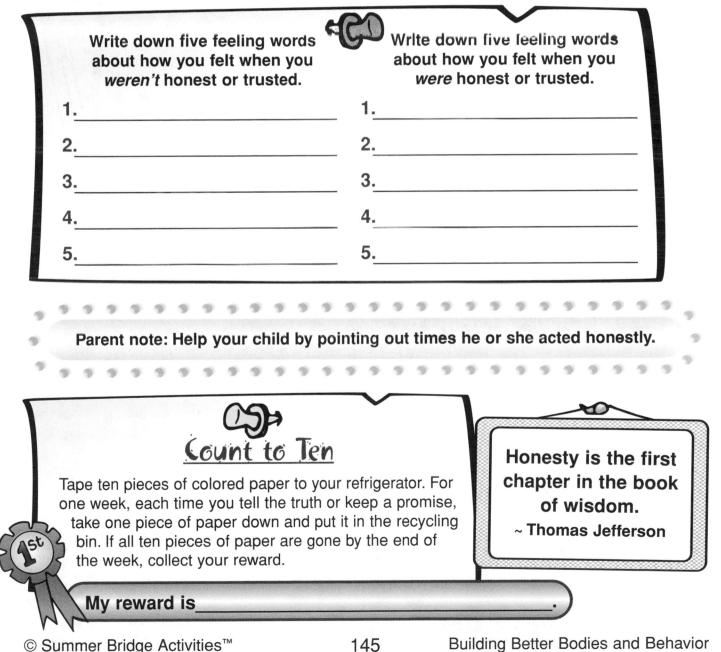

Write down five feeling words about how you felt when you *weren't* honest or trusted.

1._____
2._____
3._____
4._____
5._____

Write down five feeling words about how you felt when you *were* honest or trusted.

1._____
2._____
3._____
4._____
5._____

Parent note: Help your child by pointing out times he or she acted honestly.

Count to Ten

Tape ten pieces of colored paper to your refrigerator. For one week, each time you tell the truth or keep a promise, take one piece of paper down and put it in the recycling bin. If all ten pieces of paper are gone by the end of the week, collect your reward.

Honesty is the first chapter in the book of wisdom.
~ Thomas Jefferson

My reward is _____.

Happiness

Happiness is a feeling that comes when you enjoy your life. Different things make different people happy. Some people feel happy when they are playing soccer. Other people feel happy when they are playing the cello. It is important to understand what makes you happy so you can include some of these things in your daily plan.

These are some actions that show you are happy: laughing, giggling, skipping, smiling, and hugging.

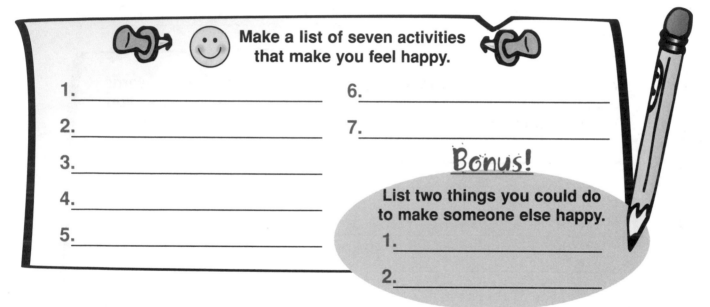

☺ **Make a list of seven activities that make you feel happy.**

1. _____
2. _____
3. _____
4. _____
5. _____

6. _____
7. _____

Bonus!

List two things you could do to make someone else happy.

1. _____
2. _____

Activity

Write down a plan to do one activity each day this week that makes you happy.

Try simple things—listen to your favorite song, play with a friend, bake muffins, shoot hoops, etc.

Be sure to thank everyone who helps you and don't forget to laugh!

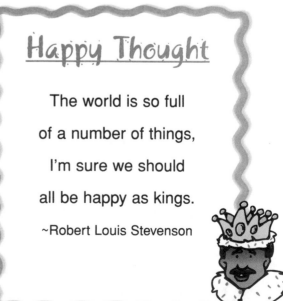

Happy Thought

The world is so full

of a number of things,

I'm sure we should

all be happy as kings.

~Robert Louis Stevenson

Notes

Five things I'm thankful for:

1. _____
2. _____
3. _____
4. _____
5. _____

Notes

_____
_____
_____
_____
_____
_____
_____
_____
_____
_____
_____
_____
_____
_____
_____
_____
_____
_____
_____

5 Five things I'm thankful for:

1. _____
2. _____
3. _____
4. _____
5. _____

Notes

_____
_____
_____
_____
_____
_____
_____
_____
_____
_____
_____
_____
_____
_____
_____
_____
_____
_____
_____

5 Five things I'm thankful for:

1. _____
2. _____
3. _____
4. _____
5. _____

Notes

_____

_____

_____

_____

_____

_____

_____

_____

_____

_____

_____

_____

_____

_____

_____

_____

_____

_____

5 **Five things I'm thankful for:**

1. _____

2. _____

3. _____

4. _____

5. _____

Fraction Table

1

$\frac{1}{2}$	$\frac{1}{2}$

$\frac{1}{3}$	$\frac{1}{3}$	$\frac{1}{3}$

$\frac{1}{4}$	$\frac{1}{4}$	$\frac{1}{4}$	$\frac{1}{4}$

$\frac{1}{5}$	$\frac{1}{5}$	$\frac{1}{5}$	$\frac{1}{5}$	$\frac{1}{5}$

$\frac{1}{6}$	$\frac{1}{6}$	$\frac{1}{6}$	$\frac{1}{6}$	$\frac{1}{6}$	$\frac{1}{6}$

$\frac{1}{7}$	$\frac{1}{7}$	$\frac{1}{7}$	$\frac{1}{7}$	$\frac{1}{7}$	$\frac{1}{7}$	$\frac{1}{7}$

$\frac{1}{8}$	$\frac{1}{8}$	$\frac{1}{8}$	$\frac{1}{8}$	$\frac{1}{8}$	$\frac{1}{8}$	$\frac{1}{8}$	$\frac{1}{8}$

$\frac{1}{9}$	$\frac{1}{9}$	$\frac{1}{9}$	$\frac{1}{9}$	$\frac{1}{9}$	$\frac{1}{9}$	$\frac{1}{9}$	$\frac{1}{9}$	$\frac{1}{9}$

$\frac{1}{10}$	$\frac{1}{10}$	$\frac{1}{10}$	$\frac{1}{10}$	$\frac{1}{10}$	$\frac{1}{10}$	$\frac{1}{10}$	$\frac{1}{10}$	$\frac{1}{10}$	$\frac{1}{10}$

Protractor

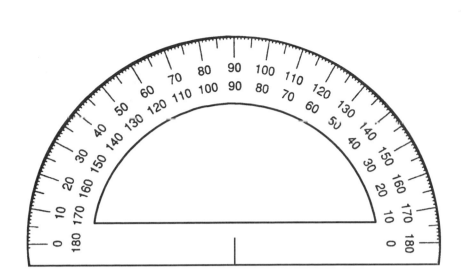

Napier's Bones

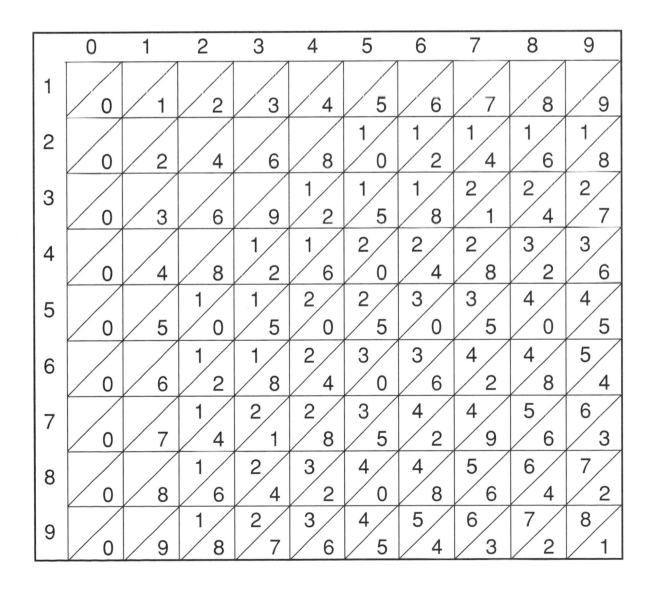

Yardstick

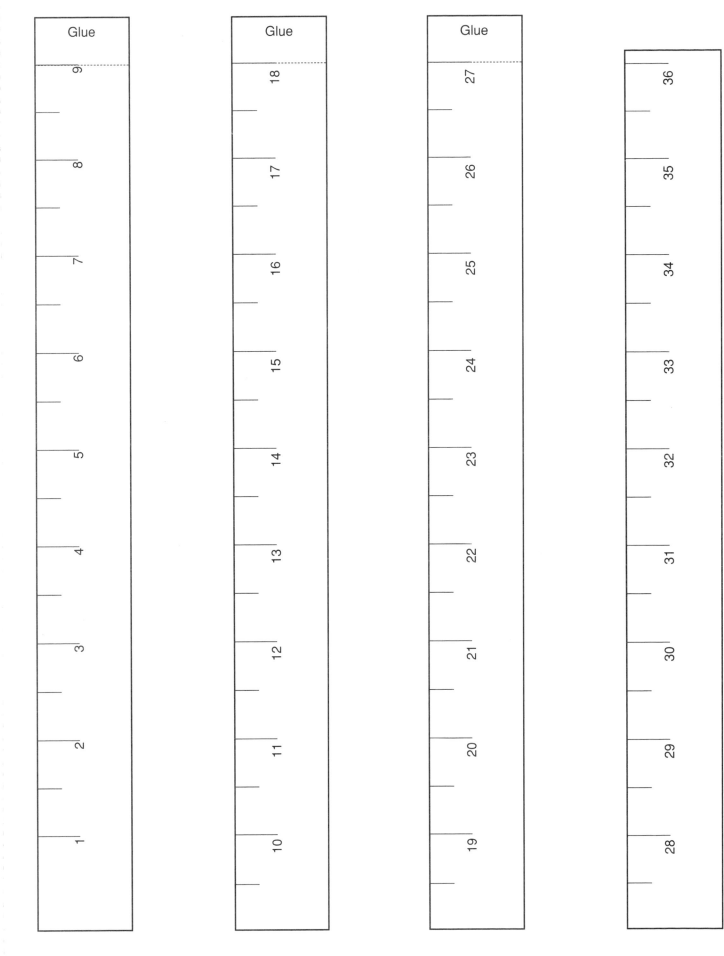

Inch Rulers

Centimeter Rulers

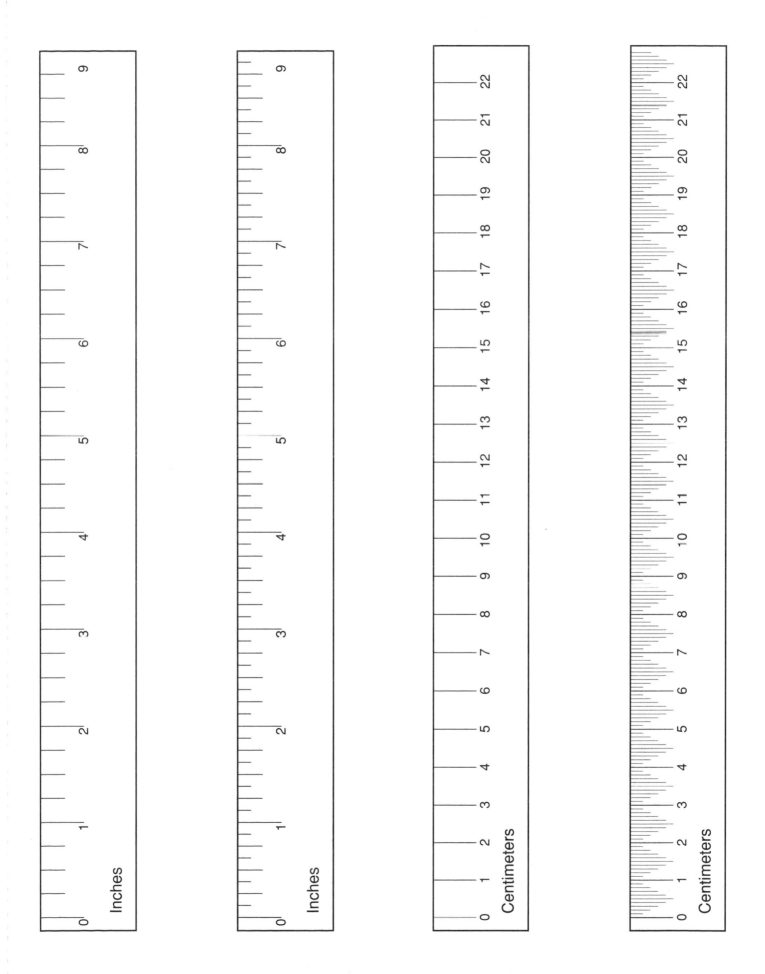

Meterstick

Glue	Glue	Glue	Glue	
20	40	60	80	100
19	39	59	79	99
18	38	58	78	98
17	37	57	77	97
16	36	56	76	96
15	35	55	75	95
14	34	54	74	94
13	33	53	73	93
12	32	52	72	92
11	31	51	71	91
10	30	50	70	90
9	29	49	69	89
8	28	48	68	88
7	27	47	67	87
6	26	46	66	86
5	25	45	65	85
4	24	44	64	84
3	23	43	63	83
2	22	42	62	82
1	21	41	61	81
0	0	0	0	0

Certificate

of

Completion

Awarded to

for the completion of Summer Bridge Activities™
5th grade to 6th grade.

Ms. Hansen
Ms. Hansen

Mr. Fredrickson
Mr. Fredrickson

Parent's Signature